INDIAN GIVERS

Books by Jack McIver Weatherford
Tribes on the Hill
Porn Row
Narcoticos en Bolivia y los Estados Unidos

INDIAN GIVERS

GIVERS

▲ ▲ HOW ▲ ▲
THE INDIANS
▲ ▲ OF ▲ ▲
THE AMERICAS
TRANSFORMED
▲THE WORLD▲

JACK WEATHERFORD

CROWN PUBLISHERS, INC.
NEW YORK

Published by Crown Publishers, Inc., 225 Park Avenue South, New York, New York 10003 and represented in Canada by the Canadian MANDA Group

CROWN is a trademark of Crown Publishers, Inc.

Manufactured in the United States of America

Library of Congress Cataloging-in-Publication Data

Weatherford, J. McIver.
  Indian givers: How the Indians of the Americas transformed the world.
  Bibliography: p.
  Includes index.
    1. Civilization—Indian influences. 2. Civilization, Modern—His-tory. 3. Indians of North America—Colonization. I. Title.
E59.I53W43 1988   970.004'97   88-3827

ISBN 0-517-56969-8

10 9 8 7 6 5 4 3 2 1

First Edition

For
Walker Pearce Maybank

CONTENTS

Acknowledgments.   ix

1. Silver and Money Capitalism   1

2. Piracy, Slavery, and the Birth of
   Corporations   21

3. The American Indian Path to
   Industrialization   39

4. The Food Revolution   59

5. Indian Agricultural Technology.   79

6. The Culinary Revolution   99

7. Liberty, Anarchism, and the Noble
   Savage 117

8. The Founding Indian Fathers 133

9. Red Sticks and Revolution 151

10. The Indian Healer 175

11. The Drug Connection............. 197
12. Architecture and Urban Planning.... 217
13. The Pathfinders.................. 235
14. When Will America Be
     Discovered?..................... 249
     References..................... 257
     Index 267

ACKNOWLEDGMENTS

The writing of this book involved the assistance of many colleagues and friends to whom I am grateful. My family contributed to my work on this project by helping me in the field when possible and by covering for me while I was gone. I thank my wife, Walker Pearce, for her help in Asia and Europe, and I must credit her as being the person who insisted steadily for twelve years that I should write this book. I thank Roy Pearce Maybank for his work with me in South America and Minnesota, and I appreciate the help of Walker Pearce Maybank in Central America.

Much of the travel and many of the contacts for this project came through the assistance of the W. K. Kellogg Foundation, where I particularly thank Larraine Matusak, Patrick McDonough, Anna Sheppard, and the members of Class V of the Kellogg National Fellowship Program.

I thank the administration of Macalester College for giving me the opportunity to work on this book, and funding from the Bush Foundation and the Joyce Foundation. I particularly appreciate suggestions and help in the research by Anne Sutherland, David McCurdy, Anna Meigs, Kay Crawford, Chris Cavender, and James Stewart. Many students also helped me in this work, but I particularly appreciate the help of David Warland's computer skills and the field assistance of Douglas Kleemeier in Africa and South America.

My Spanish teachers through the years have worked patiently to open up to me the Indian world of Latin America. I thank Antonio Lasaga, Maria Doleman, Fabiola Franco, and Jorge Vega for their efforts to educate me. In Bolivia I am particularly thankful to Luis Morató-Peña and his family, with whom I lived and worked so often, and I appreciate the assistance of the families of Johnny Villazon in Cochabamba and Federico Kaune in La Paz.

Others who have read and assisted with comments on the manuscript include Twila Kekahaba-Martin, Götz Freiherr von Houwald, Marc Swartz, Zaida Giraldo, Lee Owens, Rochelle Jones, Hans Christoph Buch, Lavon Lee, Evelyn Hu-DeHart, Joyce King, and Ali Salim. I owe a great debt to my agent, Lois Wallace, and my editor, James Wade.

I appreciate the help of the Newberry Library of Chicago, the Library of Congress in Washington, D.C., and the Macalester College library in St. Paul, Minnesota.

No government money was used for any part of this work.

INDIAN GIVERS

▲ ▲ 1 ▲ ▲

SILVER
AND
MONEY
CAPITALISM

Each morning at five-thirty, Rodrigo Cespedes eats two rolls and drinks a cup of tea heavily laced with sugar before he slings his ratty Adidas gym bag over his shoulder and leaves for work. Rodrigo lives in Potosí, the world's highest city, perched in the Bolivian Andes at an elevation of 13,680 feet above sea level. At this altitude Rodrigo stays warm only when he holds himself directly in the sunlight, but this early in the morning, the streets are still dark. He walks with other men going in the same direction, but like most Quechua and Aymara Indians they walk along silently. The loudest sounds come from the scraping noise of the old women who laboriously sweep the streets each morning. Bent over their short straw brooms, these women look like medieval witches dressed in the traditional black garments woven in Potosí and the tall black hats native to the area.

Rodrigo reaches the main road and joins a line behind forty to fifty men waiting to board one of the dilapidated but once brightly painted buses that leave the Plaza 10 de Noviembre at a quarter before the hour. In the dawning light, he stands across the street from a small dump in which a handful of old women, two dozen snarling dogs, and a few children fight over unrecognizable chunks of food in their daily battle for garbage. When he finally boards the bus, Rodrigo squeezes agilely into the dense pack of silent and stooped men. Very slowly the old bus begins its labored climb up Cerro Rico, the mountain towering over the city. After ascending the mountain for only a few minutes, the bus passes the entrance to the original colonial mine founded on Cerro Rico in 1545. Workers long ago boarded it shut after exhausting that vein, and then they moved to higher veins more difficult and less profitable to mine. After another twenty minutes and a hundred meters' rise in elevation, he passes the dilapidated entrance to the massive government-operated tin mine and the scene of many bloody confrontations between miners and management. Once owned by the "Tin King" Simon Patiño, these mines were nationalized by the revolutionary regime of Victor Paz Estensoro after the revolution in 1952, and now COMIBOL (Corporación Minera de Bolivia), a government-owned and highly unprofitable company, operates them as a way to keep the miners' leftist union tranquil. The bus chokes to its first stop at the mine opening, and most of the men leave the bus.

Even though the bus has less than half a load now, the old engine wheezes and belches up thick black diesel fumes as it struggles on to an altitude of fourteen thousand feet. Few vehicles anywhere operate at a higher altitude, and this bus probably plies the highest daily bus route in the world. Barely able to climb any higher, the bus coasts to a stop near the Heart of Jesus, a large abandoned church covered with graffiti and filled with the strong smell of stale urine, all topped by a giant concrete Jesus. The edifice and its large statue jut out on a cliff a little over halfway up the mountain. Here Rodrigo and the remaining men leave the bus, which then descends for another load.

Without a glance at the Heart of Jesus and without raising his eyes toward the immense mountain above him, Rodrigo begins to climb the long familiar path. For the next two hours he looks only at his feet and he keeps his chin tucked into his jacket and out of the mountain winds that whip around him in freezing but bone-dry swirls even though he is only a few degrees south of the equator. He does not need to look around, for as long as his legs are climbing up the mountain he knows that he is heading in the right direction. He need not fear bumping into a tree, because he is far above the timber line and because over the last four centuries millions of brown hands have already removed every bush, weed, and blade of grass searching for rocks with traces of silver, tin, tungsten, or bismuth. He need not worry about bumping into a large boulder, because generations of Indian workers have long since pounded, hammered, and shattered every boulder into millions of rocks smaller than a child's fist. He need not fear falling into a crevice, because women carrying baskets of rock and dirt have long ago filled in all the crevices with refuse from the five thousand mines that have pierced Cerro Rico in the past five centuries. If Rodrigo did look up, he would see nothing but the endless pile of rusty brown rocks that he climbs every day.

The monotony of the mountain face is interrupted only by the mine openings that pock it like the ravages of some terrestrial cancer. Rodrigo finally stops just short of the summit of 15,680 feet; the trip from his home below has taken two and a half hours. He sits down just outside the mouth of the mine he works, opens his bag, and fishes out a flat, round roll like the ones he ate for breakfast. As he chews the roll, he looks down at the city spread out below him. Because the air is so crisp and clear at this dry altitude, he can clearly pick out the block of houses where he lives in the city of 100,000 people with lives much like his own. He is now half a mile above the city and three miles above the ocean, which, of course, he has never seen. In the distance a small black ribbon of railroad track connects Potosí with the outside world, hauling the tin to Arica, the port on the Chilean coast of the Pacific. The line also connects Potosí to the capital of La Paz. Twice a week passengers can ride the day trip to La Paz on the narrow-gauge railway. Straining to cross the Condor Pass at 15,705 feet above sea level near Río Mulato a few hours out of Potosí, this train operates the world's highest passenger railway. But all of this is far removed from Rodrigo's life.

Swallowing the last of his dry roll, he reaches deep inside his jacket and shirt and brings out his distinctively handwoven *chuspa*, a brightly colored bag of coca leaves that he always keeps on a string around his neck. Picking a few leaves, he carefully inserts them one at a time, together with a little lime, into his mouth with a well-practiced turn of his wrist. After only a few minutes of inactivity at this altitude, he begins to feel the cold, but the mildly narcotic effect produced by chewing the leaves will soon numb that. It will also alleviate his hunger, his thirst, and the sheer drudgery and monotony of the coming eight hours in the mine. It will ease but not stop the pain which slowly begins to torture him in the morning and by the close of the shift has engulfed his whole body from head to toe.

With his quid of coca securely between his cheek and gum, Rodrigo silently joins the other miners and begins his shift, hammering out small pieces of rock for eight hours without even a meal break. They work without the aid of automated machines or even of animals to haul the heavy wagons of rock. Because Rodrigo works in a mining cooperative, he receives pay only for what he produces and not for the time it takes to produce it. Unemployed miners form cooperatives that take over old mines when the government and the private mining companies judge them too unprofitable to operate. As twenty generations of Indian miners have done before him, Rodrigo chips away at a little more and a little more of the mountain each day. The mountain is now so honeycombed that the Indians say it is nearly hollow and soon will collapse upon itself.

At the end of his shift in the mine, Rodrigo reverses his climb. Even though he does not ride the bus during his descent, the trip down takes him only two hours. He returns home exhausted from the ordeal of twelve and a half hours. Rodrigo repeats this routine seven days a week for a wage of approximately a dollar a day and under the constant threat of unemployment because his health might break down or the world economy might take some turn on commodities for reasons incomprehensible to him. He pauses in this weekly routine only for an occasional fiesta or funeral, and on those days he loses that dollar.

Rodrigo knows that the colonial town of Potosí and the mountain on which he works have a long and supposedly glorious history stretching back to Inca times. He has heard that history acknowledged many times by the priest, by politicians in speeches, and by the union officials, and he also knows many of the stories about the fabulous riches, the horrible disasters, the massacres, the revolts, the swindles, the strikes, and the wars surrounding the history of these mines. He easily and vividly relates the stories about the disasters, whereas the stories about the lives of the rich and powerful are only vague accounts of limitless food in large, warm rooms. But Rodrigo has little time to dwell on such topics; perhaps if he lives past the average life expectancy of forty-eight years he can find out more about it.

This mountain on which Rodrigo lives and works is the richest mountain ever discovered anywhere on earth. Beginning in 1545, this mountain produced silver for the treasuries of Europe at a rate and in a volume unprecedented in human history. The Cerro Rico, which means "rich hill," was a mountain of silver over two thousand feet high. Eighty-five percent of the silver produced from the central Andes during the colonial era came from this one mountain. The name Potosí became a synonym for fabulous and inexhaustible wealth after Miguel Cervantes used the phrase *vale un Potosí*, "worth a Potosí," in *Don Quixote de la Mancha*. For a while the expression was even used in English and became the name of towns in Wisconsin and Missouri as well as two mountains in Colorado and Nevada and another mine in Mexico.

The Indian miners say that they have extracted enough ore from this mountain to build a sterling-silver bridge from Potosí to Madrid. It produced so much silver ore and required the labor of so many Indian slaves that for a while Potosí was the largest city in America. It was the first real city of the New World, reaching 120,000 inhabitants by 1573 and 160,000 by 1650. Potosí rivaled such Old World cities as London and Paris in size. The vain Spaniards who ruled it chose to advertise their wealth even in Potosí's coat of arms, which ostentatiously proclaimed: "I am Potosí, the treasure of the world and the envy of kings."

According to Quechua myth, the Inca emperor Huayna Capac first mined Cerro Rico a generation before the Spanish arrived, but the Incas called it Sumaj Orcko, "beautiful hill." The emperor stopped the operation, however, when a voice thundered out of the mountain saying: "Take no silver from this hill. It is destined for other owners." The prophecy certainly came true, for the people of Bolivia have never profited from their great riches. The silver of Potosí was destined for others.

The story of the silver of America seems at first to be less important and dramatic than that of gold. The early invaders of America did not show as much interest in silver as they did in gold. Only after they had thoroughly looted all the gold they could find in America did Cerro Rico begin to play its unprecedented role.

Prior to Columbus, most of Europe's gold arrived from the place the Europeans appropriately called the Gold Coast, in present-day Ghana, Benin, Togo, and Guinea on the west coast of Africa. Two-thirds of the gold in use in Europe prior to the discovery of America came from West Africa [Wolf, p. 39]. It arrived in Europe by a long and torturous route through the tropical jungle, across the Sahel and on through the Sahara. Much of this traveled by caravans and was traded from merchant to merchant through Gao or Timbuktu in present Mali on to Fez in Morocco and then to Spain. Another route crossed the Sahara to Tunis or Tripoli, whence merchants traded the gold with Italian merchants. The Europeans traded cloth, beads, and craft items, which then made their way down the same trail. Timbuktu became so rich from this trade that it was known as the Golden City. When the Malian king Mansa Munsa undertook a pilgrimage to Mecca in 1324, five hundred slaves accompanied him and a caravan of one hundred camels supposedly laden with gold. Even though the amount of gold is unknown, he supposedly gave away and spent so much of it that he caused a gold inflation on the Cairo market. This earned his kingdom and his trade cities of Gao and Timbuktu a reputation for fabulous wealth.

The Europeans sought desperately for ways to increase the trickle of gold that flowed up so slowly from the Gold Coast to Europe, and they wanted to find ways to circumvent the numerous Moslem merchants who monopolized the trade at each stage. Spain's need to find new sources of gold was made all the more desperate by the frequent disruption of the gold trade during the campaigns of Queen Isabella and King Ferdinand against the Moors. The expulsion of the Moors and the Jews from Spain in 1492 worsened the problem.

Every step in the discovery and conquest of America was spurred on by a greed for gold that overshadowed the quest for silver, spices, or souls. Columbus gave evidence of this in his diaries with the oft-repeated statement "I was anxious to learn

Bracketed notes specify page numbers of books listed in References section.

whether they had gold" [Pendle, p. 17]. In the end, Columbus brought back only a small amount of gold, but it was enough to whet the appetite of all Europe.

When Hernando Cortés conquered the Aztecs he immediately demanded gold from their leader, Moctezuma Xocoyotzin; the conquistadores tortured and killed many Aztecs, including the next and last Aztec leader, Cuauhtémoc, to obtain more gold. On *la noche triste*, the sad night, in the summer of 1520 when the Spanish army fled from Axayacatl's palace via the Tlacopán causeway, so many of the conquistadores carried their loot of gold bars, chains, and idols that the tactical retreat became a bloody rout. About one-fourth of the army died on that one night. The Aztec soldiers easily killed and captured the slow-moving Spaniards burdened by their gold, and many of the conquistadores drowned because the heavy gold dragged them down when they fell from the causeway into the lake. As recently as 1981 one of the gold bars was found by excavators in what is now downtown Mexico City [Berdan, p. 169].

When the Spanish entered what is today Colombia, they heard the legend of the Indian nation around Lake Guatavita located at an elevation of ten thousand feet in the mountains. Each year their king covered himself in gold dust, took a barge loaded with golden objects out into the middle of the lake, and sacrificed the gold to the god of the lake by throwing the objects into the water. The leader himself then dove into the lake and swam around to wash away and thus sacrifice his "golden skin." This became the legend of the Golden Man, or El Dorado. The reputed location varied, but the legend remained the same: somewhere there was a city filled with the gold of this Golden Man. The conquistadores soon explored almost all of America from Kansas to Patagonia searching for this treasure of gold.

Many of the Indian nations prized gold, but they did so more in an aesthetic or religious sense than in a mercenary one. As the Inca Garcilaso de la Vega wrote in his commentaries on the life of the Incas, "there was neither gold nor silver coin, and these metals could not be considered otherwise than as superfluous, since they could not be eaten, nor could one buy anything to eat with them." He explains further that in a nation without markets or a money economy, gold and silver "were esteemed only for their beauty and brilliance" [Vega, p. 162]. The best use the Incas could make of them was to decorate temples, palaces, and convents. Inca goldsmiths of Cuzco lined the walls and columns of the great Temple of the Sun in Cuzco with beaten gold, and they decorated the temple with five golden fountains. The emperor owned gardens in which stood examples of almost all his empire's animals and plants cast in gold and silver. This included even golden lizards, butterflies, and snakes darting among the golden flowers and corn stalks [Vega, p. 190].

When Francisco Pizarro invaded the Andes and seized the Inca emperor Atahualpa in 1532, he demanded a room filled with gold as ransom, and the Incas paid it. Bearers from all over the empire gathered jewelry and stripped their temples to fill the room. The gold of Atahualpa formed the greatest ransom ever paid. Even though the Incas complied, Pizarro nevertheless killed Atahualpa and continued to loot the country in search of even more gold.

Hernando de Soto crisscrossed the southeastern part of the United States from Florida and the Carolinas to the Mississippi River in search of gold. Francisco Vásquez de Coronado wandered through the modern states of Arizona, New Mexico, and California searching for the seven lost cities of gold. Francisco de Orellana sailed two years through the Amazonian jungle searching for El Dorado. No matter how hot, cold, wet, dry, or high the place, some conquistador went there searching for gold.

Today, we can still see a small fraction of the gold treasure of the Indians. The most extensive collection, belonging to the Peruvian industrialist Mujica Gallo, is in Monterico, a suburb just outside Lima. On a tree-lined street of affluent suburban homes, surrounded by a massive wall and armed guards, is a large building that looks like a cross between a ranch-style home and a bomb shelter situated in the middle of a beautiful park. On the ground floor of this private museum, Gallo displays his large collection of military arms from around the world. Japanese suits of armor guard the walls next to samurai swords. Small pistols, muskets, and pikes dangle in midair and rest in numerous display cases. The pride of the collection of arms, however, is the sword that Francisco Pizarro himself used in the conquest of Peru.

To see the gold that inspired Pizarro, one must leave the ground floor and descend into a gigantic subterranean vault with massive walls covered by sheets of seemingly impermeable steel. Visitors enter the room today with the hushed voices and subdued movements of mourners at a funeral. In the eerie underground cavern, they walk silently from one of the thirteen thousand golden pieces to another, staring at the small gold beads, golden masks, ear plugs, and goblets. One of the commonest figures in the collection is the *tumi*, an object possibly used as a scepter, made in the form of a human figure standing atop a curved blade. One of the most unusual is a set of elbow-length gloves beaten from thin sheets of golden foil decorated with geometric designs.

Protected in their well-lit cases and set against dark backgrounds and with few placards to distract the eye from the gold itself, the artifacts seem to float in space. The pieces also seem suspended in time, for no apparent history or chronology is attached to the objects. The museum presents them for the maximum aesthetic appreciation of the art aficionado and the gawkers at beauty or wealth. The displays focus on the direct aesthetic appreciation of the objects, and this helps account for the hushed tones of the awed visitors. Usually experts know nothing about the artisans who created the objects, when or why they were made, who owned them, or even who discovered them or where they were found. Most of the pieces came to the collection from grave robbers or their intermediaries, who conceal the location of their crimes for fear of either prosecution or competition. Whenever a group of such robbers finds an object, they usually cut it into equal parts on the spot so that each man can be assured of getting his share. Each man then sells his pieces wherever he thinks he can get the best price. In this way most of the objects arrive in the museum cut into pieces, and in some cases parts of the pieces are never found. Even the famous golden gloves arrived with the fingers cut off, and Gallo had to buy each piece separately and have them painstakingly reassembled. Thus objects arrive in a historical and archaeological vacuum.

The Gold Museum of Bogotá boasts about thirty-five thousand pieces of gold, much of it from the Chibcha people and the coastal peoples of Colombia. Estimates place the value of this collection at approximately $150 million, by weight alone, without factoring in the artistic and historical value of the items. The archaeological museum of the Banco Central in Quito, Ecuador, also boasts a small but elegant collection of golden objects. The Banco Central of Costa Rica in San José also has an exhibit of golden objects, mostly of small animals. The total value of the metal in the collection is around $6 million.

But to find the Indian gold one must look not in the banks and museums of America but in the banks, museums, and churches of Europe. The conquistadores immediately melted it, and sent it to Spain as golden bars. They shipped intact some of the more unusual objects, such as the golden sun from Cuzco, to inform the emperor about the valuable crafts of his newly conquered land. Charles V sponsored a traveling exhibit of these objects through his empire as a propaganda device to glorify his reign by displaying the wealth from his new realms of Mexico and Peru. After the public exhibit, the emperor had all the pieces melted down for use in his treasury. He minted new coins from the gold, paid some of his debts with it, gave some of it to churches, and used it to finance the expansion of his army and his palaces.

Between 1500 and 1650, the gold of the Americas added at least 180 to 200 tons to the European treasure [Braudel, Vol. I, p. 467]. This amount of gold has a contemporary value of over $2.8 billion, far more than the meager hoards in Gallo's museum or in the banks of the other Latin American capitals. The churches of Europe still groan under the weight of American silver and gold jealously guarded but ostentatiously displayed. Once-simple churches such as those in Toledo suddenly soared to new heights, expanded, and had new windows installed to let the sun pour down on the vast collection of gold and jewels from the New World. The cathedral of Toledo boasts a five-hundred-pound monstrance made in the fifteenth century from gilded silver said to have been made from the Indian booty brought back by Columbus himself. Córdoba, Avila, and every other city in the south boast similar artifacts, even though they do not always brag about the source of the precious metals. Gold became so common in European palaces and churches that architects developed a novel style of decoration emphasizing entering light that could illuminate the gold and make it dazzle the observer. Thankful conquistadores and an appreciative monarchy filled the churches with golden crucifixes, golden statues of saints, gilded frames of paintings, golden reliquaries, and gilded tombs. The Spaniards melted the American gold to fashion golden chalices, trays, and other religious articles that still survive in the churches in Spanish cities such as Seville and Toledo.

I first saw this wealth of silver and gold in a Holy Week procession in Córdoba. The crowd in the darkened courtyard of the cathedral of Córdoba quieted as a group of young men swung open the twenty-foot-high doors of the former mosque. Out marched the members of the Pious Brotherhood of Penitents and Union of Nazarites of the Holiest Christ and Our Lady of Tears in Sorrow. Dressed in their long robes of purple and white topped by tall conical hats from which hung veils covering their faces, they looked like marchers in a Ku Klux Klan rally. The first one carried a six-foot-high cross of silver. Twelve young boys, without masks but wearing twisted lace collars several inches thick, followed him; each of them carried a golden trumpet four feet long and a foot wide at the mouth. From each trumpet hung a banner of the Hapsburg eagle, which also served as the emblem of this confraternity. Following the trumpet players marched more boys with tall silver crosses and more men with covered faces.

Slowly and clumsily, like a dinosaur with too many legs, forty young men followed in tight formation carrying on their shoulders a float of Christ on the cross. The float was awkwardly pulled through the Moorish doors and into the night air, which immediately extinguished most of the several dozen candles burning in four golden candelabra that reached up to five feet in height.

As the forty men awkwardly swung their load back and forth, they entered the ancient courtyard of the cathedral where mullahs taught the Koran to generations of Spanish boys before the discovery of America. The branches of the orange trees whipped against the float, dropping leaves over the Christ and spreading the sweet smell of orange blossoms throughout the crowd. More hooded men marched behind the float with a band that alternately played marching songs and mournful dirges. Behind the band followed the float of the weeping Virgin Mary, bedecked with white gladioli and orchids and far more gold and silver than the float of Christ.

Every night during Holy Week at least three such processions wended their way through the narrow streets of Córdoba, through the mosque-turned-cathedral, past the old synagogue of the ancient Jewish quarter, and through the alleys of the Arab merchant section. A few of the floats were made of wood, but most were either gilded wood or solid silver. Córdoba alone had twenty-nine such processions, each with two floats, and in the region of Andalusia over three hundred such processions marched during Holy Week, the largest and most emotional of all being in the regional capital, Seville.

These processions offered more than an opportunity for men to hide their identity while marching through the streets as an act of penitence for their sins of the year. Holy Week gave each neighborhood parish the chance to compete with the others in decorating the most beautiful floats and in using the most costly materials.

The processions and the churches of Europe offer the most visible reminders of the deluge of American gold that showered Europe in the sixteenth century, but the remains of this golden wave still shine in the secular buildings as well. Church and lay authorities found themselves with so much gold that they decorated their palaces with it. They put gold leaf on the ceilings, added golden cherubs in the corners, strung vines of golden grapes between them, and puffed up golden clouds to fill any unadorned spaces. The gold of America gave Europe the baroque and finally the rococo styles of ostentatious decoration for public buildings, churches, palaces, and even the homes of the rising new merchant class.

By comparison with the golden treasure, the silver of Cerro Rico provoked a less ostentatious response among the Europeans, but the eventual impact of the silver proved to be far more extensive and more profound. The exploitation of the silver in America followed very quickly that of the gold.

Once extracted, this silver did not stay in Bolivia. In the imperial mint of Potosí, craftsmen hurriedly minted the silver into sterling bars or coins that were shipped across the mountains to the sea, up the coast to Panama, across the Isthmus by mule, and onto galleons bound for Seville. In 1637 an English Dominican saw one of the mule trains carrying the silver to Porto Bello on the Caribbean coast of Panama. He described them as "laden with wedges of silver; in one day I told two hundred mules laden with nothing else, which were unladen in the marketplace, so that there were heaps of silver wedges like heaps of stones in the street" [Pendle, p. 64].

Never before in the history of the world had so much silver money been in the hands of so many people. Kings, emperors, czars, and pharaohs had always accumulated great wealth in their jewels, their hoards of gold, and their coinage, but the total amount of gold and silver was quite limited by the scarcity of the precious metals. A royal treasury guarded a hodgepodge of whatever valuable items could be collected. This changed with the opening of the Americas. Now for the first time people had massive amounts of silver and gold. Quickly and inexorably the traditional mercantile system of Europe changed. With so much money, the old system mutated into a true money economy in which large numbers of people could buy large amounts of goods, and private citizens could start their own hoards of coins. Production increased, and people began to accumulate capital in quantities undreamed of by prior generations.

The silver treasure unearthed in the bowels of Cerro Rico made this possible. Gold serves well for making jewelry, decorating palaces and churches, and making some very valuable coins, but for the thousands and millions of small daily transactions necessary to make a money economy, silver proves much more practical. A baker buying barrels of flour, a weaver selling new bundles of cloth, a fish merchant buying the catch of small fishermen, all need coins of small but consistent value. The discovery of Cerro Rico brought them into the world economy; it let them have plentiful coinage and thereby made them active players in the monetary world.

The ancient world had never enjoyed access to enough silver to assure a plentiful supply of coins. Even in Roman times the shortage of silver led to periodic debasing of the currency by alloying the silver with less valuable metals. At times the Roman emperors even resorted to silver-plating baser metals and circulating the coins or paying their armies with them under the pretense that they were sterling silver [Garraty and Gay, pp. 223–24].

In the first fifty years of the conquest of America, the amount of silver and gold circulating in Europe trebled, and the annual output from America was ten times the combined output of the rest of the world [Crow, p. 267-73]. Royal customs agents in Seville, Spain's only official port of entry for goods from the New World, recorded sixteen thousand tons of silver entering during this time [Braudel, Vol. I, p. 467], $3.3 billion worth in today's silver market; illegal trade and pirating may have brought in another five thousand tons or more.

Even though Potosí was the major source, the Spanish also opened silver mines in the western mountains of Mexico. In 1546, Juan de Tolosa discovered another major silver vein in the territory of the Chichimec people, called Zacatecas; he named the mine La Bufa. Being much larger than Bolivia, Mexico yielded many more mines. After La Bufa the Spanish opened mines at Guanajuato in 1548, Taxco in 1549, Pachuca in 1551, Sombrerete and Durango in 1555, and Fresnillo in 1569 [Wolf, p. 135]. Although no single find in Mexico ever attained the unprecedented output of the fabled Cerro Rico, the total output there surpassed that of Potosí.

At the time of the discovery of America, Europe had only about $200 million worth of gold and silver, approximately $2 per person. By 1600 the supply of precious metals had increased approximately eightfold [Webb, p. 138]. The Mexican mint alone coined $2 billion worth of silver pieces of eight [Crow, p. 267].

The silver coins flowing through Europe at first promised to strengthen the feudal order, but in the end they forged whole new classes and changed the fortune of many countries. The new coins helped to wash away the old aristocratic order in which money games could be played only by the privileged few; massively larger amounts of money opened up new games to new people. Even though all the silver and gold went into Spain, it did not stay there. From Spain the money spread throughout Europe. The Hapsburg monarch Charles V occupied his throne both as emperor of the Holy Roman Empire and as the king of Spain; this facilitated the spread of the money from Spain to the Hapsburg holdings in the Spanish Netherlands and across Germany, Switzerland, Austria, and the Italian states. Three-fifths of the bullion entering Spain from America immediately left Spain to pay debts, mostly those incurred by the profligate monarchy; as Cervantes wrote in *Don Quixote*, Spain had become "a mother of foreigners, a stepmother of Spaniards" [Wolf, pp. 140, 114].

Precious metals from America superseded land as the basis for wealth, power, and prestige. For the first time there was enough of some commodity other than land to provide a greater and more consistent standard by which wealth might be measured. This easily transported and easily used means of wealth prepared the way for the new merchant and capitalist class that would soon dominate the whole world.

The impact of this new money showed clearly in the port of Antwerp, which had belonged to the Duke of Burgundy before he became Emperor Charles V. Writing in 1560 about the great trading city of Antwerp, a Florentine diplomat, Ludovico Guicciardini (1483–1589), wrote that he found in the market "innumerable kinds of merchandise, precious stones, and pearls of various quality and prices, which the Spaniards bring from their West Indies and from Peru called 'America,' and the New World." In particular they bring in "a large amount of gold, of pure silver in bullion and hand-wrought, which is likewise for the most part from that new and happy world" [Ross and McLaughlin, p. 185]. By 1555, Antwerp had grown to a city of over 100,000, even though at the time of the discovery of America it probably still had less than 20,000 [Wolf, p. 114].

Jean Bodin (1530–1596), a French lawyer, writing in 1568, first realized the inflationary effect of the American money. He concluded that there were several reasons for the rising prices in the sixteenth century but that "the principal and almost the only one (which no one has referred to until now) is the abundance of gold and silver, which is today much greater in this kingdom than it was four hundred years ago" [Ross and McLaughlin, p. 202].

The tremendous volume of new currency influenced the economy of all Europe. For example, in Naples there were only 700,000 ducats in circulation and in savings in 1570. In less than two centuries, by 1751, there were eighteen million ducats. These eighteen million ducats, moreover, could be used many times in a year for various types of transactions. The total number of ducats used in buying and selling would be approximately 288 million. Similarly, in France, which received its wealth from the New World much later than Spain, approximately 120 million francs circulated in 1670, but by 1770 there were two billion in circulation, a fifteenfold increase in a century [Braudel, Vol. I, p. 464].

The American silver traveled around Europe very quickly, and it made a quick and heavy impact on the economy of neighboring parts of the Old World, such as the Ottoman Empire, which controlled Turkey and Greece and most of the Near East, North Africa, and large parts of eastern Europe in the sixteenth century. The Ottoman silver *akce* coin suddenly fell to half its former value before the end of 1584 in a bout of uncontrolled inflation. The coin lost its important place in world trade and never regained it [Garraty and Gay, p. 613]. After centuries of struggle between the Moslems and the Christians, American silver probably did more to undermine Islamic power for the next half a millennium than did any other single factor.

In *The Wealth of Nations*, Adam Smith discussed at great length the impact of American silver in causing worldwide inflation. He wrote that within a generation of the opening of the mines of Potosí, the silver from them started an inflation that lasted for approximately a century and caused silver to fall to its lowest value in history [Smith, pp. 191–202]. The new wealth in the hands of Europeans eroded the wealth of all the other countries in the world and allowed Europe to expand into an international market system.

The silver of America made possible a world economy for the first time, as much of it was traded not only to the Ottomans but to the Chinese and East Indians as well, bringing all of them under the influence of the new silver supplies and standardized silver values. Europe's prosperity boomed, and its people wanted all the teas, silks, cottons, coffees, and spices which the rest of the world had to offer. Asia received much of this silver, but it too experienced the silver inflation that Europe underwent. In China, silver had one-fourth the value of gold in 1368, before the discovery of America, but by 1737 the ratio plummeted to twenty to one, a decline of silver to one-fifth of its former value [Weber, p. 5]. This flood of American silver came to Asia directly from Acapulco across the Pacific via Manila in the Philippines, whence it was traded to China for spices and porcelains.

Asia experienced a temporary gain from the discovery of America, but Africa suffered. America had all the silver and gold Europe needed, and this destroyed the African gold markets and the dependent trade networks. Cities such as Timbuktu and the Songhai Empire of which it was a part crumbled as merchants abandoned the ancient trade routes. To replace the Mediterranean trade of cloth, beads, leather, and metals upon which the Africans had become dependent, the Africans now had only one commodity that the Europeans wanted—slaves. For centuries the African merchants had sold a small but steady number of slaves to the Middle East, but with the decline of their traditional European trade and with the opening of America, the slave trade became a boom. The Africans thus became victims of the discovery of America as surely as did the American Indians.

In the first few years after the discovery of Potosí, the Spaniards brought in six thousand African slaves to work the mines, but they soon died at that high altitude. The colonial administration then turned to the Indians to work the mines without pay as a form of forced labor, or *mita* as it was called in Quechua, the Inca language. Indians had to walk from hundreds of miles away in every part of the highlands of Peru and Bolivia. They worked for approximately one in each four years, even though by law they were not required to work more than one year in each seven. Each miner's family supplied him with his food and with the candles he needed for light inside the mines. The Indians entered the mines on Monday morning and did not emerge again until Saturday. Each man had to chisel out his daily quota of one and a quarter tons of ore. He then loaded it in bags of a little over one hundred pounds and carried it up to the main tunnel. This required that he drag and push the bag through a labyrinth of small tunnels barely large enough to squeeze through, and then carry it up ladders at odd angles for hundreds of feet. In the first decades of this system, four out of five miners died in their first year of forced employment in the mines [Crow, p. 269].

In the modern era, with a battery-powered light on my head, I had great difficulty maneuvering through the older channels even without trying to haul a quintal of silver ore. As I climbed ladders from one level to another, mud constantly dripped down on me from the boots of the man ahead of me. I had to grasp the rungs tightly to keep my hand from slipping off in the mud, but slivers of wood then embedded themselves in my fingers. When I could walk, I was constantly standing in water up well above my ankles, and even though I wore modern miner's boots, the moisture still managed to get through to my socks. All the while the temperature inside was so cool that I could see my breath whenever the dust subsided enough for the air to clear. All of this was made all the more difficult by the thin air at well over fourteen thousand feet above sea level, almost three times the altitude of Denver, Colorado.

Despite these working conditions, if the Indian worker failed to fill his quota the Spanish overseers forced him to work on Sundays, held him over for a longer *mita*, or forced his family to pay in goods or other services for the work he had not been able to do. Thus several members of a family, including women and children, often worked to fulfill what was supposedly the obligation to supply a single person [Werlich, p. 43].

Even though the Indians made possible the greatest economic boom in the history of the world and even though this boom gave rise to the great capitalist world economy, they still languish in poverty. They live in a struggling country in which prices sometimes increase by the hour, and where the value of a day's pay can plummet by a fourth overnight.

Today a second mountain rises up from the valley floor next to Cerro Rico in Potosí. This artificial mountain arose from the millions of tons of crushed rock residue that remained after the precious metals were extracted. The people call this artificial mountain Huakajchi, the mountain that cried. This new structure of refuse is a giant mountain turned inside out and made from the core of Cerro Rico. It too is being mined now, or more precisely "picked over." Now that the wealth of the Cerro Rico has been nearly exhausted, the Indian women who still live in the area have turned to searching through the mountain of rubble for small bits of metal that were overlooked in the original mining. They are forced to scavenge from the garbage of their ancestors.

Potosí, the city which supplied the silver for the rise of capitalism, is now out of silver, and the miners mine only tin, but the price of tin has dropped to almost nothing as the plastic revolution spread around the world. The great mint of Potosí that swallowed eight million Indian miners and turned out billions of coins from the sixteenth century into the twentieth century operates now as a museum for visiting schoolchildren [Galeano, p. 50]. Bolivia has no more coins. Now robbed of its wealth, Bolivia uses only cheap paper money that must be imported. In the middle and late 1980s, with inflation running at an annual rate fluctuating between 2,000 and 15,000 percent, paper currency in denominations of millions of pesos printed by companies in Germany and Brazil composed Bolivia's main import.

Europe also paid the price for its greed. Spain, the greatest beneficiary of the Potosí silver, soon bankrupted itself. By 1700, Spain was reduced to a minor power of neither economic nor political importance, and even the Hapsburg dynasty lost Spain to the Bourbons. Since then Spain has continued to sacrifice occasional generations of its young men in bloody foreign and civil wars. Spain, which had ruled an empire larger than any in the world today, degenerated into a poor hinterland of Europe. It lost huge chunks of its American holdings to Portugal, England, France, and even Sweden and the Netherlands, and the admittedly vast areas to which Spain retained a nominal claim were being ransacked by merchants and companies from England, the Netherlands, and France. By the time of the American Revolution, the English-speaking colonies of North America had more Mexican silver dollars circulating within them than Spain itself did [Fehrenbach, p. 294].

The silver of Potosí helped to destroy Spain, almost as though it carried with it a curse written in the blood of the legions of Indians who died to supply it. And the curse did not stop with Spain. The money passed into the hands of the greedy Dutch, British, and French traders and pirates, and for a while it seemed that they were able to use it more wisely and profit from it more than the Spanish had done. They used it to build large modern navies and armies that colonized almost every country in the rest of the world, dividing Africa, Asia, and the Pacific islands among themselves to make vast new empires on which the sun never would set. But they also fought with one another in war after war. By the middle of the twentieth century, these empires too had fallen, leaving the British no better off than the Spanish. By then, economic power on the European continent had shifted to Germany and the Soviet Union, the two nations that had participated in and profited the least from the blood money of Potosí.

Cerro Rico stands today as the first and probably most important monument to capitalism and to the ensuing industrial revolution and the urban boom made possible by the new capitalist system. Potosí was the first city of capitalism, for it supplied the primary ingredient of capitalism—money. Potosí made the money that irrevocably changed the economic complexion of the world.

▲ ▲ 2 ▲ ▲

PIRACY, SLAVERY, AND THE BIRTH OF CORPORATIONS

 The gray-haired clerk and her teenage assistant sat silently behind the sales counter gazing out the window at the abandoned building on the far side of Victoria Street. It was a quiet May afternoon in Thunder Bay, Ontario, in the pause between the thawing of the ice and the first appearance of buds and birds. On one side of the store stood assorted stacks of serious winter equipment, including fur parkas, heavy mittens, and gargantuan scarves. On the other side hung the pelts of rabbits, muskrats, raccoons, and squirrels interspersed with miniature tomahawks crowned with bright blue and red feathers, little buckskin dolls dressed as Ojibwa or Cree children, and small drums stamped "Souvenir of Canada." A black velvet painting depicted a naked Eskimo woman reclining seductively on a bed of white fox fur.

One case displayed delicately made boxes of birch bark decorated with colored porcupine quills that had been woven into flowers and bordered in sweet grass that saturated the boxes with a fragrance pungent enough to pierce the layer of dust covering them. Eskimo soapstone carvings lined the edge of the shelf, mixed with miniature totem poles in garish colors. On the wall hung a shelf of caps with epigrams on the bill such as "Wine, Women, and Walleye," honoring the walleye pike common in Canadian lakes and rivers. On the walls hung racks of steel mosquito traps for the "giant Canadian mosquito" and clamp pins made to resemble a pink panther and his pastel animal friends, and plastic Indian beads ready for the customer to make a personal "genuine Indian" belt or necklace.

The store scarcely differed from hundreds of other souvenir shops littering North America. It sat in a slightly deteriorating part of town only a block from the nicely renovated downtown mall and the Scotia Bank and only blocks from the northern shore of Lake Superior. The local chapter of the American Hockey Association occupied the building next door, and a cluster of small retail clothing shops took up the remainder of the block. And on the corner by the shopping mall a mixture of Nordic and Indian teenagers loitered in small clusters, apparently waiting for nothing in particular but thoroughly enjoying being outside after another long and freezing Canadian winter.

But this store is special. It belongs to the Hudson's Bay Company, the oldest company in the world. The company has operated continuously since May 2, 1670, when King Charles II chartered it as the Honourable Company of Adventurers of England Trading in Hudson's Bay; it was both the last of the great mercantile companies and the first modern corporation. The origins of this tawdry little store and its parent company go back ultimately to the silver trade from Potosí and the British pirates who stalked and harassed it. Even though the company encountered difficult financial times and sold off some of its retail stores in the 1980s, it is still the world's largest dealer in furs.

Some of the modern Hudson's Bay stores in cities such as Winnipeg operate as completely contemporary department stores with indoor parking garages and merchandise ranging from televisions and personal computers through fine jewelry and imported clothes. Other retail outlets in the more remote corners of Canada stick to simple kitchen utensils and work tools along with basic food items and, of course, the traditional Hudson's Bay blanket.

The present city of Thunder Bay houses approximately 150,000 people, who were united when the two towns of Port Arthur and Fort William consolidated their governments. Today Thunder Bay is Canada's third-largest port, and it is Mile Zero on the St. Lawrence Seaway, which wanders two thousand miles through the Great Lakes and up the St. Lawrence River before spilling into the North Atlantic. The main exports channeled through Thunder Bay today are wheat from the vast plains of Saskatchewan and Manitoba and lumber or wood products from the large forests of northern Ontario. Until recently, iron ore and potash were also major exports, and before that the port specialized in the export of fur.

The site was founded exclusively for the fur trade. In 1803 the North West Company of Montreal built Fort William as the collection point for pelts from all of western Canada as far as the Pacific coast and the Yukon. A group of Scots fleeing from the United States during the Revolutionary War founded the North West Company in 1797. They deliberately sought to copy and to compete with the much older Hudson's Bay Company. The North West Company wanted to undermine the fur trade by concentrating on a southern route through the St. Lawrence River and the Great Lakes. Unlike the Hudson's Bay Company, which set up its main post at the mouth of the Hayes River, flowing into Hudson Bay, and then waited for the Indians to come with furs, the North West Company went directly to the Indians by establishing a network of trading posts throughout the west. The new strategy worked for a while, but the powerful Hudson's Bay Company devoured its younger competitor in an 1821 merger. The Hudson's Bay Company thereby acquired all of the North West Company's trading posts, such as Fort William, as well as the new strategy for itself. This enabled the Hudson's Bay Company to compete much more effectively with the American Fur Company, founded by John Jacob Astor, the richest man in the United States in the first half of the nineteenth century.

The trading post of Fort William stood very close to the present site of the Hudson's Bay Company store on Thunder Bay at the point where the Kaministikwia River empties into Lake Superior. Even though the name connotes a military enclave, it operated strictly as a trading fort manned exclusively by the army of private enterprise. The company built the center like a fort and surrounded it with a square stockade and lookout towers, but the towers served to herald approaching cargo canoes rather than war parties. Only during the times of hostilities with the United States, as in the War of 1812, did the company have to protect its fort from possible attack.

The fort sat deserted most of the year, operating only in the summer, when the lakes and rivers thawed and allowed as many as two thousand of the company's voyageurs from throughout western Canada to assemble. As agreed in their contracts, the voyageurs transported to Fort William the stock of thick winter pelts trapped by Indians. Representatives of the company office in Montreal came to the fort to take away the pelts, and they brought with them the supplies of sugar, rum, tobacco, cloth, and beads that the voyageurs needed for the coming winter to supply themselves as well as to trade for the next season of pelts.

The Scottish masters and clerks of the company did not allow the French-speaking voyageurs to come inside the stockade except on official business. The voyageurs camped around the fort close to the camp of the Indians who gathered to trade corn, birch bark, and other local items needed by the company. Several hundred Indian women also served as the fort's manual laborers, performing such heavy tasks as canoe building. Even though men supervised such tasks, Indian women performed most of the manual labor. They stripped the birch bark and made it pliable before sewing it onto frames with cedar roots and coating it with resin to make canoes. The canoes were large, capable of hauling several tons of supplies. The Indian women also served as wives to the voyageurs and the Scots, who also kept European wives and families back in Montreal. The three castes of Scots, French Canadians, and Indians were united only through their common marriages to Indian women.

The main commodity traded at the fort was beaver pelts, which the men pressed into small bundles of approximately ninety pounds each and shipped to London via Montreal. The entire process took two years from the trapping of the animal to the arrival of the fur on the English market. Workers removed the unwanted long hairs and saved only the soft, short hairs, which they matted into a thick felt. The downy underhairs made a pliable and strong felt ideal for the manufacture of the top hats that men prized at the beginning of the nineteenth century. Beaver fur surpassed other fur for making felt because the hairs stuck together so well, did not loose their shape, and remained waterproof, a property of great importance in rainy Europe before the invention of the umbrella. By comparison with the beaver, other furs were weak, drooped, and easily became misshapen or leaked when soaked with rain. Although made of beaver the hats did not resemble fur at all and were dyed in numerous shades of brown, gray, and black to match the colors of men's suits. Because of the pliability of beaver felt when first made and its firmness after finishing, haberdashers experimented with a variety of shapes. They used the beaver felt to make everything from the three-cornered military hat to top hats with a variety of curled brims.

Trappers also brought in cheaper furs such as muskrat to Fort William; these went into making lower-quality felt hats for sale to poorer men. Other pelts, such as wolf, fox, rabbit, mink, bear, wolverine, otter, raccoon, and even squirrel, could be used by tailors to line coat pockets; more expensive furs lined the insides of coats. Fashion of the time dictated that fur should always be on the inside, as it was considered too barbaric in appearance to be worn on the outside unless it had been processed into another material, such as felt.

The fur trade began strictly as a luxury trade, but the operations of the Hudson's Bay Company grew so extensive and furs became so plentiful that in time even the middle classes could afford beaver. Unlike the scarcer Eurasian furbearers such as ermine, sable, and marten, which had been overhunted through the centuries, the American furry animals still thrived in vast numbers. The extensive trapping and use of the beaver fur led it to be called the "democratizing fur," because even though its trade started as a trickle in 1600, it became a stream by 1650 and a flood by 1700 with the Hudson's Bay Company [Davis, pp. 168–74]. Almost everyone in Europe could now afford at least a few items of fur clothing.

The romantic story of the Indian trappers, frontiersmen, voyageurs, and traders struggling against the elements and against each other has overshadowed the essentially commercial and well-organized nature of the early enterprises such as the Hudson's Bay Company. The voyageurs or frontiersmen have been memorialized as fiercely independent men who lived a rugged life and who struck out from the civilized world in a quest for individual freedom and self-fulfillment. They entered the American heritage as idealized ancestors. Even if they drank too much, bathed too little, and cohabited too casually with Indian women, novels and films glorify them as genuine heroes of North American history.

In reality, these men lived as paid laborers under contract to the company that kept their wages back in the eastern cities and supplied them with everything the company thought they should have. The company even issued them the regulation buckskins, moccasins, and hats which grew into the very symbols of independence for later generations. The company recruiters selected men for their strength, since by contract they had to portage between rivers carrying at least two packs, each weighing ninety pounds, on their backs. The men received bonuses for carrying extra packs. When not backpacking on land, the voyageurs had to paddle a cargo canoe in unison at a rate of more than one stroke per second, with a ten-minute rest after each fifty minutes of paddling. Recruiters sought men of uniform height and weight, because the portage of the canoe between rivers required four men, and a shorter or taller man would have slowed the portage. Although their legs needed to be very strong, they also needed to be reasonably short in order to leave maximum space in the canoe for the pelts. The fur trade was a highly organized and precise business that called for substantial standardization of workers as well as standardization of product.

According to the contract, the voyageur would be paid his accumulated earnings when he returned home at the end of his term. Few men could leave, however, because of accumulated debts to the company, which charged them for extra sets of clothing and for part of their supplies. The company also found it convenient to insist that men who took Indian wives also leave a deposit to provide for the financial support of the wife and children. Since the men frequently lacked funds for such a deposit, they had to continue working. Even if the man was careful to accumulate no debts, wives, or children, he might be jailed and beaten by the company men until he "voluntarily" renewed his contract. In their choice of workers and in their corporate policies, the Hudson's Bay and the North West companies operated as thoroughly modern corporations. They pioneered many labor techniques which proved effective in the development of industrial society and the modern factory in the nineteenth century.

Today in Thunder Bay, a new version of Fort William has been built on the edge of town, and throughout the warm months young men and women flock to it to relive the life of the frontier. They take the names of historical and mythical characters associated with the fort, dress in nineteenth-century costumes, and live the historical role for the warm months of the year. They build canoes, paddle up and down the rivers, hold mock sales of furs, have a stately dinner each day for the owners of the company, fire cannons to signal the arrival of a new group, entertain Indians who set up tipis outside the fort, and in general recreate the life of this early trading post. Fort William has become the most popular tourist attraction in Thunder Bay after ski season. Overweight women flapping along in little rubber thongs pull on the arms of bored children sticky with melted ice cream as the camera-carrying father of the family dutifully records his children against the backdrop of this living history tableau on the shores of Lake Superior. The scene is markedly different from the other world of Potosí, high in the Andes so many thousands of miles to the south.

The connection between the Hudson's Bay Company and modern corporations appears direct and obvious. Just as direct, but not nearly as obvious, are the historical and economic links back to the Spanish silver and the mines of Potosí. The modern corporation is built on the British quest for American silver and gold. Spain used conquistadores to loot America, the British used pirates and private companies.

Spain created the Casa de Contratación, or House of Trade, in Seville to monitor, license, and tax all commerce, immigrants, and travelers to America, but this operated more as a medieval institution than a modern company. Because the Spanish thought themselves far too noble to engage in either manufacturing or commerce, the money of Potosí quickly passed into the accounts of French, Dutch, and British companies set up to supply Spain with cloth, cannons, leather, and other items needed for colonization. These goods passed through Seville but did not originate in Spain. By 1595 the Dutch had assumed effective control over the House of Trade in what has been called a "silent takeover" [Braudel, Vol. III, p. 208]. In addition, many non-Spanish freebooters made great profits smuggling goods into America. Even though the Spanish crown outlawed any American commerce outside the House of Trade, by the second half of the seventeenth century two-thirds of the commerce with colonial Spanish America was in the cargo of French, Dutch, and English smuggler ships [Helms, p. 159].

The commodity most in demand by the Spanish in the New World was slaves, because the Spanish had already killed most of the Indians of the Caribbean and other coastal areas, and they found that Indians from the highlands died immediately of diseases such as malaria and yellow fever when brought into the lowlands. The Spanish ships were too busy hauling off the loot of America and bringing back Spaniards and supplies to be able to go to Africa for slaves. But many British and Dutch companies quite willingly rushed to perform this service for them. The first such British enterprise sailed under the command of John Hawkins in 1562 [Williams, pp. 30–39] with the patronage of Queen Elizabeth herself. Among the commanders working for Hawkins, twenty-seven-year-old Francis Drake performed exceptionally well as commander of the slave ship *Judith* in 1568. This adventure started a close economic relationship between Drake and Hawkins that was to last for many more years, until Drake surpassed his mentor in riches and glory.

From these early trips, Drake realized quickly how much wealth the Spaniards looted annually from America, and he knew that he would never obtain more than the smallest crumbs of it by legal trade alone. Thus in 1571 Drake made his first illegal raid on Panama, attacking it from the less inhabited Atlantic side. During this venture onto land, he glimpsed the Pacific Ocean and vowed to sail it one day in search of the Spanish treasure that he may or may not have known was pouring out of Potosí. To pursue this dream, Drake assembled a syndicate of investors in 1577 to finance a series of raids aimed at the mysterious source of the Spanish wealth on the Pacific coast of South America in the virtually unknown Spanish realm of Peru. The slavetrader John Hawkins quickly signed on as one of the primary investors, and some of his own kinsmen sailed with Drake. John Hawkins also supplied the ship *Pelican* for this financial venture, but Drake later changed the rather plebeian name *Pelican* to the more aristocratic *Golden Hind*. Thus was launched one of the early

British companies that was organized for a short time and for a specific return. This syndicate operated with the approval of Queen Elizabeth, who was quite probably an investor; even though she reigned as queen she lacked the money to finance such undertakings alone [Morison, p. 677].

On February 7, 1579, Drake, sailing along the coast of what is today Chile, reached the port of Arica, where the Spaniards transferred the silver from llamas and mules to ships. He easily captured the poorly defended town, which had never before been visited by an English ship and was completely unprepared for attack by anyone. Drake confiscated some silver bars and one trunk of pieces of eight; then he set off in pursuit of the treasure ship that had already sailed north toward Lima and Panama. He soon captured the unsuspecting crew of *Nuestra Señora de la Concepción*, better known by her nickname, *Cacafuego* ("Shit-fire"). In the greatest act of piracy then known, Drake seized unknown millions of dollars' worth of booty from this one ship. According to the account left by Francis Pretty, one of the "gentlemen" serving with Drake, they stole "thirteen chests full of reals of plate, fourscore-pound weight of gold, and six-and-twenty ton of silver" [Pretty, p. 11].

Traveling on up the coast, Drake paused to plunder various Spanish settlements of present-day Chile, Peru, Central America, and Mexico. Pretty mentions that in one encounter they found "a Spaniard lying asleep, who had lying by him thirteen bars of silver, which weighed 4,000 ducats Spanish." Pretty then adds, "We took the silver and left the man" [Pretty, p. 10]. Even though he affected the manner of a great gentleman and paraded his chivalry and munificence in dramatic gestures such as bestowing lavish gifts on noble prisoners, Drake plundered the rich and the poor unmercifully. He targeted Catholic churches as a special source of lucre on the excuse that the Catholics often persecuted the Protestants. Drake's men stole everything they could and even pulled precious metals and emeralds from crucifixes. What they could not carry away they destroyed on the grounds that it was Catholic and therefore idolatrous and evil.

The *Golden Hind* soon strained so fiercely under the burden of silver that she began bursting at the seams and leaking. Drake then headed for the unknown California coast north of all Spanish settlements in search of a secure place to hide and repair his ship in the summer of 1579 [Morison, p. 699]. Just where Drake landed has long been a topic of debate, but there is some evidence that Drake took his ship into the bay of San Francisco. Drake claimed the land in the name of Queen Elizabeth and called it Nova Albion after the Latin name of England, making California the original New England.

After repairing and resupplying the ship with the aid of the Indians, Drake sailed westward across the Pacific for home. He arrived back at Plymouth a year later on September 26, 1580, the first Englishman to have followed Ferdinand Magellan in circumnavigating the earth. Scholars still debate exactly how much booty Drake brought home from that trip, because the crew secretly unloaded much of it under cover of night. Some of the booty went directly into the royal treasury, some went for storage in the Tower, and a few wagons of it went directly to the queen, who was off visiting in the country. Estimates of value varied from 332,000 to as much as 1.5 million contemporary English pounds; the financial backers of the project supposedly reaped profits as high as 1,000 percent on their investment. The queen gave Drake ten thousand British pounds as his reward for his work, and she knighted him. In turn, Sir Francis gave her a crown and a cross made from the silver of Potosí and studded with the jewels he had looted from the Spanish churches [Morison, p. 720].

Soon these fledgling British companies, such as the one operated under Drake's management, made permanent beachheads in the Caribbean, until then a Spanish lake. Today, the effects of that remain clearly visible in the English-speaking communities that dot the Caribbean islands and run the length of the coastal areas of Central America. Jamaica, the Bahamas, Trinidad, the Cayman Islands, Anguilla, Barbados, Grenada, Dominica, and dozens of smaller islands mostly owe their British character and English language to the early pirates who stalked their waters.

Just as John Hawkins rose as the first of the great English slavers, Drake became the first of the great English pirates. The men worked together closely to extract the Indian silver from Spanish coffers and move it into British ones. Whenever practical, they did this "legally" through the sale of human flesh, but they often resorted to piracy. These British pirate companies lasted as long as the flow of gold and silver continued, about a century. Then the British had to seek new sources of income. The companies that had been formed to transport slaves and to loot the Spanish ships and ports then turned to organizing new companies for other commercial purposes. These British companies established their own plantations in the Caribbean and supplied a steady cargo of slaves to meet the insatiable need for plantation workers.

Trade eventually replaced piracy among the British, and the enterprises changed from single forays into long-term undertakings by permanent companies. Thus, by the time of the foundation of the Honourable Company of Adventurers of England Trading in Hudson's Bay, the king had already given a charter in 1663 to another Company of Royal Adventurers as a monopoly on the slave trade for a thousand years. In 1672 he rescinded this and recreated the company as the Royal African Company, but with the same mission of selling slaves for profits to the New World [Williams, p. 31]. The governor of the Royal African Company was James, Duke of York, better known by his later name King James II. He also served as the second governor of the Hudson's Bay Company following the death of Prince Rupert, and he functioned as the governor of the Royal Fisheries Company [Newman, p. 102]. When James became king the office of governor of the Hudson's Bay Company passed to John Churchill, Duke of Marlborough, who held it from 1685 until 1692.

The original investors of the Hudson's Bay Company numbered nineteen. This included Anthony Ashley Cooper, Earl of Shaftsbury. Shaftsbury had served as chancellor of the Exchequer and as a member of the Privy Council, and he also invested heavily in both the Royal African Company and the Royal Fisheries Company. In 1663 he served as one of the lord proprietors of the Carolinas, and the two rivers that empty into Charleston Bay received his name as the Ashley and the Cooper rivers. Throughout all of this he worked on various schemes of social improvement. This interest led him to employ as his secretary the philosopher John Locke, who managed to write his *Essay Concerning Human Understanding* while attending to the details of his employer's slave investments and writing the socially innovative constitution for the new Carolina colony.

These companies operated on the fringes of the law, performing feats and implementing politics that the king desired but could not officially sanction in his role as monarch. The companies then became the agents to kill innocent Celtic peasants in Ireland or Scotland, sell Indians and Africans into slavery, and raid Spanish treasure ships from America. The king saved money by not having to pay for such activities, and he still reaped a substantial part of the profits.

The goal of these companies was to go into the New World and extract something for trade and profit. To accomplish this, the companies frequently had to build a permanent trade center in the New World. Thus, at the beginning of the seventeenth century, the New France Company founded Montreal and the Virginia Company of London founded Jamestown in Virginia. The Dutch West Indies Company founded both New Amsterdam (later New York) and Albany in New York in 1614. The Massachusetts Bay Company founded its colony in 1630, a decade after the Pilgrims' arrival [Wolf, p. 161].

In all cases the companies that founded these centers did so for commercial profit, a point often ignored by later generations in looking back on the colorful tide of explorers, swashbucklers, frontiersmen, pilgrims, and adventurers who washed up on North American shores. The Pilgrim Fathers first left England to settle in Leyden, Holland, where they found ample religious toleration but few economic opportunities in an already advanced mercantile nation. They consequently decided to move on to America in search of the profits that had proved so elusive in the Netherlands. Their first shipment back to Europe contained furs and lumber to sell [Turner, p. 13]. They were no less motivated by greed than the Spanish conquistadores, and they seemed no more religiously motivated than the Spanish conquistadores, who made a point of carrying priests and establishing a church in every community. By contrast, the subsequent waves of Puritans in their search for profits quickly uprooted all natives and sold many of them into slavery without bothering to extend to them the right to become Christian before being sold or killed.

If an area lacked easily exploited goods such as furs or if the Indians could not produce enough of a needed commodity such as tobacco, the companies sent in their own contract employees, indentured servants, convicts, and slaves to cultivate the land themselves. The Virginia Company of London first settled Jamestown in the search for gold. Like the stockholders of the Hudson's Bay Company, the stockholders of the Virginia Company wanted to find a new Potosí [Hecht, p. 56]. Next they turned to furs, and only as a last resort did they turn to crops. Thus the companies established many different kinds of plantations throughout the Caribbean and along the North American shore to grow sugar cane, tobacco, indigo, rice, maize corn, and some cotton.

By 1670 all of the important parts of North America and the Caribbean had been allotted to one company or another to explore, control, and exploit. Only the forbidding Hudson Bay remained; even though it opened out onto the frozen Arctic, ships could reach it from the Atlantic during the warmer summer months. This became the base for the last great mercantile company unleashed by the Europeans on America. It soon owned land more extensive than all of western Europe and ten times the size of the Holy Roman Empire, which was then the largest political division in Europe. Charles II, who chartered the company, and the stockholders who financed it wanted to find in North America what the Spanish monarchs had found in Mexico and South America—silver and gold. They wanted a new Potosí in the frozen mountains of northern Canada. Because of this hope of finding gold, Prince Rupert, who was already governor of the Mines Royal for the king, became the first governor of the Hudson's Bay Company. But they never found the silver or gold. The bounty of the north was fur.

The British started the Hudson's Bay Company specifically to challenge the French traders already operating from Quebec or New France. The same men who founded it also decided to challenge the Spanish operations in St. Augustine, Florida, by opening trade through a settlement at Charleston, South Carolina. Southern beaver pelts were far too thin to rival those of Canada, so the traders of Charleston specialized in deerskins, which were as commonly available throughout the southeast as the beaver was in Canada. The merchants of Charleston soon met with more success in their competition with Florida than did the Hudson's Bay Company in its competition with the French.

The British traders of Charleston had a number of advantages, the greatest of which was that they sold considerably cheaper goods than the Spanish. The York factory on Hudson's Bay and Charleston on the Carolina coast entered American history as the two first "discount stores" set up in the backyard of the more established merchants of Montreal and St. Augustine. In addition to offering lower prices, the British pursued a single, clear goal: profits. The men of Hudson's Bay and Charleston did not try to convert the Indians to Christianity or to a "civilized" way of life. By contrast, both the Spanish traders in St. Augustine and the French traders in Montreal worked under special constraints by their respective crowns and bishops to assist the Jesuits and the Spanish Franciscans in spreading Catholicism. For these colonies, trade often became only a means of proselytizing and consolidating their religion, since they traded almost exclusively with baptized Indians.

In addition to the money earned through the sale of slaves and deerskins, the Carolinians derived income from service as a primary station for the pirates, who still played a major role in the Caribbean. Charleston, like Belize City and Kingston, gave them a safe port in which to hide and to resupply their ships, as well as a recruiting ground for sailors willing to raid the Spanish galleons hauling the silver of Potosí across the Atlantic to Seville. Whereas the Hudson's Bay Company showed a more modern organization in that it did not engage in either piracy or the slave trade, Charleston combined the newer mercantile practices with the two traditional pursuits of piracy and slaving well into the nineteenth century.

Just as the Hudson's Bay Company's trade extended all the way to the Pacific Ocean, the trade of Charleston extended as far as the Mississippi River and the Gulf of Mexico. Other British trading settlements from New York and Philadelphia down to Annapolis and Jamestown could extend inward for only about a hundred miles before hitting the seemingly impenetrable barrier of the Appalachian Mountains. The Indians on the western side of the mountains turned their backs on most of the British settlements because they could more easily trade with the French through the Mississippi and Ohio river systems, which linked them to the Great Lakes and Montreal. The expeditions from Charleston, however, marched directly into the interior of the continent by passing under the southern edge of the mountains. They found an intricate network of rivers and creeks that made transportation as easy on that coastal plain as was transportation on the network of plains rivers that emptied into Hudson's Bay. Because they were not encumbered by mountains, the traders of the Hudson's Bay Company and those of Charleston played special roles in the development of the North American continent. Like giant pincers, they pierced the middle of the continent and opened it to commercial enterprises and profits while slowly choking off both the Spanish and the French.

Today the great slave market of Charleston, like the Hudson's Bay Company store in Thunder Bay, caters to a mixture of tourists and locals, and Fort Sumter, like Fort William, is staffed for the entertainment of people who wear oddly colored shorts and travel the country in camper vans. The long, low brick building that once housed the slave market has now been made into a series of boutiques and restaurants where the tourists can eat while soaking up a little history. The same types of plastic and wooden tomahawks for sale in Thunder Bay can also be bought in the boutiques of the Charleston slave market, along with tom-toms, Indian belts, and other "native" handiwork, much of which is manufactured in Asia. Unlike the Hudson's Bay Company store, the Charleston slave market sells very large baby bonnets made of lace, the Pawley's Island hammock, and handmade baskets sewn and woven by the descendants of the very slaves who were chained and sold in that building. The ancestors of possibly as many as two-thirds of all the blacks in the United States today entered through this one port, and much of the buying and selling was done with silver coins minted in Mexico and Potosí.

After the establishment of settlements in the Carolinas and along the eastern seaboard, waves of settlers moved deeper inland from the coasts, and older settlers started new companies for the exclusive purpose of selling land and thus settling new areas along the American frontier. The myth of the pioneer family or lone frontiersman venturing into virgin forest to hack out a meager homestead is belied by the thoroughly organized commercial nature of such ventures. The main figure in the settlement of the west was the land company, which frequently operated not only on the edge of civilization but on the edge of legality as well. One of the first was the Loyal Land Company, chartered in Virginia in 1749 to sell land to the south and west of the settled areas. This was followed in other years by the Ohio Company, the Vandalia Company, the Mississippi Company founded in Virginia, the Susquehanna Company, Lyman's Mississippi Company, and the Ohio Company of Associates founded in New England [Turner, p. 123]. These companies blazed a commercial trail through the frontier in much the same way as the Massachusetts Company, Hudson's Bay Company, and Virginia Company had started the settlements on the coast.

As settlers killed or pushed back the Indians, their business concerns changed from trading to starting plantations in the South or large wheat farms in Canada. The commercial interests of large banks and investment corporations of England exercised a close control over the early plantations of both the Caribbean and the North American mainland. As Thomas Jefferson said, an American plantation is "a species of property annexed to certain mercantile houses in London" [Braudel, Vol. III, p. 401].

The Americans drove out many of these British companies in the American Revolution, but the British companies soon found new soil in Latin America. After Simón Bolívar led the South American colonies in their long and bloody revolt against Spain, British companies quickly moved in to fill the economic and sometimes the political void. In the war of independence, the mines of Potosí lay abandoned, but in 1825 a group of British investors chartered the La Paz and Peruvian Mining Association and sent out Edmund Temple to revive the silver mines on Cerro Rico. But the silver was virtually exhausted, and the mines supplied tin rather than silver [MacShane, p. 93].

Other British corporations met so much success in Latin America that whole nations such as Argentina became economic colonies of British corporations that controlled the railroads, shipping, and buying of produce. These companies also monopolized the importation into Argentina of most of its manufactured goods. France also tried to push into the new Latin American world, but it relied more on politics than on corporations. Emperor Napoleon III installed a puppet regime under the so-called Emperor Maximilian to rule over Mexico, but Benito Juárez executed him in 1867 by firing squad as a foreign invader of Mexico and as a criminal usurper of Mexican sovereignty. By contrast, the corporate imperialism of the British thrived and expanded even while political imperialism such as that of the French met strong rebuffs.

England was not the only country to pursue its colonial policies through supposedly private companies. Businessmen in Holland founded the Vereenigde Oost-Indische Compagnie, or Dutch East India Company, in 1602 and the Dutch West Indies Company in 1621. The French followed with the Company of New France or the Company of One Hundred Associates in 1627, and the French India Company in 1664. Edinburgh merchants entered the competition with the Company of Scotland (later the Darien Company) in 1695. But in the long run the English companies, backed squarely by a strong crown and navy, reaped the greatest success, eventually taking over India and Burma in Asia as well as most of North America, southern and eastern Africa, and the South Pacific. These companies also spawned a new, modern banking system through the birth of super banks such as the Bank of Amsterdam and the Bank of England in 1694, as well as the stock market. The first such exchange opened in Amsterdam in 1602, established expressly to finance the East India Company [Newman, pp. 92–93].

By the start of the eighteenth century, the financial institutions of the modern capitalist world operated with well-established joint stock companies, extensive banking networks, and even stock exchanges. The entire economic transformation of the world had taken approximately two centuries from Columbus's discovery of America. The capitalists constructed their new systems in America from their strongholds in England and the Netherlands, but they carried them around the world in their colonial holdings in places such as Hong Kong and Singapore. In The Wealth of Nations, published in 1776, the year of American independence, Adam Smith wrote that the discovery of the New World and the ensuing opening of trade with Asia began "to raise the mercantile system to a degree of splendour and glory which it could never otherwise have attained to" [Smith, p. 591]. For Smith these two events were the most important in all of human history, for it created a world economy. The discovery of America created what he called a "revolution in commerce" [Smith, p. 405].

The capitalists built the new structure on the twin supports of the slave trade from Africa to America and the piracy of American silver. Karl Marx echoed and amplified Smith's assessment when he wrote that the "discovery of gold and silver in America, the extirpation, enslavement and entombment in mines of the aboriginal population, the beginning of the conquest and looting of the East Indies, the turning of Africa into a warren for the commercial hunting of black-skins, signalised the rosy dawn of the era of capitalist production" [quoted in Wallerstein, p. xv]. All of these enterprises depended directly or indirectly on the money coming out of the mines of Potosí and the other Spanish mines of America. From the early commercial syndicates that supported the slave and pirate ships developed the later companies of exploration and exploitation. The Hudson's Bay Company of today is a visible corporate survivor.

These great trading companies helped create what Immanuel Wallerstein calls the "world-system." They made a single economy out of the previously diverse regional economies of the Far East, sub-Saharan Africa, India and South Asia, the South Pacific, and Europe together with the Americas. Goods could now be produced in any part of the world and transported to virtually any other part of the world, and all of this was accomplished using the standardized values of the gold and silver supplied by the Indians of America.

3

THE AMERICAN INDIAN PATH TO INDUSTRIALIZATION

 The German village of Kahl lies where the small Kahl River flows into the Main River at the northern border of Bavaria with Hesse. If you stroll along the smaller river, you pass through a bucolic setting reminiscent of the era of the Grimm brothers, who collected their fairy tales in this area nearly two hundred years ago. The little river meanders across a meadow, past the garden plots of the villagers, around the old mill, and past a few half-timbered farmhouses and barns from which cows and goats amble down to the water's edge for an occasional drink. Children going to and from school cross the river on a small footbridge, often stopping to play or throw stones into the shallow water below them.

If you choose to stroll along the Main River, however, you will see the other face of Kahl. Large barges chug up and down the river; trucks noisily enter and leave a fenced compound on the edge of the river; workers clear some tracts along the river to build monotonous rows of worker housing. And just on the edge of town by the river looms Germany's first atomic-powered electric plant, which opened in June 1961. By the standards of modern atomic power plants with their giant cooling towers and large containment domes, the Kahl plant seems almost a miniature; yet by the standards of the village church and thatch barns, it is monstrous in size and form.

People have lived in Kahl since about 1000 B.C., and for thousands of years before that nomadic groups of hunters made occasional encampments in the area, apparently having found the two rivers a good place to find game. The length of the encampments grew longer, and in due time the hunters established a permanent village and gradually changed from hunting to farming as the main source of their subsistence. Different Germanic tribes such as the Chatten, Franks, Alemannii, and Burgundians invaded and took over the site, sometimes through peaceful intermarriage and sometimes by violent conquest and eradication of the former inhabitants. The Romans came and went, and ownership of the village passed through a long succession of emperors, kings, counts, archbishops, and princes. In more modern times the village fell prey to the French, the Swedish, the English, the Austrians, the Hessians, and finally the Bavarians, who still control it today.

Despite all this coming and going, the way of life of the villagers changed very little for thousands of years. Once the neolithic hunters settled down to farm crops, life took on a fairly consistent form. The daily routine for the villagers during the Roman times differed little from life under the Holy Roman emperors or the archbishop of Mainz. The peasants grew their crops, paid their taxes to their lords clerical and secular, and sent their sons to fight in the wars of both lords. The names of the rulers changed from century to century, but little else did. Great intellectual movements passed them by, and even the great religious changes of the world had minimal impact on their lives. The ancient peasant worshiping the pantheon of Germanic gods such as Thor and Donner differed very little in life-style from the later peasant worshiping the Roman pantheon of gods such as Jupiter and Mercury or the calendar of Christian saints such as the Virgin Mary and St. Peter.

Farm life in Kahl remained much the same regardless of whether the village was inhabited by the Celts, the Chatten, the Romans, or the Franks. A peasant would probably have felt equally at home farming in the Kahl of 700 B.C. or A.D. 1700. In this time the basic subsistence pattern of agriculture—the crops grown, the animals used, and the tools for growing and processing them—remained basically unaltered. The houses of the peasants from the two eras differed little, the peasants moved around by the same modes of transportation, and they ate roughly the same meals.

Suddenly in the last few centuries, life changed radically after millennia of great technological stability. The peasants stopped working in the fields and started to work in factories. They illuminated their houses and other buildings with electricity, and they replaced their horses with bicycles, tractors, and trucks. They altered their diet, and the way they built their homes and educated their children. Within a few generations, virtually every aspect of life changed.

After thousands of years of agricultural life, this sudden leap into the industrialized world seems difficult to explain. Why had the Greeks, with so much mathematical and philosophical learning and such outstanding architectural techniques, not been able to make and use machines? Why were the Romans, with all of their technical and practical knowledge of engineering and their vast array of engines of war, not industrialized? Why could the people of the Renaissance, who demonstrated their mechanical wizardry by making elaborate toys, not make the leap into machine production? What happened to the world in the 1700s and 1800s to make it industrialize after thousands of static years of technological stability?

If we look back over the last few thousand years of the history of Kahl and some of the surrounding communities, we see a clear historic pattern. The rapid sequence of changes which culminated in the building of an atomic power plant began at the end of the eighteenth century with the widespread introduction of New World crops. The American Indian potato provoked the first radical change in the diet of the people and of some of their animals. But the potato precipitated disastrous changes to the economy of Kahl.

Because Kahl was surrounded by so much water, the village had been a major milling site in the area for many centuries. Peasants from surrounding villages brought their various grains to be milled into flour and to be pressed for making oil. With the introduction of the potato, however, the demand for the mill services of Kahl declined precipitously. People ate more potatoes and milled less flour. Kahl entered a period of economic decline and physical deterioration as the mills decayed from neglect.

Early in the nineteenth century, after Kahl recovered from the disasters of the Napoleonic conquests, imaginative entrepreneurs discovered new uses for the mills of Kahl. The mills offered a great source of energy, and this energy could be applied to other purposes than the mere grinding of grains or pressing of oils; the energy could be harnessed to power looms to make cloth. Gradually the mills throughout the area were converted into small factories producing textiles, matches, electrical fuses, and felt, and eventually they were renovated to produce electricity, felt-making machines, and more complex electrical equipment. Finally there was a nuclear power plant, financed by the Versuchsatomkraftwerk Kahl GmbH. In a little more than a century the wooden waterwheel had been replaced by the nuclear reactor. All of this began with the adoption of the potato, but obviously the process involved many more factors than the mere potato, since the Peruvians have had potatoes for thousands of years but still do not have atomic energy.

Around the time the potato arrived in Europe, a cornucopia of other New World crops and products also poured in. The potato freed the mills but gave them nothing new to process. Into this vacuum poured one of the inedible American products—cotton. Some Old World types of cotton had been grown in India and the Near East for centuries, but only very small quantities of it ever reached Europe. This cotton was not only expensive, but weak and difficult to weave because of its short strands. Asiatic cottons, *Gossypium herbaceum* and *G. arboreum*, had a strand length of only about half an inch, but American upland cotton, *G. hirsutum*, usually grew to a full inch or more. Meanwhile, *G. barbodense*, the tropical American cotton that became best known as Sea Island cotton (from the plantations that grew it on the coast of South Carolina and Georgia), could grow to two and a half inches. In Europe the short strands of the Old World cotton served primarily for padding jerkins under the coats of mail worn in battle. In time the uses of cotton expanded to the making of fustian, which was a coarse material built on a warp of stronger flax and a woof of Old World cotton. Not until American cotton arrived in England, however, did the phrase "cotton cloth" appear in English; the *Oxford English Dictionary*'s earliest date for it is 1552.

The long-strand cotton of the American Indians so surpassed in quality the puny cotton of the Old World that the Spaniards mistook American Indian cloth for silk and interpreted its abundance as yet further proof that these new lands lay close to China. For thousands of years before the European conquest of America the Indians had been using this carefully developed cotton to weave some of the finest textiles in the world. Many remnants of these early cloths survive to the present day, their colors and designs intact, after several thousand years in the desert burials of Peru, Bolivia, and Chile.

Traditionally, Europeans wore wools supplemented by leather. They wove everything, from their underwear to their hats, from wool. Only the very rich could afford luxury fabrics such as silk or linen. But the quantity of wool was determined by the number of sheep, and this was determined by the amount of grazing space. Using only sheep to produce cloth ensures a slow and inefficient system that consumes a large parcel of land to clothe each person and limits the amount of clothing available.

As long as Europe depended primarily on wool for clothing, peasants could spin it and weave it with simple home technology. The bottleneck in cloth manufacture was the amount of wool that the land was capable of producing, not the ability of the weavers to make cloth. Since the number of sheep determined the amount of wool for weaving, peasants lacked incentives to develop machines or more efficient ways to make clothing.

This situation changed with the massive influx of cotton from America. Suddenly, the peasants and the weavers had more fiber than they could weave. They lacked the labor to process so much fiber. Europe desperately needed more energy than it had in human and animal power, and the most readily available source for creating new energy lay in the waterwheels already in place throughout the continent. Thus were born the first textile factories.

Cotton production far surpassed the production of wool and other fibers, but several steps in the manufacture of cloth slowed the process. After the cotton bolls were picked from the plant, the seeds had to be removed to free the cotton. This work proceeded at a slow and laborious pace, requiring more time than the actual picking of the cotton. Thus the slaves picking cotton spent more time picking cotton seed out of the bolls than picking the cotton from the plant. This problem was solved, however, when Eli Whitney (1765–1825) of Westborough, Massachusetts, invented a mechanical gin to do this task in 1793. The invention of this twenty-eight-year-old teacher allowed one worker to separate up to fifty pounds of cotton per day.

This one contraption did not produce the whole revolution in production. The change depended on nearly simultaneous developments that increased the rate at which thread could be spun from the cotton and the rate at which the thread could be woven into cloth. Together, the mechanization of ginning, spinning, and weaving the cotton launched the industrial revolution.

American cotton output increased from only three thousand bales in 1790, just before the invention of the cotton gin and the mechanization of the spinning and weaving process, to 4.5 million bales in 1860, on the eve of the American Civil War. In the decades just before that war, cotton alone accounted for the major part of exports from the United States, and it went primarily to the textile mills of England [Wolf, pp. 279–80]. This demand for so much cotton greatly increased the demand for appropriate land and thus pushed the southern planters out of the Carolinas and Georgia and all the way across to Texas within a few short years. In the process the United States annihilated or scattered the Choctaw, Chickasaw, Creek, and Cherokee nations as well as most of the Seminole and some smaller nations.

After the invention of the cotton gin, manufactured cotton cloth became an item that even common people could afford. Until that time it had been a luxury fabric for the rich; the common people continued to wear homespun wool. Soon cotton textiles spread so widely and the technology for making them became so refined that the Europeans were selling them around the world in another escalation of the capitalist enterprise. By 1800, cotton accounted for one-fourth of Britain's annual exports. By 1850 this had risen to over half of all her annual exports, and British factories produced cotton cloth in such abundance that the price fell to only a quarter of what it had been in 1800 [Braudel, Vol. III, pp. 572–73].

Cotton is still the most important and widely used vegetable fiber in the world, and the overwhelming majority of the cottons grown are of American origin.

In addition to the cotton fiber, manufacturing requires a large variety of other raw materials. Just within the textile industry, for example, dyes posed a problem for the Europeans. For centuries they traded dyestuffs, according them the same importance as rare spices. Without a consistent source of cheap yet high-quality dyes, the textile industry would scarcely have developed. The American Indians, however, had also developed a complex technology for producing superior dyes, and the Europeans immediately adopted it. At the time of European contact, the Peruvian artisans used 109 distinct hues that they produced in seven color categories. These craftsmen used only dyes made from natural substances, and they produced dyes of such strength and brilliance that museums still exhibit brightly colored Peruvian textiles over two thousand years old.

One of the first dyes found was the red and purple dye called brazilin, a crystalline compound taken from the brazilwood tree, *Caesalpinia*, of South America. Europeans prized brazilwood both for making furniture and for the dye derived from it. This tree is sometimes confused with *Bertholletia excelsa*, which produces the so-called Brazil nut, but they are completely distinct types of trees. The Spanish called the land where the valued tree was found *tierra de brasil*, a phrase the Portuguese later shortened to Brasil.

Cochineal quickly emerged as the most important of Indian dyes in North America. The Indians of Mexico produced cochineal on special farms and in highly specialized workshops. The dye came from the bodies of the females of the scale insect *Dactylopius coccus*, which grows exclusively on a particular type of nopal cactus, *Nopalea coccinellifera*, a close relative of the prickly pear cactus. One pound of dye requires the processing of up to seventy thousand insects. After the conquest of Mexico, the Spaniards immediately seized control of the cochineal plantations and built new ones in Oaxaca. The European merchants then began marketing the dyes all over Europe. After silver, cochineal led American exports to Europe in the second half of the sixteenth century [Wolf, p. 140].

Cochineal became a staple of the British textile industry, and it provided the scarlet dye for the brilliant British army uniforms, which earned the English soldiers the nickname "redcoats." In time, manufacturers used the dye in food products and cosmetics, in which it still plays a major role as a completely natural dye, but in the textile factories synthetic dyes replaced cochineal at the start of the twentieth century.

The Aztecs also cultivated the small annatto tree, *Bixa orellana*, for its red-and-pink blossom, used to flavor foods. From this plant's seeds, called achiote, the Mexican Indians refined a bright yellow or a reddish-yellow dye that made an excellent cloth dye. Like so many of the natural dyes of America, achiote has also found extended applications in the processed foods of the modern era. Achiote today colors oleomargarine and other artificial dairy products, giving them the brilliant yellow coloring that makes them brighter than butter.

Based on the Indian technology, other dyewoods found in America allowed for new levels of quality in making purple, brown, and even black dye. These found widespread application not only in textile and food use but also in making glass, staining wood, processing leather, making ink, and printing. These remained the world's most important sources of dyes until nineteenth-century German chemists using coal deposits (such as those around Kahl) managed to synthesize new dyes from coal tar.

At each step in the process of industrialization, starting with the supply of early cottons and dyes, the Americas played an active and significant role. In the nineteenth century, industry made great leaps forward with the simple addition of two new products from America—sisal and rubber. Indians used sisal, the tough cord extracted from the agave plant, *Agave sisalana*, to make cords, ropes, and rough bags or rugs. The industrial revolution generated needs for more types of cord and rope binders to hold together large quantities of raw materials or finished products, and sisal proved to be the ideal product. It offered a smoother and finer product than Asian hemp; only the long fibers of jute surpassed it in quality. Sisal became especially important in the development of harvesting machines to mechanize agriculture in the United States. These machines required a superior and very consistent cord with which to bind the grain and hay harvested, and sisal best met the need.

The American marvel rubber, or *caoutchouc*, as the Quechua Indians called it, provoked a series of technological innovations. The Indians of America used rubber for untold millennia in a variety of ways. The Indians first extracted the sap or latex growing in the rubber tree, *Hevea brasiliensis*, and cured it over fire before using it. They made raincoats or rubber-coated ponchos to protect themselves from the rain, rubber-soled shoes for walking, rubber balls for playing games, rubber bottles for transporting liquids, and rubber ropes for carrying and fastening. Even though the Indians used it for centuries and the Spaniards knew of it, Europe had no practical use for this curious substance, for the first few centuries after discovery. Columbus himself was reputedly the first European to see rubber, but he did not mention it in his writings. Early chroniclers described rubber as a sap made into balls which bounced and looked "as if they had been alive" [Poatgierter, p. 87]. For them rubber was no more than a curiosity, and Europe quickly forgot about it in the quest for gold, silver, tobacco, and other more profitable products.

The French scientist Charles de La Condamine rediscovered rubber in 1735, on a research expedition to Peru and the Amazon sponsored by the French National Academy of Science to measure the equator and establish a universal unit of measurement. Suddenly in the nineteenth century at the start of the industrial age, the Europeans found myriad uses for the mysterious substance.

The Indians who first used rubber heated it and mixed it with sulfur to make it strong and resilient while at the same time removing its stickiness and its foul odor. In other words, the Indians *vulcanized* their rubber. When the American inventor Charles Goodyear accidentally discovered the same process in his laboratory in 1839, the way was clear for the multiplication of uses for rubber. In 1827, before the perfection of the vulcanization process, Brazil produced only twenty-seven tons of rubber, but by the end of the century it was putting out twenty thousand tons annually [Wolf, p. 325].

Applications of rubber followed one another in quick succession as rubber ushered in a new wave of inventions. The Englishman

Thomas Macintosh used rubber to make water-resistant clothes and thus invented the raincoat which still bears his name. Shoe manufacturers applied rubber to make waterproof footwear that soon developed into rubber-coated tennis shoes and an array of other sports shoes that have steadily increased in popularity for daily wear. Articles of this material found their way into the making of boots, gloves, hats, canteens, knapsacks, supply bags, blankets, tents, life preservers, air mattresses, and wagon covers [Burke, p. 202]. Such articles had a special appeal to the military, to explorers, and to pioneer settlers in new areas. With this new equipment, expeditions penetrated into the Arctic and other cold regions. European armies launched expeditions into the fiercest jungles of the Congo and the deserts of Mongolia and the Sahara, as well as up the highest mountain peaks of the Himalayas. The rubberized goods loaded onto a wagon enabled pioneers to cross the Great Plains of the United States, push deeper into southern Africa, and open up the new continent of Australia.

Rubber also found use in making tires to cushion the wheels of the bicycle. Without rubber tires, the bicycle was only a novelty, too bumpy and unstable for any practical use. Once it acquired rubber tires it quickly spread around the world as one of the most popular and inexpensive forms of transportation. The same tire then freed transportation from iron wheels on iron tracks and allowed the development of the automobile and all other modern wheeled vehicles.

Rubber went into machine parts that needed flexibility and elasticity. Some of the earliest uses included hoses for machines and rollers for printing. Rubber was also found to be the best available means of insulating electrical wire. Electricity had been known for a century, since the experiments of Benjamin Franklin and others, but until scientists insulated metal wires with rubber, they lacked a practical way to harness it and make it useful. Rubber insulation then inaugurated the era of electrification which began late in the nineteenth century and was responsible for the opening of the first electrical fuse mill in Kahl in 1888.

Tar and asphalt had nearly as great a role in making the modern world as did rubber. From modern Pennsylvania to California, the Indians of North America applied asphalt to baskets or cloth to make them waterproof in much the same way that South

American Indians had applied rubber. The California natives carried water in these containers, which were lighter than pottery and were unbreakable. The tar-coated cloths made excellent tarpaulins for protecting people and goods from rain, and the Indians of southern California even used asphalt to caulk their boats and to waterproof their roofs. Pennsylvania Indians used a number of open pits as early oil wells, and based on these applications the white settlers of the Quaker State opened the first oil wells there in the nineteenth century, thus launching the oil industry.

America furnished more than the raw goods that served as the impetus for a technological revolution. America also supplied much of the new technology itself. The industrial revolution did not begin in villages such as Kahl, in the workshops of skilled urban craftsmen, or even in the factories of Manchester and Liverpool—it began in the mines and on the plantations of America.

The Americas in the sixteenth and seventeenth centuries promised vast resources—gold, silver, and furs, as well as the seemingly inexhaustible agricultural potential for crops of tobacco, sugar cane, rice, coffee, indigo, and hundreds of other plants. But a major obstacle constantly slowed the extraction of both the metals and agricultural treasures from the ground: the persistent shortage of labor. The Spanish quickly impressed the Indians into slave labor, but in some areas, such as the Caribbean islands and Central America, the Indians died very quickly from diseases, malnutrition, overwork, or simple culture shock and grief. In other cases the natives lacked sufficient experience in agriculture or mining to be acculturated into the new Spanish system as workers.

No matter how many slaves the British and Dutch shipped to America, the plantation and mine owners demanded more laborers. Because of the lack of sufficient manpower, the Americans improvised whole new mechanical technologies to help tap the natural resources and potential wealth.

These technological innovations first arose in the mining industry. The Spanish brought with them the most advanced mining technology that Europe had, but it proved unsuited to the unusual conditions of this highland desert. Spanish smelting technology did not work, because the thin air lacked sufficient oxygen at such altitude to make fire hot enough to melt the ore. The Spanish turned to Inca craftsmen, who introduced a device known as a *guayra* or wind oven that had been used traditionally in the Andes. The Incas produced fifteen thousand *guayras* for the Spaniards, who understood the technology so little that for the first two years they left the working and management of the mines entirely in Indian hands. The Spanish seemed content to reap the profits and allow the Indians to use whatever technology and organization worked best [Cole, p. 3]. However, the scale of mining at Potosí, the unusual environment, and the type of ore required a whole new approach and organization to mining.

The next major innovation came in the silver mines of Mexico in 1556, when a miner discovered an amalgamation process using mercury to extract the silver. The application of mercury to crushed rock promoted easier extraction of a larger amount of silver. In 1572, Spain implemented this Mexican technology in Potosí after Francisco de Toledo opened mercury mines at Huancavelica in southern Peru. By 1575 the new mills had been established under Spanish rather than Indian management, and the mercury amalgamation process not only permitted the more efficient extraction of silver from the newly mined veins, but allowed the Spanish to begin reprocessing all of the tailings, or residual rock, from earlier mines. In order to crush the massive amounts of rock extracted from the giant mountain, the workers used Eurasian technology to build hydraulic wheels and install them at the base of the mountain. Within the first century of mining in Potosí, the workers built 132 such ore-crushing wheels. To supply energy to turn these wheels in the virtual desert conditions of the high plateau, the Spanish forced thousands of Indians to excavate a series of thirty artificial lakes in the surrounding mountains to capture the small amount of rain in the area as well as the snow that melted and ran off from the higher elevations in the summer [Crow, p. 271]. Canals carried the water, which then cascaded down a series of sluices to turn the wheels. The churning wheels crushed the rock into a fine gravel, and the energy from the waterwheels also powered a series of giant hammers that pounded the gravel into a fine sand the consistency of flour. The "flour" became *pasta* when the Indians walked on it and mixed it with mercury.

The workers made thousands of bars from the silver in an assembly-line process; they sent these bars into the center of town, to the Casa de Moneda or imperial mint, to be made into coins. In Europe, craftsmen struck coins using hammers and manual dies that they impressed on blank slugs of metal. Such technology sufficed there, where the supply of precious metals for making money had been decisively limited. But in Potosí, the silver poured forth in such large quantities and there was such a dearth of skilled craftsmen that the old ways proved inadequate. In 1773 the Spanish opened the modern Royal House of Money, a series of buildings and workshops devoted exclusively to the manufacture of money. The innovators of Potosí adapted an indoor version of the waterwheel to supply extra power. Because of the lack of water, men and animals propelled the wheel by trudging in an eternal circle. This closely resembled the threshing mills used in many Old World areas that lacked running water. The wheels in the mint, however, turned a series of wooden gears up to eight feet in diameter as well as much smaller wheels. When all of the wheels moved in concert, they produced a whopping blow of a hammer much like the hammer used at the base of the mountain to pulverize the ore. Because of the scarcity of wood, craftsmen substituted the more abundant metals for machine parts wherever and whenever practical.

Using these comparatively primitive machines, the mint at Potosí struck three million silver pesos. Even more coins were struck at the Casa de Moneda established in Mexico in 1732 by the Spanish king Philip V. These coins were shipped out in great convoys that crossed over land and sea. This created the persistent problem of guarding the coins from the very men who transported and stored them. The Spanish crown needed foolproof shipping containers and secure locks that only the right authorities might open. To meet this need, locksmiths and cabinetmakers invented various mechanical trunks that required multiple keys to open and which had a whole series of locks. In some cases as many as twenty-four locks on one chest could be opened by a single key. The large number of very minute gears and levers required for such contraptions pushed the locksmith's traditional craft beyond what had been sufficient in the past.

From extracting the ore and pulverizing it on to minting coins and transporting them, the traditional Old World technology that had sufficed since the days of the ancient Phoenician mines or the mines of Solomon failed to meet the new situation. The Spanish learned little about metallurgy from the Indians, although in many regards Indian technology was equal to and in some cases superior to European techniques. But the great magnitude of the mining enterprise in America demanded new techniques in order to produce silver at a rate that the Indians had never before attained. So much new information about mining developed in these years that in 1640 Barba published his *Art of Metals*, summarizing this new knowledge and thereby building the foundation for a modern metallurgy that became increasingly important with the development of industrialization [Picon-Salas, p. 107].

Potosí grew into something far greater than just the world's largest mining town. It became a massive and integrated operation for the manufacturing of silver coins; it was a money factory. As such it may well qualify as the first modern factory. In other mines at Guanajuato, Taxco, Pachuca, Sombrerete, Durango, and Fresnillo in Mexico as well as Porco in Bolivia, similar factories developed for the production of silver or gold. Later these gave way to mines for the baser metals of tin, copper, zinc, bauxite, and uranium, each of which had its own role to play in later stages of the industrial revolution.

At the same time that the Spaniards were making Potosí into a large money factory, other Spaniards developed similar models of production on the plantations throughout the Caribbean and along the northeastern shore of Brazil. These plantations produced native crops such as cotton and tobacco as well as imported crops such as sugar cane, coffee, and rice from other tropical and semitropical zones of the world. Of these, sugar cane was one of the first, having been introduced to the island of Hispaniola by Christopher Columbus himself. It quickly became the most widely cultivated and most lucrative of the plantation crops.

Sugar cane, *Saccharum officinarum*, has the peculiarly problematic characteristic that its sucrose starts to decay immediately after the cane is harvested. This required the farmers to press the sweet juice from the cane as soon as possible after cutting the cane. Shipping the cane for processing to a nearby urban area, let alone all the way to Europe, as was done with cotton, would destroy the product. Each plantation needed its own sugar mill to grind the cane and to boil the residue down to a crystalline brown sugar. The plantation functioned more like what we today think of as a factory than like the traditional European farm or manor. In the organization and timing of crops, the plantation workers developed novel procedures. Since the sugar cane took one and a half years to mature, the plantation operators had to break the traditional cycle of seasons characteristic of European agriculture. Because of the need to process the cane immediately after harvesting, the harvesting had to be staggered so that not too much cane came ripe at the same moment. This made sugar-cane culture even for the field workers a continuous rather than a seasonal or sporadic activity.

Stanley Mintz describes the sugar plantations as a "synthesis of field and factory" in a form that was "quite unlike anything known in mainland Europe at the time" [Mintz, p. 47]. The cane had to be crushed, and then go through the stages of reduction, clarification, molding, and crystallization in a carefully synchronized and very exact procedure involving mills, giant furnaces, and boiling caldrons. This highly skilled part of the work required about 10 percent of the total workers of a plantation. Mintz describes this as "the closest thing to industry that was typical of the seventeenth century" [Mintz, p. 48]. Even though the final refining of the sugar into a white substance was completed in England, the plantations of the Caribbean were essentially early sugar factories.

Sugar plantations often had attached to them not only the sugar mill but also a distillery for fermenting rum from the cane syrup. Thus the plantations functioned as factories of alcohol as well as of sugar, syrup, and molasses.

The close connection of sugar-cane plantations to factories is seen even in the nomenclature. In Portuguese, sugar mills are called *eghenos de assucar*, which means "engines of sugar." Even in English the term sugar *mill* emphasizes the industrial rather than the agricultural aspect of the enterprise.

The process for making sugar closely resembled that for extracting silver from ore and for making coins from ingots. The shortage of labor and the high cost of slaves impelled the plantation owners to mechanize as many of the steps as practical. The rough terrain of the fields in the era before tractors limited the use of machines in the fields, but the craftsmen on the plantations adapted machines to take over the manufacturing part of the process, thus freeing more hands to work in the fields in cane cultivation. Whereas in the case of the mechanized mines there were only a few dozen major ones operating, there were thousands of plantations, each one an individual factory.

Plantation society pushed the complexity of economic organization to a new level because of the scale of human organization. By comparison, the early factories of Kahl usually employed only ten to twenty workers, and those of England rarely had more than a hundred prior to the nineteenth century. But well before this the sugar-cane, tobacco, and rice plantations employed workers by the thousands. Aside from the army, the mines and the plantations used the largest organizations of human beings of any enterprise known. This type of economic activity represented such a marked departure from past modes of production that it has been called "military" agriculture [Wolf, p. 315].

European companies and their governments insisted that as much of the manufacturing as possible be removed from the plantation and performed in Europe, because America lacked the labor that Europe had in excess and also because the colony-owning governments of Europe favored moving the manufacturing to the home country as a source of local employment and revenues. The tobacco and cotton went to Europe to be made into finished products—snuff, cigars, cigarettes, textiles.

Just as the plantations consisted of a small nucleus of slave barracks clustered around central warehouses and the production area, the European factory clustered workers' houses around a centralized manufacturing site. This new spatial arrangement replaced the traditional organization of manufacturing in Europe, in which individual craftsmen worked in individual workshops or homes. The new European factory modeled itself on the American plantation. The centralization of workers obviated the need for costly transportation to distribute raw materials to scattered households and workshops and to pick up finished goods. Centralization also helped the owners impose uniformity of work and production on industrial laborers much as the plantation owners had already done with the African and Indian slaves.

Some people erroneously assume that the European factory grew naturally out of the traditional European craft system as some sort of inevitable cultural evolution. As Peter Kropotkin pointed out quite decisively, the factory system competed with the crafts system and did not derive from it. He showed how the Swiss watchmakers doggedly resisted the sale of machine-made watches and how the Lyon silk workers fought adamantly against manufactured silks [Kropotkin, p. 132]. The technology of mass production of goods completely contradicted the principles of the craft tradition, which relied on the apprentice working first toward journeyman and then craftsman status. Kropotkin pointed out that in contrast to that tradition, the factory system depended on unskilled labor that even a child could and often did perform [Kropotkin, p. 136]. In the end he realized that the crafts would continue only as a source of goods for the aristocracy while factory goods would be for the working-class people. Kropotkin decried the unnecessary centralization and urbanization of industrialization and strongly advocated a highly industrialized but decentralized mode of production instead. This he felt would be much more in keeping with both the agricultural and the craft heritage of European manufacturing history [Kropotkin, p. 177]. Kropotkin did not explain the origins of this alien mode of production—the alien factory which bore so little resemblance to anything else then existent in European society.

Kropotkin recognized in the emerging factories a condition closer to slavery than to the craft heritage. Slavery *per se*, however, proved to be an inefficient and expensive way to maintain a factory, as was shown in the few attempts made to use slaves as industrial workers. One of these attempts took place in South Carolina.

Along the west bank of the Saluda River just outside Columbia, South Carolina, stand a series of abandoned canals and decrepit locks and a labyrinth of ruined brick walls. Suburban housing has grown up on every side, and young children swim and play among the ruins during the day, while young lovers swim and play there during the night. Partway up the steep embankment from the river is a small cave, partly protected by a large rock across the entrance. A small opening inside the cave makes a tunnel leading down to an underground stream that surfaces sixty feet away from the cave. Local residents call the place Sherman's Cave, because of a dubious story that General William Sherman stayed in it while his artillery shelled Columbia on the far side of the river. A thick semitropical growth has reclaimed most of the area immediately around the ruins, and long vines hang from the trees. Teenage boys climb up the walls and swing on the vines, dropping deftly into the water while avoiding the large rocks that long ago crumbled from the building foundation into the water.

These imposing ruins that now offer such an idyllic playground on the edge of the city once served as a factory staffed by slave workers. Using waterpower from the Saluda River, the factory operated with much the same technology as factories being built at the same time in New England, Great Britain, and even Kahl. The major difference was that African slave labor rather than paid workers was used to operate the factory.

This unusual factory tried to take advantage of the simple contradiction first made explicit by John C. Calhoun. He recognized an inherent conflict between labor and capital—that is, between those who worked and those who owned the tools, machines, and other means of production. For Calhoun, the solution to this tension came in the simple remedy of unifying capital and labor: the person who owned the factory should own the workers as well [Parrington, p. 76].

The slave factory system failed, in part because the owners could not compete with the much cheaper goods manufactured in New England and Europe. The capitalist system relied on paid laborers to run the factories, and these proved much cheaper than slave laborers. Factory owners had to pay only the one person, often a child, in the family who worked, and had to pay for only as many years as the worker actually produced. Slavery proved too expensive a system to operate in a factory.

In contrast to the failed slave factory in the United States, Kahl's local enterprising merchants began to gather young women together to work in the mills by the middle of the nineteenth century. One of the earliest of such enterprises manufactured cigars from tobacco leaf, a form of production that required little skill and for which there was little available machinery. The cigar factory was soon supplemented by the other manufacturing factories that gradually took over all the mills of the village, making them into factories for cloth, barrels, and eventually even electrical goods. One form of mechanization pushed other forms.

Soon the new manufacturing in Kahl surpassed the capacity of the waterwheels to supply power, and the villagers began excavating local deposits of low-quality brown coal to produce electricity and thus increase the power available to them. After they exhausted the coal veins, the village switched to nuclear power to generate electricity. Throughout this process the emergent industries stimulated development of collateral businesses such as construction and thus heightened demand for lumber, stone, brick, sand, gravel, cement, and other raw materials.

The industrialization of Kahl illustrates in miniature the process that occurred throughout England, Germany, and the other European nations. America supplied the raw materials for the revolution, and the sugar-cane plantations of the Caribbean and the mines and mints of Mexico and the Andes supplied the prototypes for the first factories. This initiated the industrial revolution in Europe; later in the nineteenth century a new stage based on coal and its derivatives replaced the first stage. This in time was superseded by the oil revolution when petroleum products became not only major sources of fuel but the source of many new raw materials, such as dyes, plastics, synthetic fibers, and a side array of chemicals.

Had Europe and America not come together through Columbus or some other connection, the industrial revolution would never have happened in the way that we know it. The peasants of Europe, Asia, and Africa would have continued tilling their fields while the craftsmen produced small quantities of needed goods in their workshops. Life would probably have continued as it had for thousands of years. But once the two great civilizations of the Old World and the Americas collided, technological progress exploded, making a true revolution in the mode of production. Soon cities such as Manchester and Paris and villages such as Kahl in Germany and Fort William in Canada plunged into the flurry of development that radically altered the traditional way of life of the whole world.

Without European technology and organization, the industrial revolution would never have started in America; without American precious metals and methods of processing, the industrial revolution would never have spread to Europe.

4

THE FOOD
REVOLUTION

There is only one Machu Picchu, but it guards many mysteries. The ruins of this ancient Peruvian city sit perched eight thousand feet above sea level on a mountain overlooking the Urubamba River. Even though in size Machu Picchu barely surpasses a village, the ruins show a complexity indicative of a much more important place. The stone houses with trapezoidal doorways and simple lintel construction do not resemble the houses of the *puric*, the common peasants, and the public buildings surpass any administrative or religious building one might expect to see in a town of comparable size. The ruins show precision-crafted buildings with the neat regular lines, beveled edges, and mortarless seams that characterize the best of Inca architecture.

The spectacular setting combined with the exquisitely wrought buildings evoked much speculation and much romantic rubbish about the purpose of the city. The North American discoverer Hiram Bingham erroneously assumed that he had found Vilcabamba, the holdout capital of the Inca Empire after the fall of Cuzco. Lacking an explanation, many people assume that the purpose must have been religious and thus have dubbed the place "the sacred city of the Incas." Others claim that it was built as a city to protect the noble women from the Spanish, or that it served as a monastery associated with the sacred coca plant, or as a cult center.

None of this agrees with what we know about the Incas. Unlike the superstitious Aztecs, the Incas did not build large pyramids to perform massive blood sacrifices or pursue long wars to please their gods. Unlike the mystical Mayas, they did not build observatories to watch the endless patterns of the stars or write long, philosophical poems on the creation of the world. They displayed an austere practicality in every aspect of their lives, and they show little hint of religious fervor, no penchant for meditation, no tendency toward either the sentimental or the superstitious.

The supposedly practical peoples of ancient Rome, traditional Germany, and the contemporary United States seem almost like mystics compared to the Incas, and ancient Sparta seems like the home of the frivolous. The Incas' practicality shows in the precise and very angular style they used to construct buildings, in contrast to the more haphazard and rounder style of their predecessors. This same practicality and passion for organization shows in their economic system, which lacked money, markets, or merchants and yet managed to avoid the famine that stalks so many great empires.

In light of this practicality the very existence of Machu Picchu seems all the more puzzling. Why would the Incas build a city and line the mountain with terraces even though there was very little soil there? The builders used the best techniques known to them to make terraces that would last for eternity. Then the workers added layers of rock and clay as subsoil, and from the river below them they hauled up rich dirt over steep embankments half a mile deep. This task would be the equivalent of hauling dirt from the Colorado River to plant fields on top of the Grand Canyon.

The Incas built hundreds of the terraces, all of them quite small for any kind of extensive agriculture. Some of them narrow to as little as six inches in width. Yet these terraces climb up and down the mountain to great distances, and the Incas even built small terraces high up on the facing peak of Huayna Picchu, an hour's steep climb from the city. Such an arrangement makes no more sense than if Americans today decided to start farming the face of Mount Rushmore with plots the size of large flower boxes.

A hint of the possible function of Machu Picchu came to me while hiking around the area for two days with Charles Laughlin, a plant scientist from the University of Georgia. On one of our excursions, we returned to the ruined city by way of the Inca trail from the south. This trail enters the city through Inti Punuc, the stone gate of the sun, perched high up in the saddle of the mountain dividing the Machu Picchu side of the mountain from a dry inland valley. Standing in the gateway one sees two worlds, the brown and lifeless valley to one side and on the other side the lush, emerald-green valley watered by the thick fogs and mists of the Urubamba River far below the city ruins.

As we descended toward the city from this high pass, I stared out at the spectacular landscape. Why had the Incas built the city here at this point? Was it to guard the river? But what was there to guard? Perhaps it was a place to trade coca. But why would they need a monumental city for that? Why had they built the city up so far from the water of the river?

All the while I searched up and down the long vistas of the Urubamba and the surrounding mountains, Chuck was looking at the vegetation and naming everything growing along the path. I found this distracting from the big picture, but as we descended the mountain and passed from one terrace to another, the plants that he named changed. We were passing through a series of ecological layers, as one does on many mountains in the Andes. The mountainside is laid out in strips of vegetation and micro-zones. The place is a scientist's dream—the perfect place for all kinds of controlled experiments. Viewed in that context, the small terraces took on new meaning as experimental patches at a range of altitudes and built at so many different angles facing the morning sun, the evening sun, constant sun, or no sun. They are like a scientist's set of experiments all laid out in a field.

In my mind, Machu Picchu suddenly became an agricultural station. In that sense it was a sacred spot, because agriculture was a sacred activity for the Incas, who worshiped the life-giving Pachamama, the earth mother, and Inti, the sun, who together made the plants grow.

The ancient Peruvians had been among the world's greatest experimenters with agriculture, and they built numerous experimental areas where crops could be grown in different ways. It would not be surprising if they devoted a place such as Machu Picchu to just such activity. Whether this site actually functioned as an ancient experimental agricultural station or not, the Indians of the Andes probably did more plant experiments than any other people anywhere in the world.

Starting thousands of years before the Incas, the natives ascertained how to produce extremely high yields of potatoes from small plots of land. In the modern world, producing high yields has come about primarily through developing plants that can grow in different types of environments and, when necessary, through the manipulation of the immediate environment of the plant to ensure that it has just the right amount of moisture, nitrogen, and other requirements for maximum growth. Peruvians seem to have approached the problem in the opposite way. They sought to develop a different kind of plant for every type of soil, sun, and moisture condition. They prized diversity. They wanted potatoes in a variety of sizes, textures, and colors, from whites and yellows through purples, reds, oranges, and browns. Some tasted sweet and others too bitter for humans to eat, but the latter were useful as animal fodder.

They did not seek this diversity merely for the aesthetic pleasure of having so many shapes, colors, and textures, but rather for the practical reason that such variations in appearance also meant variation in other, less noticeable properties. Some potatoes matured fast and some slowly, an important consideration in a country where the growing season varies with the altitude. Some potatoes required a lot of water and some required very little, which made one variety or another more adaptable to the highly variable rainfalls of different valleys. Some potatoes stored easily for long periods of time, others made excellent food for livestock.

In addition to the potato, the Incas produced other tuber and root crops, such as *oca, añu, achira, papa liza, luki,* and *maca,* none of which even have names in English. The Peruvians grew corn in just as many varieties and diverse habitats, and they cultivated the native American grain crops that in Quechua they called *kiwicha* (or amaranth, *Amaranthus caudatus*) and quinua (or quinoa, *Chenopodium quinoa*).

The success of these early experimenters remains visible today, not only in the variety of food crops but in the extensive agricultural ruins of the Urubamba Valley stretching from Machu Picchu to the Inca capital city of Cuzco. As one goes along the valley, one is constantly in sight of Indian ruins remaining from the Spanish conquest. Crumbling watchtowers dot the high ridges like a row of decaying teeth, and empty citadels loom over nearly deserted villages. Irrigation canals once brought water down from the melting snows high in the mountains to the terraces. But the terraces now lie broken, and rock or mud long ago filled in the canals. It taxes the mind to imagine how magnificent this valley must have been before the conquest. Green terraced fields continued for miles, punctuated by filled warehouses; now, parched parcels of land, crumbling terraces, and destroyed bridges are all that remain to be seen.

As the Spanish armies, clergy, and diseases swept through the river valley, whole villages died or were taken away to work the mines of Potosí, and the rich valley soon gave way to decay and dim memories. This valley of the Urubamba River, which may have supported millions, now has only a fraction of its former population. While these fields lie neglected, the government of Peru, the land of the potato, imports potatoes from the Netherlands to feed the people.

Indians of the Andes have cultivated the potato on their mountain slopes and in their valleys for at least the last four thousand years. Apparently the potato descended from a tuberous *Solanum* that grew wild throughout the Americas and was used by Indian groups as far north as the southwestern United States, where the Navajos made it a major part of their diet. The Indians of the United States and of Mexico apparently were in the process of domesticating their own varieties of this potato when the Spanish arrived in the sixteenth century [Salaman, p. 1].

At the time of the Spanish conquest, Andean farmers already were producing about three thousand different types of potatoes in the Andes. This contrasts with the mere 250 varieties now grown in North America, and of those no more than twenty varieties constitute three-quarters of the total potato harvest in the contemporary United States. Under the guidance of the Indian farmers of the Andes, the potato became the basis for several great Andean empires, the last of which was that of the Incas whose empire fell to Francisco Pizarro in 1531.

The Andean farmers also devised and perfected the first freeze-dried method of preserving the potato. At night, farmers put their potatoes out in the freezing air of the high mountains. During the day the sun thawed the potatoes, and the farm family walked over them to press out the melting moisture. After several repetitions of this process, the potato dried into a white chunk which very much resembled modern plastic foam. In this very light form the Incas easily transported great numbers of potatoes to distant storehouses, where they could be preserved for five or six years without harm. When needed, the potato could be reconstituted by soaking it in water, and then it could be cooked. Cooks also ground it into meal for making soups and other dishes. Today this entire procedure continues exactly as before in thousands of hamlets scattered throughout the Andes. The resulting ch'uño, as the dried potatoes are called in Quechua, still serves as a staple of Andean cuisine throughout the year.

The Incas also used drying techniques on a variety of other vegetable crops and even on meat. The dried meat, or charqui as it was called in Quechua, also found favor among the Europeans as a convenient and light way to preserve and transport meat. The name charqui was taken over and corrupted into "jerky," one of the few English words derived from Quechua.

Just as the silver of Potosí spread to Europe and then on to the Ottoman Empire, Timbuktu, and China to cause a major change in the world's economy, the humble potato spread to the rest of the world. The potato spread far more slowly than the silver, but in the end the potato and the other native crops of America have produced a far greater impact than the mountain of silver.

It is difficult to imagine what Ireland would be today without the potato. What would the Russians, the Germans, the Poles, and the Scandinavians eat? Without the potato the Soviet Union might never have become a world power, Germany would not have fought two world wars, and northern Europe and the Benelux countries would not have one of the world's highest standards of living.

Before the discovery of America, the Old World depended primarily on grain crops of domesticated grasses such as wheat, rye, barley, and oats in Europe and the Near East, rice in the Far East, and millet and sorghum in Africa. All of these plants, however, face numerous problems in their growing cycle. Because they grow on high stalks above the ground, they are easy prey to the destructive elements of wind, hail, heavy rain, and snow as well as to birds, insects, and animals.

For centuries the northern countries such as Russia and Germany suffered periodic famines when the grain crop failed because of unsuitable weather. For as long as the Old World depended on grain crops, the great population and power centers remained in the warmer southern nations around the Mediterranean, where the grains flourished. Greece, Rome, Persia, and Egypt all had successful empires primarily because of their control of grain production. Even a nation as far north as France was able to become a world power and a reasonably good producer of grain. But the unpredictable weather and food supply sat as a permanent burden on the German states, England, and Scandinavia, and on Russia, which sometimes exported grain and then sometimes imported it. These were all societies waiting for their chance to act on the cultural and political stage of world, but first they needed a consistent supply of nutritious and cheap food to sustain them.

This food finally arrived in the somewhat ugly form of the Andean potato. Together with maize corn from Mexico, potatoes were what French historian Fernand Braudel called "the miracle crops" [Braudel, Vol. I, p. 74]. The Europeans by no means greeted this new plant with general enthusiasm. The peasants of Europe despised the new plant. Aside from the occasional side dish of parsnips, turnips, and carrots, Europeans did not eat root crops. They certainly did not want to adopt one as a staple of their daily diet. For them the staples were the grains that they could mill and then bake into bread or more commonly could eat as a porridge, such as the oatmeal of the Scots and Irish or the gruel of the English. This was real food to the European peasant, not a knotty tuber grown by American savages.

European legends claimed potatoes caused leprosy because the potato grew in such a misshapen and ugly form. Some Orthodox sects in Russia called it the devil's plant and decreed it a sin to eat the potato, the tomato, and sugar, because they were not mentioned in the Bible. Even as authoritative a source as Denis Diderot's Encyclopédie of 1765 accused the potato of being tasteless and of causing excess flatulence in the peasants who eat it [Braudel, Vol. I, p. 170].

Adam Smith wrote one of the first defenses of the potato and theorized about the tremendous importance that its adoption portended for Europe. He accurately predicted that increased cultivation of potatoes would cause an increase in production, an increase in population, and an increase in the value of land. Based on his observation of Ireland, which was at that time the only country where the potato was already widely cultivated, Smith judged the tuber to be an excellent food, especially for the lower classes. In his opinion, the potato made men stronger and women more beautiful, and he based this opinion on his observations of the prostitutes and laborers imported from Ireland to London. Despite Smith's strong advocacy of potato cultivation, he doubted that potatoes would become very widespread because of the difficulty of preserving them for longer than a season [Smith, pp. 160–61].

For its first two centuries in Europe, the potato was little more than a curiosity grown in herbal gardens around monasteries and universities and eaten by the upper and middle classes as a novelty food; the masses steadfastly ignored the interloper. Not until the second half of the eighteenth century did the potato finally take root in fields of northern Europe. The peasants grudgingly accepted it only after their rulers forced them to plant it. Frederick the Great in Prussia, Catherine the Great in Russia, and similarly enlightened monarchs forced the peasants to grow potatoes or starve following a series of eighteenth-century famines, epidemics, and wars.

The archbishop of Mainz broke the dependence of the villagers of Kahl on grains through a number of strenuous laws. In Kahl and other villages, he outlawed construction of new home ovens and provided each village with only a single communal oven that the village women used in shifts. The large beehive-shaped oven still stands in the oldest part of Kahl near the church as a historical talisman uniting the contemporary villagers with the ancient community of their ancestors. The building of the communal oven markedly reduced the bread and baked goods available, because each housewife had only one turn per week at the oven, and she had to pay tax on each tray of foods she baked. Taxes on mills further reduced dependence on flour, and additional taxes on bakers and ovens raised the cost of bread. The peasants had to grow potatoes or face severe financial strain and possible hunger.

The monarchs and Adam Smith knew what the peasants would soon learn: a field of potatoes produces more food and more nutrition more reliably and with less labor than the same field planted in any grain. Even today, a hectare of land planted in potatoes produces 7.5 million calories. The same land planted in wheat produces only 4.2 million calories. The cultivation of potatoes also consumes far less calories or energy than does that of wheat. This means that each farmer could produce more hectares of food per worker, or that some of the workers could be freed for other tasks. The potato needed only three to four months to grow compared to almost double that for grains. The potato also needed far less attention and care while growing, and it grew in a variety of soils that were not otherwise productive [Farb and Armelagos, p. 76]. Farmers found that the potato required none of the extensive milling and processing of grains, which necessitated a large capital investment in equipment and transportation. By contrast, potatoes could be pulled from the fields for immediate consumption or stored in the basement for nearly a year before being cooked.

The potato could be used for bread, although that was usually not necessary, since enough grain existed for the making of bread. Instead, cooks could make the potato into many new dishes to replace the limited breads, noodles, gruels, and porridges that could be made from grains. The potato could be served baked, boiled, roasted, or fried or could be made into soups, pancakes, dumplings, soufflés, and pies.

Once introduced into the fields of the European farmers, the potato thrived. Accustomed to the cool and often damp highland valleys of the Andes, the potato adapted easily to the cool and damp climates of Ireland, Germany, Poland, Russia, Scotland, England, the Netherlands, Belgium, and Scandinavia. Of the approximately three thousand varieties of potato grown in America, comparatively few were transplanted to Europe, but there were enough varieties to ensure that whatever region of Europe wanted a potato, at least one type possessed the traits that made it ideal for that climate and soil condition. In Europe only the warmer areas of the Mediterranean proved inhospitable to the potato; there the natives continued with their traditional grains.

In the northern climates, where long winters without fresh vegetables were the rule, the potato offered a new source of vitamin C that greatly improved the health of the population. For a reason still not adequately understood, potatoes do not produce tooth cavities nearly as much as grains. When eaten as processed flour, the finely ground starches from grains stick to the teeth and rot them. On the other hand, when eaten as tough grains, they are very abrasive and wear out the teeth. By eating more potatoes, the northern Europeans retained strong teeth until an older age, and this improved their general health. Nutritional diseases declined steadily, and by early in the eighteenth century, they virtually disappeared as causes of death in Europe except during war [Petersen, p. 442].

In its gradual conquest of Europe the potato moved primarily from west to east. Ireland was the first nation to make an enthusiastic conversion to potato farming. As is often the case when reliable historical information is scarce, various legends arise to account for the origin or introduction of the potato. According to one such legend, Sir Walter Raleigh introduced the potato to Ireland in the sixteenth century on his way back to England from the Caribbean. Another legend claims that the Irish peasants discovered the potato in galleys of the ships of the Spanish Armada washed up on Irish beaches in 1588 after the Armada was attacked by the English navy and dispersed by a great storm. The timing for both legends seems more or less accurate; the latter half of the sixteenth century is usually accepted as the date of introduction. But another century passed before the plant took hold and won the widespread and fanatic devotion which the Irish have had for it ever since. By the end of the seventeenth century, it was the staple food of Ireland [Salaman, p. 222].

From Ireland, the potato as a staple crop of the field, rather than as a mere curiosity of the garden, spread through England, Scotland, and Wales, across the low countries and France, and through Germany and eastern Europe. The Russians did not adopt it very widely until the 1830s and 1840s, but then became no less devoted converts than the original Irish.

Despite the difficulties of introducing the potato to Europe, once the peasants became accustomed to it they loved it. In Flanders, between 1693 and 1791, grain consumption fell from 758 grams per person per day to 475 because of the introduction of potatoes. This meant that potatoes replaced about 40 percent of the cereal consumption of Flanders [Braudel, Vol. I, p. 170]. The nutrition of the people improved markedly and the population grew accordingly.

One major problem encountered when tracing the history of the potato derives from its being misnamed from very early in the English-speaking areas. The Indians of the Andes have called it and still call it the *papa*. The word "potato" first came into English as the name of a very different plant imported from the Caribbean islands. The word *batata* came from the Taino Indians of what is now the Dominican Republic and Haiti; the Spanish made it *patata*, whence came the English "potato." This plant has since been called the "sweet potato" in English, but at the time of its introduction it was known simply as the potato. When the *papa* arrived from the Andes the English mistook it for the Caribbean sweet potato and consequently have called it "potato" ever since. To distinguish between the two unrelated tubers, one is often called the "sweet potato" now and the other is the "common potato" or sometimes the "white potato." In reading the early chronicles of plants and agriculture, it is often impossible to ascertain which of these plants is designated by the name "potato."

With the new calorie source and the new source of nutrition, the potato-fed armies of Frederick of Prussia and Catherine of Russia began pushing against their southern neighbors. During the Age of the Enlightenment these northern cultures wrestled free from the economic, cultural, and political domination of the south. Power shifted toward Germany and Britain and away from Spain and France, and finally all were eclipsed by Russia. Russia quickly became and remains the world's greatest producer of potatoes, and the Russians are among the world's greatest consumers of the potato. Their adoption of the potato as their staple food preceded their rise as a world power.

American foods brought about the miracle that centuries of prayer, work, and medicine had been unable to do: they cured Europe of the episodic famines that had been one of the major restraints on the population for millennia. Even France, the richest country of Europe, suffered acutely from numerous general famines and even more regional ones. The number of general famines in France varied from as few as two in the twelfth century to as many as twenty-six in the eleventh century. Even as recently as the eighteenth century, France succumbed to sixteen general famines, bringing the total number of famines to 111 for the years between 1371 and 1791 [Braudel, Vol. I, p. 74].

As little as an acre and a half sufficed to nourish the average family if they planted the land in potatoes and supplemented these with milk, butter, or cheese. With the revolutionary crop, the population of Ireland expanded from 3.2 million in 1754 to 8.2 million less than a century later in 1845. During this same century an additional 1.75 million Irish left Ireland for the New World. Thus in the first century after the introduction of the potato, the population of Ireland effectively tripled [Crosby, p. 183]. Then when the potato blight hit, thousands of Irish starved or emigrated, because without the potato Ireland could not support such a massive population. Had the Irish followed the Indian technique of planting many different types of potatoes rather than just a few, the effect of the blight probably would have been considerably lessened.

Despite the Irish famine, the population of each country boomed as it adopted the potato. Possibly it was because of this effect of the potato on population that so many people accepted the notion that the potato was an aphrodisiac. The reputed aphrodisiac powers of the plant may also have been due to the tuber's somewhat phallic shape. Its erotic reputation further grew because of its similarity to the truffle, an extravagantly expensive delicacy associated with the rowdy and gluttonous life of the rich and aristocratic.

If we look at the larger population picture since the spread of American crops around the world, we see much the same process. In the three centuries between 1650 and 1950, the population of Europe (including the Soviet Union) climbed from just over 100 million to almost 600 million, a sixfold increase. In 1650 the population of Africa was probably about the same as that of Europe, but Africa's population only doubled, from 100 million to about 198 million in 1950. This comparatively slow growth reflects the slower incorporation of American food crops as well as the depopulation caused by the slave trade and colonization. Asia's population did not increase as rapidly as Europe's but did grow faster than Africa's. Asia went from 327 million to 1.3 billion in the same three centuries. In all, the Old World of Europe, Asia, and Africa increased in population from about half a billion people in 1650 to over two billion by 1950. In addition, tens of millions of people left Asia, Africa, and Europe to live in the New World as colonists or slaves [Crosby, p. 166].

On the world scene, the total population in 1750 has been estimated at 750 million. It reached a billion in 1830, two billion in 1930, and four billion in 1975 [Farb and Armelagos, p. 75]. In recent decades, medical advances have accounted for some of the increase in population, but most of the population growth preceded the medical innovations. Improved nutrition accounts for most of the growth prior to this century. Only later did improvement in public health and sanitation have an impact, and only in the past century have any real gains in medicine affected the population.

The potato alone cannot claim full responsibility for the great population and health boom of the Old World. The American Indians cultivated over three hundred food crops, and many of these had dozens of variations. The people of the Old World gradually transplanted many of these crops from America, and each in turn contributed in various ways to improving the world diet in both quantity and quality of foods. The Indians gave the world three-fifths of the crops now in cultivation. Many of these grew in environments that had formerly been inaccessible to agriculture because of temperature, moisture, type of soil, or altitude.

Some of these plants spread through the world by way of Europe, but most of the tropical plants crossed directly to Africa and Asia. The African slave trade sent hundreds of ships laden with humans across the middle Atlantic to Brazil, the Caribbean, Virginia, and the Carolinas, but they had less cargo with which to return. In carrying food and supplies with them on the return voyage to Africa, the crews also carried American Indian foods and spices, many of which quickly took root in the similar soil and climate of Africa. At a slightly slower pace the tropical American foods spread to Asia aboard Spanish ships sailing from Acapulco, Mexico, to Spain's major Asian port at Manila in the Philippines. Other products were brought to Asia from the opposite direction by the Portuguese, who carried products from their Brazilian colony to their scattered holdings in Africa, around to Goa in India, and on to their easternmost colony of Macao in southern China.

The protein supply of the Old World also increased with the great variety of beans brought in from America, principally from Mexico, where beans, corn, and squashes had been the mainstay of the Indian diet. Different parts of the Old World eagerly adopted one or more of the American beans, including kidney beans, string beans, snap beans, the Mexican frijole, the common bean, butter bean, lima bean, navy bean, and pole bean. In addition, American Indian beans included many which took on very un-American names, such as the French bean, Rangoon bean, Burma bean, and Madagascar bean [Crosby, p. 172].

In Africa the American peanut or groundnut also helped to increase the protein intake. The peanut found a large following in Asia as well as in Africa, but in Europe it never became anything more than a novelty snack, a source of oil, and animal fodder. Even a food as common in the diet of the United States as peanut butter never found a European following, but it became common in West Africa, where peanut butter is mixed with hot peppers and sold in the streets as a tasty and nutritious snack.

Farther north in Europe where the cold hampers peanut cultivation, large amounts of oil and animal feed are made from another American staple, the sunflower, which is native to the

United States plains and was domesticated by the Indians of North America. Next to the potato the sunflower is probably the most important plant that America gave to Russia. Neither olives nor oil-producing grains grew very well in Russia, and thus the sunflower finally gave the Russians a reliable source of edible oil. As with the potato, the Soviet Union is today the world's largest producer and consumer of sunflowers.

Of the many types of American grains, only maize corn found a use among the Europeans. The European farmers learned to grow corn, but most of them never learned to eat it. Only in a few areas of southern Europe, such as Italy, Greece, Yugoslavia, and Romania, is it sometimes used as a substitute for grains in making soupy porridges. Otherwise, the Europeans have largely ignored it. But corn did have a role to play. Many important products such as oil can be made from it, and it makes a nutritious food for most domesticated animals. Potatoes may be eaten by some animals, such as pigs, but not by others, such as cows or chickens. Corn, however, could be fed to all of these animals. Corn did for the animal population of Europe what the potato did for the human population. The new animal food not only increased the supply of meat and lard but also increased the supply of eggs, milk, butter, cheese, and all the animal products that constitute so important a part of the European diet. These foods substantially increased the European intake of protein.

The population impact of maize corn was much stronger in southern Europe than in the north. During the eighteenth century, when corn and other American crops were being widely cultivated in southern Europe, the population of Italy grew from eleven million to eighteen million, and the population of Spain doubled [Farb and Armelagos, p. 76]. The impact on Africa is more difficult to measure, but corn grew more reliably than did the traditional African staples of millet and sorghum.

Corn grows easily in soils that receive too much or too little moisture for wheat or rice. While rice grows best in semitropical zones and wheat flourishes primarily in temperate zones, maize corn thrives in both. Indians cultivated rapid-growing varieties in areas as cold as Canada and Chile, while other types of corn flourished in the heat of the Amazon. Inca farmers cultivated it on the terraced sides of Andean mountains, and Hopi farmers irrigated it and made it grow in the hottest and driest deserts of the United States.

Even though the whites adopted corn slowly in comparison with the Chinese and Africans, they have not stopped finding new uses for it. The many varieties can be eaten directly or made into flour, starch, or syrup for cooking in other products. Particularly in its use as dextrose or as corn syrup it has steadily replaced cane sugar in processed foods. Unlike cane sugar, corn syrup can hold its moisture and thereby prevent crystallization of itself as well as any other sugars with which it is mixed. This unique resistance to drying out and crystallizing creates unusual uses for corn syrup, as in motion-picture studios, where special-effects artists dye it red and use it for blood in their films, since it will retain the appearance of fresh blood for hours of rehearsals and film shootings. This same quality has more practical applications, making corn syrup the ideal ingredient for sweetened drinks from baby formulas and chocolate milk to colas as well as for ice creams, catsup, syrups, candies, salad dressings, pies, and any dish for which moisture is desirable. Corn syrup can also do all of this much more cheaply than other sugars.

In Africa, maize corn and cassava together underlie the great population explosion which started in the last century and has continued throughout the twentieth century. Cassava assumed a particularly important role in Africa because it grows in poor soils that will not produce any other food crop; thus it does not compete with corn or the grains for land. Cassava has the added advantage that its roots can be harvested at any time within a two-year period after becoming mature. Thus they make an excellent food bank that can be preserved in the ground for times of scarcity. The climate and the numerous animal and insect pests of tropical Africa make food storage precarious. Cassava has one major drawback in that unlike the potato and corn it lacks substantial nutrition. Since the cassava root is almost pure starch, one hectare of land planted in cassava produces almost ten million calories, compared with less than half that for grains and three-fourths that for rice and potatoes. Cassava became a major source of calories and an important crop in preventing famine, but it did not improve the nutrition of the African diet.

Asians adopted the sweet potato with the same eagerness that Africans adopted cassava, and it had much the same impact on their diets as the common potato had on the Europeans'. Even though rice offers more nutrition than most grains, it still suffers from many of the shortcomings of the grains. It also showed high susceptibility to both droughts and floods, which caused frequent famines in China. The sweet potato enabled the Chinese to ameliorate the cycle of feast and famine that their dependence on rice had so long made inevitable. The sweet potato yields three to four times as much food as would rice planted on the same area of land, and the sweet potato thrives in weather and soils that kill rice [Crosby, p. 172].

Even though the stereotype of Oriental food is that it is all rice-based, the common people depend heavily on the sweet potato as well. China is the world's largest producer of sweet potatoes; the Chinese enjoy them plain or ground into flour to make noodles, dumplings, and other dishes. Rice is the prestige food of the Orient, but the sweet potato is the daily food for many of the peasants.

America also gave the world some new grains that offered more nutritional value than any of the Old World grains. For the most part the Europeans ignored the amaranth from Mexico and quinoa from the Andes. In the last years before the conquest of Mexico, the Aztec capital of Tenochtitlán received an annual tribute of twenty thousand tons of amaranth grain from its seventeen provinces (mostly in native Mexican varieties of *Amaranthus hypochondriacus* and *A. cruentus*). Because of its high protein content of 16 percent, compared with 7 percent for rice and 13 percent for wheat, amaranth is considerably more nutritious than most grains. It also has twice the lysine found in wheat and as much as is in milk, making it far more balanced in proteins than most plant foods. The Aztecs respected the grain so highly that each year they publicly celebrated it by eating amaranth cakes made with honey or human blood shaped into the forms of the gods. The Spanish interpreted this as a black mockery of the holy communion of the Christian church and consequently forbade the cultivation, sale, or consumption of amaranth under penalty of death [National Academy of Sciences, pp. 1–4]. No matter how nutritious it might be, they already had enough grain crops and did not want more.

In the twentieth century, scientists discovered that Indian farmers in the high valleys of the Andes and in remote parts of Mexico still cultivate amaranth. Now international research organizations such as the National Academy of Sciences of the United States and UNICEF encourage its dissemination to help feed the Third World nations. Amaranth went on sale in health-food stores in the United States in the 1970s, and quinoa followed in 1986, but the great potentials of these two miracle grains of the Indians have not yet been tapped.

Amaranth has become one of the most important cereals in the diets of highland peoples in India, China, Pakistan, Tibet, and Nepal. Cultivation has spread so widely in the past century that Asia now cultivates and consumes more amaranth than do the Americas.

In the marshy ponds that dot the terrain of Minnesota and Wisconsin, the Indians for centuries gathered a water-grown grain which the whites later called "wild rice", even though it is not an Old World rice. Despite the emphasis on "wild", the plant grew under human care, for during the harvesting the Ojibwa farmers dispersed the seed for the next year's crop. The Ojibwas also introduced wild rice into ponds where it had not grown. In this way they spread the plant into new areas, but they also controlled the type of plant grown in ponds by selecting for particular characteristics preferred by various groups of Ojibwas. Thus lakes and ponds became associated with particular types of wild rice.

Unlike regular rice, which grows in semitropical areas, wild rice thrives in the coldest parts of the northern great plains. It grows after passing the winter in lakes that freeze for four or more months each year. This unusual crop has become popular as a luxury food, and cooks often mix it with white rices to accompany gourmet dishes. The full food potential of the plant is yet to be explored. Just as the potato was eaten only by the rich for the first two hundred years after its introduction to Europe and only later became a staple for common people, perhaps one day wild rice may find its role in the feeding of large populations in cold swampy areas such as the Siberian tundra which have shown little agricultural potential thus far.

Today the agricultural experimentation that began many centuries ago in the Andes continues at the International Potato Institute, located in the suburbs of Lima. The modern buildings of the institute spread out over the countryside like the new campus of a community college. Immaculate beds of potatoes in small, neat rows surround and run between the buildings. The site looks almost as though the beautiful mountain terraces of Machu Picchu had been flattened out and arranged in military formations across the plain. Funded by various international agencies, the institute serves as a bank of germ plasm for the approximately ten thousand varieties of domesticated and wild potatoes found in the Andes. In addition to the beds at this lowland center, the institute maintains a highland center and one in the jungle as well. In the bins of the institute one sees yellow, red, and purple potatoes as well as white, blue, green, black, and brown ones. Some are round or oval, others horn-shaped or squash-shaped. Some have smooth skins and others have gnarled skins. No matter how beautiful or ugly a potato may be, each one is carefully protected and nourished for the future treasure it may give the world.

The full array of scientists from agronomists and anthropologists through botanists, cartographers, demographers, economists, and on through the alphabet to zoologists all work together to study every aspect of the potato and its place in the environment and in human society. They study the way it grows, how the peasants prepare the soil, how it is harvested, and the ways of storing it in diverse climates. Looking at so many scientists puttering around the potato beds, working in the lab, conferring around coffee pots, and experimenting with diagrams on computers, I could not help but think of what it must have been like at Machu Picchu five hundred years earlier. I have no special knowledge of exactly what went on at Machu Picchu then, but perhaps the work done there now continues at this institute.

Like their predecessors, these scientists work to expand the range of the potato into new environments such as the tropics, to find ways of growing potatoes from seed rather than from the root, and to develop ways to preserve its nutrition longer. They hope that one day the potato might feed the peoples of Brazil, Botswana, or Bangladesh as it already feeds the peoples of Germany, Ireland, and Russia.

▲ ▲ 5 ▲ ▲

INDIAN
AGRICULTURAL
TECHNOLOGY

The seaplane dropped out of the clouds to pass over a small cluster of houses on a high bank of the Ucayali River an hour's flight upstream from where the Ucayali joins the Amazon. All the way to the horizon on every side we could see nothing but the endless stretch of high jungle. We circled the village once as the pilot tried to make sure that this actually was the community of Genaro Herrera. His government map indicated that the closest village should be San Filipe and that Genaro Herrera lay farther upstream, and even though this air force captain had fifteen years of experience flying the Amazon and tributaries, he had never been to this particular community. Convinced that even his military maps were inaccurate, the pilot gently set the plane down in the middle of the river as a swarm of villagers rushed to the banks to watch us. This was the first visit by a seaplane in many years, and most of the children had never seen one. After nudging aside a cluster of dugout canoes and hastily devising a makeshift dock, we climbed up the muddy bank to be officially welcomed by the apparently bewildered mayor, who stood barefooted in the mud surrounded by excited children and boys clutching machetes. We had landed in Genaro Herrera, the right village.

Genaro Herrera is a small jungle village like thousands of others scattered up and down the rivers of the Amazon Basin. About a hundred thatch houses on stilts cluster around a large open field rather euphemistically called *la plaza*, and to the side of it leans a church loosely made of sticks and mud, now empty except for a large statue of the Virgin Mary. The houses are little more than platforms built on sticks and with a roof overhead. The main furniture consists of hammocks hanging pellmell from the roof beams of each house. Each yard contains a large fireplace around which the women toast their daily staple of the slightly sour-tasting cassava flour. Some enterprising families have converted their front rooms into stores where they sell a few cans of imported food and milk in addition to large quantities of noodles, rice, and flour.

What makes Genaro Herrera different from other villages is that a few kilometers back in the jungle from the village, the Peruvian government operates a small research center. Here the government has cleared small patches of land through slash-and-burn agriculture and set up *chacras*, traditional Indian farming plots. Following the techniques taught them by the local Indians, college-trained agronomists, botanists, and foresters scientifically study the natives' collection of crops and plant lore, their agricultural techniques, and even their building and storage methods.

Poking up from the cleared spaces in the jungle, different varieties of cassava strain to reach the sunlight. This tall and lanky bush that resembles an oversized marijuana plant has a calorie-packed root from which the Indians make flour. Called *yucca* in Spanish even though it bears no resemblance to the ornamental yucca plant known to North Americans, cassava originated in this area of the Amazon, and from here Spanish and Portuguese traders spread it throughout the tropical zones of the earth. Some people call it "manioc" or "mandioca," but English speakers most frequently call it "tapioca" and use it to make puddings and baby foods.

The Indians dig up the cassava root, which they peel and put in water for a few days to ferment. The fermented chunks next go into a sack, which is wedged between boards for several days to press out the water. The partially dried pieces now look something like white gravel. The Indians toast them very slowly over a large fire in pans five feet long. The crunchy flour or farina that results from this process resembles granola, and in this toasted form can be preserved for a long time even in a climate as disposed toward rot and decay as the Amazon's.

Near the fields of cassava plants grow experimental orchards of the trees cultivated by the natives. As parrots dashed overhead from one tree branch to another and noisily watched us, we wandered among the native orchards. One of the trees under cultivation produced fruits the size of large cherries and exceptionally bitter in taste, but it packed in its small fruit several times the amount of vitamin C in an orange. Intermixed with these and other exotic fruits grow several varieties of wild cacao or chocolate trees. The chocolate beans grow inside a large golden-green pod surrounded by a fleshy sweet fruit, which is eaten by the natives with more gusto than the bean.

Swarms of gigantic winged termites dash through the humid air searching for new places to nest. They creep into our ears and noses as well as between the seams of our moist clothes. When we brush them aside or try to extract them, their wings easily fall off and they stay where they are until they decide to look further for a building site. Then they lamely crawl out of hiding to wait a gush of air that will blow their wingless bodies to the ground.

To overcome problems with termites and other insects the Indians have learned to use special forest products, which the scientists now struggle to understand and to reproduce. Some trees produce wood that repels termites and other insects. In some of the jungle *chacras* the botanists now grow special varieties of local trees selected by the Indians as especially desirable for various building purposes. One tree produces wood that effectively repels most insects, another tree makes particularly strong planks, and yet another has durable yet pliable leaves good for thatching. One tree attracts a particular vine that can be moistened and then used to tie together joints. After drying, the vines form a fastener that is stronger than nails and will hold for twenty years, long after nails would have rusted in this humid climate. Still other trees have highly unusual qualities; one produces large quantities of flammable sap very similar to turpentine, and one supposedly produces a sap capable of substituting for diesel fuel in a gas tank.

These unusual plants thrive in their native habitat, but scientists have yet to unlock their many secrets and understand their characteristics or what applications they may have in other contexts. In marked contrast to these plants, some of the nearby fields grow malformed and dying exotic trees such as pine and eucalyptus imported by the Swiss in an unsuccessful effort to grow foreign trees commercially in the Amazon.

Now rather than allowing foreigners to experiment with the Indians by teaching them to raise foreign trees, the government seeks the aid of the Indians to teach researchers how to grow a wide variety of yams, potatoes, and tubers for which there exist no names in either English or Spanish. Like the wood under cultivation, some of the tubers also have unusual properties, such as the ability to make their own bug repellents or to thrive under conditions too wet, hot, or sunny for most plants.

The Indians around Genaro Herrera now teach the scientists how to cultivate and then how to utilize these plants. Traditional agricultural knowledge often lacks an understanding of these plants. For five hundred years, Indian farmers have been teaching others how to grow and process new plants. The American crops required new ways of farming that appeared bizarre to Old World farmers and violated all past agricultural principles of good farming. The scientists working at Genaro Herrera strive to unravel the complex technology of native agriculture and food processing as much as they strive to understand more about the biology of the plants themselves.

The traditional agricultural system of North and Central America centered on the small field called a *milpa*, which was not cultivated by plowing or planting in neat rows. The Indian farmer made a field of small mounds on which to plant the corn. In contrast to plowed rows, the small mound loses less soil to rain runoff and thus helps to stabilize the soil. White farmers in America adopted the practice, known as hilling, and followed it consistently from early colonial times until the 1930s [Sauer, p. 6]. Since the United States abandoned hilling in favor of dense planting, erosion has increased remarkably and thousands of tons of the best soil annually floats away down the Mississippi River system. Future generations may have to return to traditional hilling to preserve their farmlands.

One easily sees these principles in action in many Maya farm plots in the Yucatan today. The farm does not resemble what we might consider a farm but looks like an abandoned area after a forest fire. The field flows like an ink blot across the land. The partially burned trunks of trees and stumps are conspicuous amid the charred earth, and corn, squash, and various bean varieties all seem to be growing at random. Only after talking with the farmers does one see the intricate plan operating here. The broad leaves of the hardy corn plant shade the delicate bean plants from the harsh sun, and the strong corn stalk provides a living stake on which the bean and squash vines grow. The squash vines meander across the ground between the corn and bean plants, providing good cover for the earth and thereby ensuring maximum capture of rain and minimal erosion of the land from wind or water. At the same time the broad leaves and long vines of the squash plant so effectively cover the ground that they prevent unwanted plants from growing. This reduces the need for weeding while ensuring a better harvest. In turn, the beans fix nitrogen in the soil to help the corn and squash grow.

Recent scientific investigation has revealed that the combination of corn, squash, and beans also reduces herbivory, or the destruction of the plants by insects and other pests. The cultivated plants attract predatory insects that prey upon the pests. This limits corn loss without the use of chemical insecticides. Plants that at first appear to be weeds growing around the edges of the garden also attract pests away from the crop plants. Recent studies in modern Mexico have shown that this traditional polyculture increases corn yields by as much as 50 percent over monoculture [Gliessman et al.; Chacon and Gliessman.]

When the first settlers arrived in the United States and encountered this type of *milpa* agriculture, they had to learn farming anew. The European method of regimented lines of a single crop produced in neatly plowed rows proved impractical for either the Indian crops or for the Old World crops transplanted to America. The eastern coast of North America supported one massive, primeval forest filled with deciduous trees that were difficult to fell, and even after cutting they left very large stumps with extensive root systems that defied even a steel plow.

For centuries, however, the Indians farmed the forest through a simple, yet appropriate, technology. To clear a field, the Indian farmer killed the trees by a process of girdling or barking which cut off a crucial part of the tree without extensive chopping and sawing. Within a few months the field was reduced to the hulk of dead tree trunks, which, denuded of their foliage, allowed the sun to penetrate that part of the forest. The Indians then farmed the area for a few years before allowing it to return to forest and restore the nutrients to the land.

The settler farmers adopted the same system, with the exception that they did not allow the land to return to the forest. In due time the trees could be used for firewood, they fell of their own weight, and the root and stump system rotted. Thus after a few generations, the deciduous forest slowly retreated before the advance of *milpas* that eventually became fields suitable for plowing [Sauer, p. 7]. American pioneers opened the country through this adaptation of the Indian *milpa* and tree girdling more than through the ax and plow. Not until the pioneers reached the open prairies of North America and Argentina, where the plow was unencumbered by trees and roots, did it fully come into its own.

Another major innovation that the European settlers adopted from the Indians at first appears to be too minor to mention—the change from sowing seed to planting it. Most of the traditional Old World grains had very small seeds that the farmer broadcast by the handful onto the prepared ground. American Indians knew that corn could be planted only by placing the kernels firmly in the ground. The Indians selected each seed to be planted rather than merely grabbing a random handful of seeds from a bag and throwing them. This process of selecting the seeds allowed the Indians to develop the hundreds of varieties of each plant that they cultivated. Whereas the Old World grains came in only a few forms, the Indians had many forms of dent corn, sweet corn, popcorn, flint corn, and dozens of others. They ranged in color from yellow and red to blue and purple. Some ripened in as little as sixty days and others took several months. Some grew in very wet areas such as Florida and others in the deserts of the southwestern United States. Corn grew in the Andes as well as on the coastal plains, and it grew from Canada to far into South America.

Similarly the Indians grew many varieties of beans and of squashes and other gourds such as chayotes.

This diversity developed through the Indian farmers' profound understanding of practical genetics. To make the corn grow the farmers had to fertilize each plant by putting corn pollen on its silk. They knew that by taking the pollen from one variety of corn and fertilizing the silk of another variety, they created corn with the combined characteristics of the two parent stalks. Today, this process is known as hybridization and scientists understand the genetic reasons behind this process; the Indian farmers developed it through generations of trial and error.

In the case of some plants, it is difficult to determine whether the Indians actually cultivated them or simply gathered them wild. At one end of the spectrum, plants such as corn were definitely cultigens. In order to protect the kernels from pests and weather, the early Indian farmers bred corn to have a husk around it. This husk protected it but prevented it from reproducing without the assistance of a human who could remove the husk. Consequently, corn never grows wild; it can survive only under human care.

Though the cultigen end of the spectrum is obvious, the other end is not so clear. This difficulty in determining which plants are cultivated and which are wild came clearly into focus for me in the case of the prickly pear cactus, which includes several species of *Opuntia*. The fruit of this cactus, called a pear in English or *tuna* by many Indian groups and Spanish speakers, varies from green to yellow and red. Beneath a thick rind the pulp of the fruit is both very sweet and moist, making it a prized treat in the desert. Even today in many of the tropical parts of America with its large variety of fruits, the *tuna* frequently brings the highest price of all the fruit in the market. In addition to using it as fruit, Indian cooks remove the thorns from the fresh young pads of the cactus, called *nopales*, and cook them in a variety of dishes.

Without stopping to consider it, I assumed for many years that the prickly pear, like all cacti, simply grew wild. It puzzled me, however, that the cactus often bordered the yards of Indian homes in a fence of cacti thirty or forty feet out from the house. I had seen this pattern in the southwestern United States, parts of

Mexico and Central America, and right on down through the high deserts of the Andes deep into South America. The pattern held everywhere, but the residents always denied having built their homes deliberately in the middle of a large cactus grove or having planted the cactus into a deliberate hedge as Indians often do with plants such as ocotillo. The mystery cleared up only with lengthy stays in Indian communities. The fruit contains hundreds of very small hard seeds that prove too difficult to remove while eating the flesh and too hard to crack with the teeth. Indians chew the fruit lightly, in effect only mashing it with their teeth rather than masticating it, and then they swallow it. The hard shell of the uncracked seed passes through the human digestive tract and emerges whole and healthy when the person defecates away from the house. The seeds not only emerge in good condition but are surrounded by an immediate source of fertilizer for the new plant. Because people often defecate at a short but consistent distance from their homes, the cacti soon surrounded the home in the form of a perimeter fence.

Even though this does not qualify as cultivation in the usual sense, the cactus certainly does not grow wildly at random. The residents eradicate the cacti that spring up in the middle of the corn patch, too close to the house, or in other inconvenient spots. They confine the plant to long, thin patches that the Indians can easily harvest. In this form they also serve as protection against wind and predators.

Many other plants that at first may appear to us to have been merely wild plants that the Indians exploited often turn out under closer examination to have received some degree of assistance from them. Indians cleared competing plants aside, pruned branches, and sometimes even planted many of these supposedly wild plants. A copse of various fruit and nut trees interspersed with berry bushes may have been viewed as a godsend by many earlier European explorers or pioneers when in fact Indians had carefully tended the plants for generations with as much tender care as an English gardener. Unlike English garden plants, however, the plants grew in what appeared to be a natural arrangement and had not been planted, tied, bent, and pruned into rigid military formations.

****

As ingenious as the American *milpa* system is, it was not the only farming system developed by the Indians nor even the first one encountered by Columbus and his crew. In South America and throughout most of the Caribbean islands the Indians developed a completely different system of agriculture, called the *conuco* in the Arawakian languages. Unlike the *milpa* and all the Old World systems of agriculture, the *conuco* used no seeds. Instead these farmers had spent millennia perfecting the growing of crops from cuttings and from root sprouts. The plants grown here include cassava, many varieties of sweet potatoes (*Ipomoea batatas*), peach palms or pejibae (*Bactris utilis*), yams (*Dioscorea trifida*), and pineapples (*Ananas comosus*). The *conucos* also contained plants that have not been much used by outsiders, such as the racacha, *Arracacia xanthorrhiza*, which resembles a parsnip; aroids, *Xanthosoma yautia* and *X. malanga*; and arrowroots, such as *Maranta arundinacea* and *Calathea allouia*.

This form of cultivation thrives better in the tropics, where new plantings can be made throughout the year and harvested steadily. By contrast, the Eurasian winter confined planting and harvesting to specific seasons. The Indian farmers had practiced this type of agriculture for so long that in many cases the seeds had virtually disappeared or become vestigial. For the most part these plants of the *conuco* have remained tropical and spread around the world only in the warmer areas without acquiring a market in the temperate zones.

The *conuco* methods have proved quite valuable and have some novel applications, as was recently shown to me on a visit to the farm of Elias Sánchez outside of Tegucigalpa, Honduras. Like many Third World farmers, Señor Sánchez liked the hybrid tomatoes developed in recent years in the United States. Unfortunately, the developers of the hybrids charge high prices for the seeds. Because the plant is a hybrid, each generation of the plant requires the purchase of a new set of seeds. The farmers can produce the tomatoes but they cannot produce the seeds. Mr. Sánchez, however, applied the traditional *conuco* methods to reproduce hybrid tomatoes from cuttings of tomato plants, and at the time of my visit at the end of 1986, he had cloned the original tomatoes for thirteen generations with no degeneration of the plants. The potential for this technologically simple way of cloning mostly seems appropriate to the poorer countries, where labor is more plentiful than capital, but it probably has a variety of still-undiscovered advantages for temperate-climate agriculture as well.

The Indian farmers who developed these complex ways of reproducing plants through cuttings and through careful seed selection rather than broadcasting could control the variation in their plants and thus manipulate the genetic composition of them. Without question the Indians were the world's greatest plant breeders, and their knowledge rested largely on the techniques they used for planting seeds or cuttings rather than broadcasting the seeds. From this firm and practical base of plant manipulation the modern sciences of genetics and plant breeding have developed. Without the treasure of diversity created by the trial-and-error methods of early Indian farmers, modern science would have lacked the resources with which to start. The limited agricultural background of the Old World would have been far too meager and would have required centuries more of research before science reached its present level.

Together with the genetic development of so many different kinds of plants, the Indian farmers acquired a thorough knowledge of agronomy and ways to manage the soil. Peruvian farmers restored the vitality of the land through fertilizers. None of the fertilizers proved more effective than guano, the droppings of seabirds that littered the coasts of Peru. The Incas protected guano as a prized natural resource. In order to build up the guano deposits, Inca law specified death as the punishment for anyone who killed one of the seabirds or who approached their nesting areas during the laying season. The Incas divided the guano areas into districts clearly marked with boundary stones. A group of farmers was assigned to each of the guano areas. They could enter only the area assigned to them, and no one else was permitted into their area. Each farmer was allowed only as much guano as he needed for his own fields [Vega, pp. 158–59].

Through careful management, the guano fields became virtual mountains of white fertilizer. The Spaniards, however, lacked the historical and environmental perspective of the Incas and permitted haphazard exploitation and destruction of the deposits. In the early eighteenth century the Europeans finally discovered the value of the guano for their own agriculture when some cunning businessmen under Francisco Quiroz thought to ship a load of it to England for a trial sale. The nitrogenous fertilizer seemed a miraculous cure for the depleted British lands, and it caused a quick escalation in crop yields for British farmers.

Estimates at the time gave the guano a depth of approximately one hundred feet. Between 1840 and 1880, Peru exported to Europe eleven million tons of guano valued at $600 million [Werlich, p. 79]. This bonanza for the Peruvian government gave it the highest rate of exports of any South American country in the nineteenth century and inaugurated an era of prosperity and enlightenment known as the Age of Guano. In this way modern Peruvians arose from the treasured patrimony left them by their Inca predecessors.

The guano stimulated as much excitement among North American farmers as among the Europeans, but Yankee farmers resented the high prices charged by the Peruvian monopoly. Tensions between the United States and Peru reached such a strained point that the two nations severed relations in 1860, and the United States threatened to seize two of the guano islands. Had civil war not broken out in the United States and distracted both the farmers and Washington, there might easily have been a guano war between the United States and Peru [Werlich, p. 90].

Guano entered Peruvian history as the most valuable cash resource that the nation had found since the Spanish had looted its gold and silver and since they had lost Potosí to the newly formed Bolivian Republic. The "discovery" of guano by European agriculture in the nineteenth century initiated modern farming in Europe. The nitrogen-rich substance not only stimulated crop yields but increased research interest in fertilizers as well. The guano age marked the beginning of modern agriculture and eventually led to artificial fertilizers made from other resources.

The Indians understood the workings of other fertilizers as well as guano. They harvested the numerous anchovies off the Peruvian coast, and after eating the flesh, the Indians buried the heads in the ground when they planted their crops. In the twentieth century, this Indian technique has been expanded to a massive scale; the dried anchovies sold as fish meal for fertilizers and for animal fodder constitute a major Peruvian export today.

Indians not only gave the world a whole new set of crops and taught the world how to grow them, but also developed the technology for processing the plants into food. In the case of corn it was drying as a way to preserve it and then grinding it into flour. Drying and grinding formed the basic technologies of food processing throughout the Americas from the freeze-dried potatoes and the jerky meat of the Andes to the peppers and corn of North America, but, as I discovered in the Amazon jungle, this seemingly simple process often needed great elaboration for some products.

Three companions and I had an afternoon in a motorized canoe on the Mamore River near the Brazil–Bolivia border. We had gone four hours without passing a single hut since our last stop, where an Indian woman had fried us a batch of *pacu* fish. In the heat we had become steadily more thirsty and eventually quite hungry. Even though it was not raining that day, it was in the middle of the rainy season and the river rushed along at twice its normal size and was full of floating bushes, trees, and dead animals that together with the sediment in the water made it much too unhealthy to drink.

At long last our guide turned the canoe into a small creek and took us past an inland lake to a high embankment at the top of which was a small Indian village. Because most of the inhabitants were resting from the heat in the shade behind their huts, they did not come out to meet us. Contrary to what most outsiders think of as "the law of the jungle," we knew that that law permitted us to help ourselves to eat any fruit on or under the trees, but forbade us to carry any away without first paying for it or to bother any part of the harvest that was being processed in some way. We immediately picked the large pods of the cacao tree, cracked them against the tree trunk, and started eating them. These pods look like slightly oblong acorn squash in size and color, and the ribbing of the shell pops open to reveal a soft white pulp of flesh which is very moist but tastes nothing like chocolate. The creamy fruit quickly slaked our thirst and curbed our appetites.

Only after we had recovered from the hot trip on the river did we visit the Indian families in the community. The village and the orchards of cacao, oranges, bananas, and plantains all flowed into one another without any barriers between the orchards, the working areas, and the residences. All of it seemed to be one organic entity. On this day, one Indian couple and their children sat behind their hut curing cacao. The Indians gathered a large pile of cacao fruit, and sitting beneath the trees they split open each pod. Because the seeds, or beans as we usually call them, are so thoroughly intertwined in the fruit of the pod, they are too slippery to remove with the fingers. Instead the members of the family ate the fruits and extracted the seeds with their teeth. They sucked the beans from the slippery fruit and then spat them out into a small pile. One of the children took the growing pile of beans out of the shade to spread them out on a high wooden bench in the sun, where they dry for several days. The bench sat high enough to keep animals away, but insects crawled over them, eating the remaining bits and pieces of fruit still attached. After several days of drying in the sun and being turned regularly to ensure even exposure, the beans were toasted in large pans over an open fire.

The Indian woman toasting the beans that day used a delicate and precise process requiring just the right temperature and just the right speed for shaking the beans. Too much heat would have burned them and ruined the chocolate, too little would have left them raw.

When the toasted beans had cooled, the man fed them into a manual grinder that rendered them into a thick but dry paste. The children then scooped the paste into balls and wrapped the balls into packets of banana leaves. The next time the family went to market, they would take the packets of cacao with them in the canoe to exchange for other foods or manufactured items. For those Indians the chocolate amounted to cash; it was too valuable a commodity for them to eat it themselves. Even the toddlers unable to talk knew to spit out the cacao seeds when eating the fruit.

Though none of these steps demanded very complicated equipment, the processing of the cacao bean still involved a sophisticated technological procedure, from the extraction of the seeds through drying, roasting, grinding, and packaging. Just finding the cacao pods wild in the woods and eating them the way my companions and I did was far removed from making chocolate. It took the Indians many centuries not only to learn to cultivate the plant but also to develop the appropriate technology for making the fruit into a very different type of product. By and large the Europeans borrowed this technology, and even though they could often improve on it with new tools for grinding and for other steps in the process, the process remained the same. Cacao beans grown today in large plantations throughout tropical South America and the English-speaking countries of western Africa go through the same steps, even though the drying and roasting may be done in large mechanized mills rather than in small Indian villages where people sit around in the shade to make the chocolate. In Hershey, Pennsylvania, I have seen mountains of roasted and ground cacao that surpassed in quantity what a jungle village could produce in a generation, but the final product looked and tasted identical to me.

The extraction of vanilla requires an even lengthier and more complicated process than the making of chocolate. The delicate vine *Vanilla planifolia* has very small flowers, which the Indians early learned to fertilize by hand. The tasteless pods, which are often called beans, have to be cured and then are spread out to dry and age for four or five months in order to release the flavor. The Spanish were much enamored with the plant when they found it, and because of the delicate form and shape of the pod they named it *vanilla*, or "little sheath," a diminutive derivation of the Latin word *vagina*.

Similarly complex technological procedures underlie the processing of many native American crops. In Central America and Mexico the simple tortilla results from a nutritionally delicate and sophisticated process. Indian women soak the corn in water to which they add lime or ashes to produce *nixtamal*. Later the women put the *nixtamal* on a stone metate and grind it with another stone to yield *masa*, which they make into tortillas. Twentieth-century nutritional research has revealed that soaking the corn in a heated alkali solution, as these women have done for centuries, changes it into a form that allows the human body to absorb the maximum amount of niacin in the corn, increases the calcium in the corn, and makes the protein more easily used by the human body [Bryant et al., p. 46].

Many varieties of corn have thick hulls protecting each corn kernel. They are often too difficult to grind and too thick to eat when boiled; therefore they must be removed. Removing each hull by hand obviously costs too much time and effort, but some ancient Indians discovered that lye would eat away the hull and not damage the interior. Such lye could be easily obtained from wood ashes. Thus the Indian cooks learned to soak the corn in a solution of water and wood ashes. The Indians called the hulled corn *hominy* in the Algonquian language or *mote* in Latin America; it is sometimes called "lye corn" by English speakers. Indians ate the hominy as it was or dried it and ground it to make hominy grist, which became so popular in the American south as grits, a completely Indian dish.

For some reason, people in the north never learned to like either hominy or grits, but they continued to experiment with these Indian dishes. Finally, Dr. Will K. Kellogg of Battle Creek, Michigan, discovered that he could take the corn, flatten it into a flake, and then toast it. This one innovation of flaking the corn rather than grinding it created the first corn flakes and the start of the American breakfast-cereal industry. The corn flake, hominy grits, the tortilla, and the tamale all share a close historical and nutritional position in American society whether one looks at the Americas today or the Americas of a millennium ago.

Indians also developed the technology for tapping the maple tree, extracting the sap, and processing it into syrup and into maple sugar, a process unlike any used in the Old World. From the Indians the settlers learned how to make dried red pepper as well as how to extract the essences of a wide variety of mints, wintergreens, and other spices and flavorings. They developed the long process of grating, pressing, and washing the poisonous varieties of cassava in order to remove the hydrocyanic acid. These same Indian kitchen chemists found that the hydrocyanic acid could be broken down by heating it, and in this state the chemical could partially dissolve hard meats and yet preserve them from rotting. This solution from the cassava plant is still used in the United States in meat tenderizers and sauces.

America made a profound and extensive impact on the world's diet from fruits and nuts to vegetables and oils. But there is one major part of the diet in which the New World made no change: in meat and animal products such as milk, cheese, butter, lard, eggs, and gelatin. Whereas the Old World had domesticated a large array of animals, including horses, donkeys, cows, goats, sheep, pigs, water buffalo, elephants, camels, ducks, geese, chickens, and pigeons, the Americas were amazingly bereft of such animals. The few large animals in the Americas, such as the bison, bear, deer, elk, and moose, roamed wild and tended to live in the more inaccessible parts of the continent away from the clusters of human habitations. Indians hunted these animals and they traded the meat and fat, but this was only a minor part of the Indian's diet except in the few areas where farming was not practical.

Domesticated animals in America included only the turkey, duck, dog, guinea pig, and llama. Both the llama and the guinea pig were native to the Andes, but the llama found it very difficult to live outside the high altitudes. It does produce milk and meat, but in nothing approaching the volume of Old World cows and goats or even the llama's cousin the camel. In comparison to the llama, a cow is a virtual milk and meat factory.

Residents of the Andes still eat the guinea pig with great gusto, but it lacked appeal to people outside this area. The Europeans never adopted it as a food, because the European rabbit was larger and could live under more varied conditions. The Europeans also had a long-standing aversion to eating rodents except in the most dire of circumstances.

Only the American turkey found some following in the Old World, since it resembled a larger version of the well-known chicken. Even so the turkey never replaced the chicken. The turkey, like the guinea pig, acquired an exotic name reflecting an assumed origin in some faraway place such as Turkey or the Guinea Coast of Africa, although both are exclusively American in origin.

The Incas also kept ranches of domesticated rheas, the South American ostrich. Even though they ate the bird, they raised it for its long, soft feathers and for the leather made from its skin rather than for its meat. The Spanish found little use for the rhea other than hunting it, and the ranches soon fell into ruin while hunters almost made the bird extinct.

The spread of American foods around the Old World began in 1492, when Columbus gathered the first plants to take with him back to Spain, and the process has not yet stopped. Today in remote spots such as Genaro Herrera on the Ucayali River, the quest continues not merely for new crops but for new food technologies to feed the world. Day after day the local Indians, mestizos, and scientists laboriously gather and catalogue the plants cultivated in the area, plant them in various experimental formations, and try to get a stock of germ plasm which might be sent to other stations for further testing under other conditions. At the same time they catalogue all of the Indian techniques and procedures for using these plants.

At the Talavaya Center in Santa Fe, New Mexico, scientists work to recover some of the high-yield corns that the Hopis grew two hundred years ago. The Hopis became experts in cultivating corn, particularly their blue corn, which grows low to the ground, thus conserving energy and water that would be wasted producing luxuriant stalks or leaves. By channeling all of the plant's energies into the production of the corn cob, the Hopis grew a cob a foot and a half long. Scientists now study the Hopi cultivation technology in hopes of taking this blue corn that grows so well in the deserts of the southwestern United States and trying to find ways to grow it in Ethiopia and throughout the drought-ridden Sahel of Africa. In the same area scientists are looking at the dry-farm melons of the Indians as well as at their red, pink, and turquoise corns.

Scientists keep finding new varieties of plants grown in remote enclaves of land in the least hospitable parts of the Amazon, in high Mexican valleys, on Dakota Indian reservations, and along swampy creeks in Costa Rica. Only in the twentieth century did science begin to unlock the complex reasoning underlying Indian agricultural and food-processing technology. As science turns its attention more fully to these questions, it may turn out that the American food revolution has only just begun.

Despite all the technological innovations of the American Indians and their history as the world's greatest farmers, today few of them benefit from this largess. Too many of them live like the families along the Mamore River who eat chocolate fruits and spit out the seeds for people in richer countries when they should be growing more corn and plantains. International market trends have warped their world so that it becomes more difficult for them to practice their traditional agriculture.

This showed clearly in the family that I lived with for a short time on the Madre de Dios River in Peru. Hernán and his wife, Viviana, are highland Indians sent into the jungle as colonists after the failure of the agrarian reforms of the government to feed the highland population. Hernán took a piece of jungle an hour upriver from a village of four hundred Huarayos Indians and two days by motorized canoe from Puerto Maldonado, the closest town with a market and such amenities as gasoline and electricity.

After clearing the jungle along the riverbank with a machete and then burning the plants, Hernán built his family a home, a platform raised about a foot off the ground and covered with a thatched roof. Viviana cooks in a hole in the ground, and the family uses the river as toilet, bathtub, and drinking supply even though it teems with caimans, electric eels, sting rays, and piranha. Once he had built a home, Hernán started the laborious clearing of the jungle to plant his crops. A government development scheme that first lured him into the area encouraged him to grow bananas, which were a good export crop.

One night as we sat around the fire chewing chunks of a badger he had killed that afternoon, Hernán explained his situation to me. "The jungle has everything except capital. We have land and water and plants, and I have the labor, but there is no money." The government program offered him capital in the form of a small loan. But he could use the loan only to buy fertilizers, pesticides, and equipment in Puerto Maldonado. To Hernán, the town bankers, government officials, and merchants form one tight and powerful group. He received the government-backed loan but at their insistence used it to buy a pressurized insecticide applicator and a large supply of insecticides imported to the jungle by air from Lima.

The cost of the equipment far exceeded the average annual income of a farmer in the area, but the best scientific knowledge of the modern world backed it up. Today, the insecticide applicator sits like a family icon in a place of honor under the thatched roof. The applicator tank is their only piece of modern technology for a family that would love to have a gasoline motor for their canoe, a chain saw to cut down the trees, or a pump to haul water up the steep and very muddy riverbanks. Once the initial supply of insecticide had been applied, Hernán never again had the money to buy any more. He produced a fair-sized crop of bananas and plantains, and he had a choice of selling them to a passing canoe or else paying for passage on such a canoe and taking them to Puerto Maldonado to sell them. He chose the second alternative, and sold them for about three cents a kilogram. The bananas brought less money than the insecticide to protect them had cost. He was now in debt to the bank and had used what little money he had on the transportation of the bananas to Puerto Maldonado.

Today Hernán is learning from the Indians how to live in the jungle. Even though he is a colonist sent by the government to modernize jungle agriculture, he now feeds his family by hunting and fishing and gathering the large pods of Brazil nuts that grow in the jungle. But even as Hernán has learned to live from the jungle and river, he is still faced with the problem of paying the several hundred dollars he still owes the bank from his investment in modern farming. His only solution has been to chop down the hardwood trees of the jungle and drag them down to the water, where he can sell them to a passing lumberman. Even he realizes that in chopping down the forest he is destroying the source of his family's food. Already his hunting trips require most of a day to find meat that will last for three days, but without the trees no animals and no Brazil nuts will remain. "We will have to go somewhere else; perhaps we will go up another river to live."

Research projects such as the ones at Genaro Herrera and the International Potato Institute represent isolated attempts to learn from the natives. Hernán and his family represent the much more common situation of the Indian today. They have been given new crops to grow using expensive (and usually petroleum-based) insecticides and fertilizers that themselves require expensive equipment to operate. The results have often been devastating. The Indians used in this manner today often become tied into a complicated network of economic forces that keep them very poor and working to produce food for urban elites and for foreigners.

6

THE CULINARY REVOLUTION

The small port of Dire on the Niger River lies at the southern edge of the Sahara. In this part of the desert, temperatures easily reach 130 degrees Fahrenheit in the summer and at night barely dip below 100 degrees. Very little rain falls in the best of years, and some years see no rain. Severe dust storms harass the area at the end of the long, dry winter and turn day into virtual night. In April, even in years with good harvests, the young children, the elderly, and the weak start dying from malnutrition; in the years of drought, otherwise healthy people also die from starvation.

The mud houses of Dire surround a small mud mosque and a large market square filled with blue-veiled Tuaregs on their camels and with southerners who have ventured north to trade millet, wheat, and firewood for the slabs of Saharan salt and the dried dates of the nomadic Tuaregs. On a trip there I stayed in the home of one of these southerners, a successful Bambara merchant called Mamadou. He owned several small shops and ruled a large family compound. Behind unadorned and window-less walls of mud guarded by a thick metal door with locks the size of coconuts, his family occupied a dozen rooms, all of which opened onto a central courtyard. The courtyard contained a deep well, a squat privy in one corner, a kitchen and washroom, two male goats, and several large barrels of kerosene and gasoline, as well as storerooms of food and other merchandise.

Mamadou lived with his two wives and ten children as well as a woman and child euphemistically called servants in English, but belonging to a hereditary class of serving women usually called captives or slaves, although such terms are now frowned upon by the government. Even though the merchant speaks Bambara, Arabic, and French creole, as well as several local dialects, he remains unschooled and illiterate; clerical work is beneath his dignity as a successful merchant. He depends on a neighborhood youth to read him the occasional letter, government notice, or invoice that he receives.

Moroccan blankets striped in bold bands of green, yellow, and red decorate the floor in the main room of his compound. A foam-rubber mattress lies shoved into one corner piled with dirty clothes, and a single chair rests in another. In this room Mamadou entertains the frequent guests who come to trade with him. He serves them coffee or tea, feeds them, and, if they wish to stay the night, offers them the mattress in the corner. One evening when a friend and I were there with an Arab merchant from Timbuktu and his two Songhai assistants, we were all entertained in the traditional and lavish style of desert hospitality. The evening began when the women brought in a kerosene lamp and buckets of hot water, and each man in turn stepped into a small alcove to wash the dust and grime of the Sahara from his body. After all the men had bathed, the women returned with a large pot of goat meat and seven loaves of long bread. The host broke the bread and handed each guest half a loaf, and the men drew in around the communal pot and began to dip small chunks of bread into the spicy sauce, taking care not to get any of the food on their fingers. The host then fished out fatty pieces of goat that he fed to each of us in turn. A pot of sliced tomatoes with green and red bell peppers followed the meat dishes, and the meal ended with coffee thickened with sugar to the consistency of syrup. After this the men burped loudly, and one by one rolled over and went to sleep for the night as the women silently entered to remove the debris of the banquet from among the snoring men.

This scene could have happened almost as easily a thousand years ago as today. The villages that cling so precariously to life on the edge of the Sahara have barely altered their mud-brick architecture, their monotonous life, and their strict adherence to Islam. One of the few changes in recent centuries was the seemingly modest one of incorporating a few new spices and vegetables into their diets. The goat served us by the merchant was a traditional desert dish but had been cooked with a peanut sauce flowered with red chili peppers, and the vegetables were mostly peppers mixed with tomatoes. All of these are American Indian vegetables that have made their way around the world even into the most remote corner of the Sahara since Columbus's first voyage.

Unfortunately for accurate tracing of culinary history, much confusion surrounds the name "pepper." Prior to Columbus, the only known pepper was the black powder made by grinding the dried berry fruit of the plant *Piper nigrum*. If the outer shell of this fruit was removed before grinding it, the pepper would be white. Sometimes the category of pepper included other types of *Piper* such as cubeb, betel, and kava, but these plants were used more for their pharmacological and narcotic properties than for flavoring food and never found much of a market in Europe.

When Columbus arrived in America, thinking that he was in the East Indies near the Spice Islands, he erroneously called the natives Indians and assumed that if they were Indians then they must be flavoring their food with pepper. In fact, the Indians were using various forms of a completely unrelated plant, *Capsicum frutescens*. The fruits of this plant ranged from dark greens through bright oranges, purples, and yellows. Some were round, some oblong, some shaped vaguely like bells, and some the size and shape of small tears. Like the word "Indian," which today must do double duty to represent people in Asia and America, the overburdened word "pepper" must represent both a small Asian berry and a whole family of unrelated American fruits.

The importance of the American Indian peppers and tomatoes appeared much more poignantly to me in another part of Africa. On the island of Zanzibar in the Indian Ocean off the coast of East Africa, I spent a long, hot day wandering through rural villages looking at the deteriorating coconut and clove plantations after the government had seized control of the land and bungled efforts to collectivize it. The market disappointed me, because it offered only a meager display of fish and a few high-priced vegetables. This contrasted greatly with the busy and prosperous markets that I customarily encountered in tropical places.

During the day I visited with villagers who drank strong coffees and tea sometimes laced with coconut cream and served with pieces of ripe jackfruit. The simple foods of the natives of Zanzibar stood in stark contrast to the dishes I saw later in the island's only hotel. Built in the international style of the 1970s, this hotel played host to a handful of European tourists, a team of Chinese who were in Zanzibar to teach rice cultivation, some Indians who were helping to build a shoe factory, and some government officials. The cavernous dining room that usually fed less than two dozen people during my stay there offered international specialities such as lasagna, steak and potatoes, tomato bisque, and local seafood curry topped with cashews. After the meal, waiters brought over large trays of tempting desserts that included freshly sliced pineapples, bananas, and papayas, as well as rich Black Forest tortes, any of which could be served with vanilla ice cream or whipped cream.

Aside from the incongruities of dining on such luxurious food in the midst of a supposedly socialist economy where many of the people were underfed and malnourished, another irony struck me. As a part of "international cuisine," each of the dishes was easily recognizable as the national or regional dish typical of one place in the world. The lasagna came from Italy, the curry from India, the torte from the German-speaking parts of Europe. The ice cream was in the style known as "French vanilla," and the fruits were the generic tropical fruits that I have eaten everywhere from the Caribbean to Bali. What struck me at that moment, however, was that even though none of those national cuisines was based on an American Indian staple, all of them had been built around American Indian foods.

American foods did much more for the world than merely provide a bonanza of calories and new crops for fields that had been only marginally productive in the past. American food and spices made possible the development of national and local cuisines to a degree not previously imagined.

This is shown quite clearly in the curries of India. The basic ingredients of rice, coconut, and vegetables are traditional Eurasian foods, as are some of the spices, such as cumin, turmeric, and coriander. Some of the most distinctive tastes of the curries, however, come from the chilies used to spice them. The cooks of India and Sri Lanka adopted the hot peppers and cayenne very quickly and assimilated them into their curry sauces to supplement their tangy black pepper and ginger. Because of the Hindu and Buddhist bias against eating meat, the cooks of India and Sri Lanka had a keen eye for new vegetable dishes; consequently they quickly incorporated the American tomato and potato into their cuisine, as well as the peanut and the cashew.

The Asian Indians have carried these spices on around the world as they migrated with the British to South and East Africa, England, and even back to the Americas, where they settled in great numbers in the British islands of the Caribbean and in Guyana on the South American coast. Even though the style of cooking is uniquely Asian, many of the ingredients are typically American.

American spices made a much more modest impact on Korea, Japan, Mongolia, and northern China, but the southern Chinese embraced the chili quite fondly. The Portuguese probably introduced most of the new American foods through their Chinese colony of Macao. With these new spices and foods the city of Canton, upriver from Macao, quickly became known for having the best cuisine in China. The inland provinces of Szechuan and Hunan, lacking the delicate variety of the cuisine of all the seacoast provinces of China, found in the chili a dietary diversion. Chilies became essential parts of Hunanese and Szechuan sauces and elicited new flavors from the traditional vegetables. The Chinese also found a variety of ways to mix the chilies with a few other sauces and oil to make a sauce that could be preserved and used any season of the year.

The Chinese shared the Indian fondness for the peanut, which quickly found a place in a range of meat and vegetable dishes. The Chinese also transformed the new sweet potato by making it into very delicate noodles that rivaled wheat noodles in popularity.

South Asians traditionally combined elements of both Chinese and Indian cooking to make their own cuisine, and they too borrowed heavily from the new American ingredients, particularly peanuts, chilies, tomatoes, and some of the fruits. Often each province selected a particular pepper as a favorite, and depending on the local growing conditions and practices, this created a diversity of cooking styles. In Thailand the population favors a very small orange pepper that they call *prik kee nu luang*, and it is one of the world's most powerful chilis. The Thais also use chilies with vinegar to make a common sauce, *nam som*, that can be used to flavor almost any dish. In addition, cooks often add dried chili flakes, called *prik kee nu bon*, before the dish ever comes to the table, and diners add more to suit their own tastes.

In Bali, the Hindu island in Indonesia, the preference is for milder chilies that the Balinese often grind with shrimp into a paste to which they add lime juice. Called *sambal*, this sauce is commonly added to all types of rice dishes. Another favorite sauce uses peanuts, to which the chilies may be added or not as desired. Peanuts are also used to make *rempeyek*, a favorite type of crisp cookie. It is in the use of American fruits, however, that the Balinese most deviate from western tastes. They make the American passion fruit into a liqueur called *markisa*, and they mix American avocados with rum, coffee, and sweetened milk to make a milkshake.

American spices and condiments had an even stronger impact on the diets of Europeans. Prior to the introduction of American tomatoes and sweet peppers, the Italians endured a dreadfully dull diet. Cooks had few choices of sauces to ladle onto their hundreds of varieties of pasta. Affluent diners had meats and gravies flavored with black pepper. The less affluent had cheeses and cream sauces; the poor had a few herbs and vegetables. Spaghetti with carrot sauce or lasagna made with beets lacked the sparkle of their contemporary counterparts.

With the arrival of the first foods from America, Italian cuisine exploded with new ideas, and the tables of rich and poor alike groaned under the weight of many marvelous new dishes. Yellow, orange, green, and red tomatoes from cherry to almost melon size and in round and oblong shapes found their way into the Italian kitchen to be pickled, sliced, chopped, diced, dried, puréed, and made into hundreds of sauces. The Italians added as diverse a set of American sweet peppers, varying in more sizes and shapes than the tomatoes and named bell, banana, and cherry peppers because their shapes reminded the cooks of something already familiar to them. With virtually no other ingredients, the Italians had the perfect sauce for spaghetti, ravioli, lasagna, and a host of other noodle dishes, as well as for meats.

In addition, the Italians liked at least one of the American squashes. They adopted the long, thin, green one and called it *zucchini*, the diminutive of the Italian *zucca*, "gourd." And they added a few American beans to their diet, including the green bean and the kidney bean. These beans and peppers along with broth and some noodles became the standard ingredients in minestrone, the unofficial national soup of Italy.

The Spaniards also took the tomato and the pepper back home. They used it in very different dishes, such as gazpacho and other soups as well as sauces for meats, but without the flair of the Italian cooks. They also added beans and some potatoes, but overall the impact of the foods that they themselves discovered seem to be less on their own diets than on the diets of other Europeans.

Many eastern Europeans liked the sweet red peppers ground into the fine powder known as paprika. Particularly in Yugoslavia and Hungary this became a favorite spice for stews. Goulash without paprika would be virtually unthinkable, and different districts of Hungary developed their own particular blend of peppers to make just the right paprika. Paprika became the premier spice of choice in Hungary, making it almost an essential feature of Hungarian cuisine.

Never noted as good cooks, the British managed to take some of the most delicious of American foods and render them bland and unrecognizable. The potato was mashed into a purée and then baked with meat to make a dish called shepherd's pie, a plebeian imitation of Beef Wellington. The British also stuffed the potato along with a few meager spices and some occasional meat or fish into a baked dough shell to make what they called a "pasty." Other cooks chopped the potato into hunks and fried it to serve it together with hunks of fried seafood, thereby making fish and chips, one of the country's most noted dishes. They took the American bean and served it over toast, making it not only more bland but dry as well. The uses that the British made of American foods lend credence to the oft-cited claim that English cuisine is an oxymoron.

The tomato encountered resistance in the north, which had all the vitamin C it needed in the new potato. Even today, northern European cooks use the tomato primarily as a garnish when it is in season, in contrast to the Mediterranean cooks, for whom it is a virtual staple used as much in the winter as in the summer.

The French did not seize on any one particular food, but they did integrate the tomato, potato, string bean, and several other beans thoroughly into their diets. Unlike the Italians, who fondly embraced the new American foods, the French, particularly under the influence of the Médicis queens, developed a new cuisine that combined traditional European foods with a variety of new spices and foods from Asia and Africa as well as from America. Despite these innovations, the French have long had a grave mistrust of foreign influences on either their language or their food. By and large they consistently preferred mild flavors based on dairy products, the residue of fat left after cooking meat, and wines or vinegars. To these they have added mild herbs and spices but have avoided the stronger flavors so popular in the south. Many of the baked and fried potato dishes of today owe their origin to French cooks who combined them with the traditional cream sauces, cheeses, and garlic of French cuisine.

A major hindrance preventing the French and the northern Europeans from eating the chilies and pungent spices of America was their heavy reliance on dairy products. They smear butter and cheese on bread. They add milk to their soups, cook vegetables in butter, add cream sauces and cheeses to some dishes, and make milk puddings, pies, and custards. Because of their high fat content, these dishes leave a residual coat of butterfat in the mouth of the eater, and this fat destroys the taste of the chilies. For this reason, Italian cooks did not add the chili to their cream sauces; instead, they had to develop the whole new tomato base as a complement rather than as a deterrent to the chili flavor. Even though the Italians were willing to make this modification, the other Europeans were much too dependent on dairy products to do it.

In America the importance of Indian foods continued without interruption by the European invasion. Even though the Europeans did bring bread, dairy products, and new meats with them, these only supplemented but did not replace the American diet. Instead, the Europeans learned to eat American-style. This is nowhere more obvious than in Mexico, where beans and corn continued as the staples of the cuisine. Beef replaced venison, poultry, and human flesh in many of the tacos, tamales, and enchiladas, but the dishes remained fairly much the same.

Like Tex-Mex food, most regional cuisines in the United States stand on an Indian base. The bland New Englanders did not take to Indian spices very readily, but they accepted the bean and corn dishes. Rather than sharp spices, the New Englanders preferred the sweet taste of maple sugar and syrup, particularly when made into desserts, spread over bread or pancakes, or baked with Indian beans. This dish evolved into the several varieties of Boston baked beans eaten around the country today, but in time cheaper molasses was substituted for the maple syrup. The Americans often added a slab of hog fat to the dish to make the all-American dish of pork and beans, a dish shared with no one else in the world except the British.

The Indians taught the New Englanders to catch and enjoy a number of ocean foods that they had not known in Europe. The clam ranked primary among these, even though the Puritan settlers thought it poisonous until the Indians taught them to bake the clams in an earthen oven with seaweed. New Englanders still follow this same clambake procedure today.

The Narragansets taught the colonists to boil together whole corn kernels with lima beans and some mild flavorings in a mixture the Indians called *succotash*, an agglutinated plural meaning "cooked whole grains." Another mixed pot of Indian foods was adopted by the settlers under the name *squantum*, which had been the Indian name for an outdoor feast and celebration. The Indians of New England also taught the settlers to use the cranberry, particularly to accompany the Indian turkey.

In the American south, the diet became more Indian than probably in any other part of the country. Wheat grew very poorly there, and the population adopted with great gusto the various forms of corn. From the Indians, the settlers learned to enjoy the corn on the cob, stewed, in succotash, made into hominy, ground into grits, popped as a snack, and baked into bread. The commonest form in which it was consumed, however, was fried into thick cakes much like the Mexican tortilla. This fried cornbread formed the staple of southern food among the poor classes and was called by many names, including hoecake, ash bread, spoon bread, and johnnycake (possibly from *Shawnee*-cake); sometimes it was called by its Algonquian name, *pone*. Pone refers to a fried bread made the traditional Indian way without the milk and eggs so often considered necessary to European breads. Only the wealthy plantations had kitchens with ovens to bake the bread in the European style with sour milk or buttermilk. This elite version is what is now commonly called "cornbread."

Indians also dropped spoonfuls of cornmeal into pots of hot bear fat to make a fried bread that later became known to the settlers as "hush puppies." The settlers gradually substituted pork fat or corn oil for the bear fat, but the dish remained much the same. The same cooking procedure with wheat dough instead of corn dough produced fry bread or Indian bread. Indians often dipped this crispy fried bread into maple syrup or dusted it with sugar to make the precursor of the modern doughnut without the hole. The southerners also became great connoisseurs of the sweet potato, which they baked and then peeled like a banana to eat as a snack, or mashed, baked, and fried to make pies and pones.

The Jerusalem artichoke cultivated by the Indians of the south also became a popular condiment used in making southern pickles and relishes. The southerners also picked up tapioca, a residue from processing the cassava plant, as a favorite ingredient in making puddings, and as a thickener for watery dishes. Later, tapioca became more widely used in the United States as a major ingredient in many kinds of baby foods. Southerners also became very fond of the native American pecan, which they used in a number of dishes, notably pecan pie.

Southerners also adapted the custom of barbecuing food. The custom of basting fish and large pieces of meat with a special sauce and cooking them over an outdoor fire was adapted first from the Taino Indians of the island of Hispaniola. From the Taino language the word *barbecue* passed into the English language via the Spanish *barbacoa*. According to early explorers' accounts and early engravings from the Caribbean, the Indians used this method to roast whole leg of human. Even though there is no evidence that the Tainos or any Caribs ever ate human flesh, this image of the human barbecue gained wide notoriety in Europe. *Caribale*, the Spanish word for a Caribbean, soon became synonymous with man-eater and passed into English as the word "cannibal," thus giving "cannibal" and "barbecue" a shared etymology.

Different regions of the United States adapted the art of barbecuing to different styles and different sauces. North Carolina developed a vinegar-and-pepper sauce, while South Carolina still uses its own peculiar blend of mustard and molasses. The tomato sauces, however, became the most common and today are virtually synonymous with barbecue. In addition to the barbecue sauces, American cuisine uses related sauces such as catsup and meat sauces that are primarily tomato- or pepper-based.

The most distinctive of all southern cuisines, the creole and Cajun cuisine of Louisiana, is frequently associated more with French than with Indian cooks. But these foods are no more French than tacos and tamales are Spanish. Creole and Cajun foods came to us via the mixture of people who incorporated French, blacks, and Indians into their heritage. The resulting food is primarily Indian, secondarily black, and only tangentially French. The most basic ingredient of all the dishes is the Indian red bean. The base of this Louisiana cuisine comes from the mixture of tomatoes and hot peppers such as cayenne and sauces such as Tabasco made from the chilies. The other main vegetable and primary thickener is okra (*Hibiscus esculentus*), which the black slaves brought over from the west coast of Africa. People outside of Louisiana, however, often eliminate the okra in the dishes; many do not like its mucilaginous consistency. Similarly they often reduce the amounts of sharp chilies, cayenne, and Tabasco.

One of the most common spices, gumbo filé, takes its name from a combination of an African and a French word, but in content it is the sassafras flavoring made from the leaves of the *Sassafras albidum* tree and first introduced to the settlers by the native Choctaw cooks of the area. Shrimp, crayfish, and fish form the featured parts of Cajun cooking, and even though the Indians certainly take no credit for domesticating the seafoods, they did teach the French settlers which ones to eat, how to catch them, and how to prepare them.

Each region of the United States prides itself on a special stew of local produce usually mixed with tomatoes, peppers, or potatoes to make a regional specialty. In addition to the gumbos, creoles, and jambalayas of Louisiana, we have the chilies of the American west. The southern United States developed various forms of catfish stew that combined tomatoes and potatoes with this unusual American fish with a skin instead of scales. East coast communities developed various crab and chowder dishes, mostly using potato bases rather than tomatoes. Farther from the ocean, the settlers used simple corn to make their chowders. From the Ojibwas in Minnesota, the Scandinavian settlers adopted the wild rice soup, but they added lots of their beloved milk products to it.

In Virginia and North Carolina, the settlers adopted a squirrel stew that the Indians made with corn, tomatoes, and beans. They popularized this under the name "Brunswick stew," but in time the squirrel gave way to chicken and beef.

Nowhere else in the American cuisine, however, have Indian foods had such an impact as in the snack foods. Potato chips and french fries have strictly American pedigrees. Similarly, corn chips, nachos, and tortilla chips are all corn products from the American southwest, as are the tomato sauces, salsas, and guacamole that people dip them into. The jerky and dried meat sticks which Americans sometimes eat with their beer are also from the Indians. Popcorn and peanuts are both of Indian origin. Indians sometimes dipped this mixture in maple syrup to make a snack that sells today as Cracker Jack in the United States.

In the domain of sweets, Indian chocolate and vanilla rank as the commonest flavors for snack foods, while Americans universally prefer maple as the flavor of their syrups. As much as any other foods, these snacks form part of the modern diet and a part of the legacy of the American Indians to world cuisine.

Not all snack foods are as thoroughly processed as the chips and dips. Even many of the "natural" snacks are primarily a mixture of Indian foods. These include the mixture of peanuts, sunflower seeds, pumpkin seeds, pecans, and dried fruit that is often called "trail mix" in the United States or "student fodder" in Germany. Most of these ingredients originated in the temperate and tropical zones of America, where Indian farmers domesticated them over thousands of years.

Settlers in the tropical zones of Latin America maintained the wide variety of local fruits, but they supplemented them greatly with other fruits imported from Africa, Asia, and the South Pacific. Exotic Old World plants such as citrus fruits, breadfruit, and mangoes thrived in their adopted American home and supplemented the native American fruits of pineapple, papaya, cashew, and passion fruit.

On a side street in a middle-class neighborhood of Tegucigalpa, capital of Honduras, sits a house converted into a store called the Vegetable and Fruit Boutique. Under the guidance of the World Neighbors organization, the boutique sells the garden produce of the small community of Guinope, which is about an hour's drive from the city. Except for a few items such as bananas and citrus fruits, the produce of this small market is mostly traditional New World produce. There are baskets of corn, cassava, potatoes, tomatoes, peppers, avocados, peanuts, and papayas. In addition, there are mounds of products that the typical European or North American customer fails to recognize.

One shelf displays a variety of chayotes. This vegetable grows on a vine, *Sechium edule*, and resembles a yellow-green squash. Unlike squash, however, the plants are frequently cultivated on arbors, which make them look like giant grape vines with grossly exaggerated leaves and fruits. Like the squashes, the chayote is not so much a vegetable as it is a whole family of vegetables, for the chayotes come in many sizes and shapes. They vary from approximately the size and shape of a plum up to that of a medium melon. The skin texture varies from very smooth like that of eggplant to prickly and covered with thousands of very fine bristles, and still others have large folds in their skins like the folds of a brain. Color varies from nearly white through a variety of green shades to very dark.

The chayote's name came into English from the Spanish, who borrowed it from the Nahuatl language of the Aztecs, who called it *chayotli*. In the Fruit and Vegetable Boutique, however, the housewives and staff still call it by its Maya name, *pataste*. In recent years at least one form of the chayote vegetable has been sold in some North American supermarkets, but it has not yet grabbed the shopper's attention. Even those adventurous cooks who have tried it probably do not suspect how versatile this plant is. The Indians of Central America eat virtually the entire chayote plant. They prepare the hard and nutritious root like cassava, and they cook the tender leaves as greens. After eating the fruit the Maya toast and eat the large seed in the middle. Few other plants in either the Old World or the New World garden can match the versatility of the chayote. Despite this, the chayote remains relatively obscure and is enjoyed primarily by the descendants of those Indians who first domesticated and cultivated it thousands of years ago.

The boutique in Tegucigalpa offers a variety of tropical fruits that are little known outside of their home areas. The granadilla, *Passiflora quadrangularis*, known as the passion fruit in English, sells very well. The fruit is contained in an orange-green shell about the size of a chicken egg. Breaking the shell open, one finds thousands of small seeds in a gray, slimy fruit that tastes quite sweet. Because of these edible seeds, the Spanish first called it the *granadilla*, "little pomegranate." Another form called the *maracuya* is particularly popular throughout Latin America as a fruit for making juice. In this form it also entered the North American market, but advertisers billed it as Hawaiian fruit juice rather than as a native American fruit.

The fruit section of the boutique offers the small greenish fruit called *ciruella corona* as well as various kinds of papaya. These vary from some as small as pears to others as large as watermelons. Encased in yellowish-green skins, the insides vary in coloring from pale yellow through a much darker yellow and even red, with corresponding subtle changes in the flavor of the flesh. They are eaten raw or easily made into thick juices by themselves or in combination with tropical or temperate-zone fruits.

The list of Indian foods still in use today in Latin America often seems a bit exotic to people living far from the tropics. But throughout the North American continent grow nearly as many and as varied a set of cultivated plants. A Fruit and Vegetable Boutique in the United States might easily offer a large variety of products grown by the Indians of North America but today as unknown to the average eater as some of the foods in the boutique in Tegucigalpa. The larder of this boutique would include the green, leafy vegetable pokeweed, eaten primarily by the poor people in the United States in past generations, but now largely unused. Fruits would include the persimmon and the papaw, *Asimina triloba*, also known as custard apple. The papaw is a temperate-zone version of the papaya, and its name is probably a corruption of "papaya," since the fruits are similar superficially although not genetically. The passion fruit also has a North American relative, the maypop fruit from the vine *Passiflora incarnata*, which remains virtually unknown.

The pecans cultivated by the American Indians became popular in the United States, but they never spread to other parts of the world. Many other American nuts are now particularly unknown even in their country of origin. Most Americans have probably heard of the hickory because it became the nickname of President Andrew Jackson and because of its very hard wood. Few Americans, however, have ever tasted the smooth hickory nut, which formed the primary staple in the diet of many Indian groups such as the Muskogee Creek of the southeastern United States, who grew it in eleven varieties. Another such nut is the black walnut from the tree *Juglans nigra*. The strong-flavored nut grows inside a very hard and rough-skinned case about the size of a golf ball. This is in turn housed in a larger fruit about the size of a peach. While the fruit skin is easy to break, the shell of the nut almost always requires a firm blow from a hammer. Probably because of the difficulty of cracking the nut, it never became as popular as the plain walnut, which is sometimes also called the English walnut.

Acorns grew in great varieties throughout many parts of the Americas. In California, this was the staple of the Indian diet and was made into a flour by the women. Because of the abundance of acorn trees, most California Indians did not have to plant corn or grow any crops. In addition to the acorns, Indians of that area also harvested the pine nuts from various types of pine trees.

The types of berries used by the Indians surpass even the nuts. Nearly every part of North America had several varieties of berry bushes that the local Indians nurtured. Forty-seven types of American berries have been identified. Some of these types, such as the blueberry, had up to twenty variations, and the gooseberry came in at least a dozen different varieties. Other berries included sour chokecherries, *Prunus serotina*; wild currants, *Ribes inebrians* and *R. cereum*; at least four varieties of elderberries, *Sambucus melanocarpa, S. mexicana, S. neomexicana,* and *S. coerulea*; wild grapes, *Vitis arizonica* and *V. californica*; ground cherries, *Physalis pubescens* and *P. fendleri*; hackberries, *Celtis pallida, C. reticula,* and *C. douglasli*; manzanita, *Arctostaphylos pringlei, A. pungens,* and *A. patula*; and squawberry, *Rhus trilobata*.

Even a plant as well known now as the avocado was virtually ignored outside Latin America as recently as only one generation ago. The name comes from the Nahuatl language of the Aztecs as *ahuacatl*, which means "testicle," and it has been eaten in the United States at least since the American Revolution. The avocado is one of the most nutritious fruits ever domesticated. Because it was a semitropical plant with a thin skin it did not travel as well as bananas and pineapples, and farmers ignored it until the development of modern transportation made it possible to move large quantities of avocados from Florida, Puerto Rico, and California to urban centers very quickly without damage to the fruit. Popularity of the fruit increased when merchandisers thought to change its name from the English "alligator pear," which made it sound both repulsive and possibly sweet, to something closer to the original Aztec name.

Avocado production has now spread from the Americas to new homes such as Israel and Kenya, where it is grown both for domestic consumption and as a cash crop for air export to Europe. Thus far, however, the Europeans have shown little interest in the plant as anything more than a novelty food, and they show no sign of assigning to it the more extensive dietary role it has attained in the Americas.

"Squash" survives as one of the few English words from the language of the Massachuset Indians (derived from proto-Algonquian), who called it *askootasquash*. Even so the use of the word "squash" for a vegetable is still confined to American English; the same word in British English designates a citrus drink. Of the squashes only the zucchini found a reasonably wide following among Italians.

On Thanksgiving Day North Americans sometimes remember the Indians who gave them their cuisine by dining upon turkey with cornbread stuffing, cranberry sauce, succotash, corn on the cob, sweet potato casserole, stewed squash and tomatoes, baked beans with maple syrup, and pecan pie. Few cooks or gourmets, however, recognize the much broader extent to which American Indian cuisine radically changed cooking and dining in every part of the globe from Timbuktu to Tibet. Sichuan beef with chilies, German chocolate cake, curried potatoes, vanilla ice cream, Hungarian goulash, peanut brittle, and pizza all owe their primary flavorings to the American Indians.

The discovery of America sparked a revolution in food and cuisine that has not yet shown any signs of abating. Tomatoes, chilies, and green peppers formed the first wave of American flavorings to circle the globe, but the American Indian garden still grows a host of plants that the world may yet learn to use and enjoy. These plants may have practical uses, such as providing food in otherwise unusable land or producing more food in underused land. They also vary the daily diets of people throughout the world and thereby increase nutrition. Even in this high-tech age, the low-tech plant continues to be the key to nutrition and health. Despite all the plant improvements brought about by modern science, the American Indians remain the developers of the world's largest array of nutritious foods and the primary contributors to the world's varied cuisines.

▲ ▲ 7 ▲ ▲

LIBERTY, ANARCHISM, AND THE NOBLE SAVAGE

On a hot Friday afternoon in the last week of August, cars, pickup trucks, camping vans, and school buses slowly pull into a park on the edge of Fargo, North Dakota. Young people greet their friends excitedly, and old Ojibwa women solemnly shake hands with one another with greetings of "Bozhoo, bozhoo" and look over one another's grandchildren. Dakota men greet one another with the friendly "Hau, kota" before exchanging stories and jokes. Lakota families carve out small pieces of territory around their vehicles, making the park into a series of encampments, each with its own blanket on the ground, aluminum folding chairs, and grill.

As for an unknown number of generations in the past, the Indians of the Great Plains gather once again for an annual powwow. For much of the afternoon, everyone seems to be helping everyone else get dressed. A father straps a bustle of bright-colored feathers on his adolescent son, and then he holds up a mirror for the boy to adjust the roach of hair cascading down his scalp. Young girls fasten each other's deerskin dresses and help untangle the fringes of their shawls from the hundreds of jingle bells on their dresses. A group of men gather near the cars out of sight of spectators to paint one another's faces with irregular and markedly asymmetrical designs of black and red, and then braid one another's hair. Women sew their torn moccasins,

girls string pendants of embroidered beads into their hair. A young girl helps her father fluff up the feathers in his headdress, and mothers and grandmothers put headbands and small bracelets on babies they carry in their arms.

In the central arena, a young man sets up a microphone system and checks the lighting. An announcer takes up the microphone and asks if a drum group has arrived. When no one answers, he calls out the names of various drum groups from White Earth, Pine Ridge, Red Wing, Lake Nipigon, and The Cities, but he gets no response. Twenty minutes later he repeats the same request, emphasizing that some of the people are now dressed and ready to dance, but there is no drum group ready to drum.

About dusk, an older man and his adolescent grandson appear from the edge of the arena with a large drum. They set it up and wait for several more men of various ages to join them in a circle around it. The oldest man puts his left hand over his ear, cocks his head to the side, and seemingly shuts his eyes before he cries out a long high wail that sounds almost like a woman's shriek, and immediately all of the men start pounding on the drum and singing in the same high voices.

Young children dance energetically on the sidelines, but no one moves into the arena. The announcer's voice booms over the microphone for some warriors to please come forward to carry the flag so that they can begin. He repeats the call seven times before the first two men emerge, dressed in feathers and beads. These men are in their sixties, veterans of World War II, and they march out carrying the flags of the United States and Canada. They must wait for the younger veterans of the Korean and Vietnam wars, who straggle forward singly, some dressed in denim pants and cowboy hats while others wear traditional feathers and boast large beer bellies protruding over the ample loincloths that cover their bathing trunks. These middle-aged men carry the North Dakota flag and several flags from neighboring states and Canadian provinces as well as a series of colorful Indian reservation flags. Among the cloth flags some men carry staffs lined with eagle feathers. All seated people rise, and the already quiet crowd becomes absolutely silent for a few moments before the singing of the national anthems of Canada and the United States.

The men dance slowly around the arena with the brightly colored flags and then sing a special song honoring the flags themselves.

Following the flag ceremony, the same warriors lead off the first dance of the powwow, with the eldest veterans dancing first, and slowly other people join them in the Intertribal Dance. Grandmothers shuffle with their grandchildren in their arms while teenage boys dance widely around them. Beaming young women dance while flourishing long and very colorful shawls in front of them, and studiously ignore the boys. Some people in street clothes join in the ceremony, and finally nearly a hundred people slowly move clockwise around the arena, all moving at the same speed but dancing the particular steps appropriate to their gender and dress. Most subsequent dances that night permit only one of the five categories of dancers into the arena: Men's Traditional Dance, Shawl Dance, Men's Fancy Dance, Women's Traditional Dance, and Jingle-Dress Dance. Each category wears the correct clothing and follows an exact choreography. The announcer and a panel of judges award occasional prizes as high as $100 to different dancers. Between rounds of competition, someone will make the call for another Intertribal Dance in which participants of all categories as well as the audience dance together.

English predominates among the people representing a dozen different tribes, but among the smaller groups and families, people speak one or more of the Indian languages and some words of a French creole used in many of the languages of the area. All singing and praying is done in Dakota, the language of the powwow hosts.

Between one set of dances, a family comes to the fore to distribute presents in honor of their teenage daughter, who has taken her grandmother's Indian name. The young girl presents gifts of blankets, embroidered pieces of Indian bead jewelry, cartons of cigarettes, and money to people who have helped her mature to this stage in life. She then leads off a dance in their honor.

Between dances, someone occasionally rises to honor another person, commemorate an event, announce an upcoming powwow, or welcome a group that has traveled particularly far to participate in that night's festivities. Various announcers remind the assembled people that part of the money collected for admission to the powwow will be donated to a program combating alcohol and drug addiction among Indian people, and they denounce the evils that these two substances have brought to them.

On the side, a food concessionaire sells fry bread, Indian tacos, hamburgers, and bratwursts, as well as a selection of cold soft drinks and hot coffee. Vendors hawk Indian ornaments and items of dance wear made from diverse synthetic and natural materials. A man offers a selection of buttons and bumper stickers with slogans such as "Red Power," "Proud to be an Indian," "I powwowed in Fargo," "Squaw on Board," and "I'd rather be dancing."

The dancing and eating continue late into the night, when some people leave to go home or to a motel and others drift off to their vans and campers. The activities resume the next day and continue until the afternoon, when some people pack up and start the long drive home. Others settle in for another night's rest before starting their own trek.

Today the powwow blends traits of a dozen different Indian groups together with items borrowed from white culture, just as some of the Indians have blond hair and green eyes. Some have "typical" Indian names while others have Norwegian, Irish, or French names. Despite all of the blending, however, some very basic Indian values dominate.

To an outsider, such powwows often appear chaotic. Even though posted signs promise that the dances will begin at four o'clock, there is still no dancing at five-thirty. Drummers scheduled to play never arrive, and some groups drum without being on the program. Impromptu family ceremonies intertwine with the official scheduled events, and the microphone passes among a score of announcers during the evening. No one is in control.

This seems to be typical of Indian community events: no one is in control. No master of ceremonies tells everyone what to do, and no one orders the dancers to appear. The announcer acts as herald or possibly as facilitator of ceremonies, but no chief rises to demand anything of anyone. The event flows in an orderly fashion like hundreds of powwows before it, but leaders can only lead by example, by pleas, or by exhortations. Everyone shows great respect for the elders and for warriors, who are repeatedly singled out for recognition, but at the same time children receive great respect for dancing and even the audience receives praise for watching. The powwow grows in an organic fashion as dancers slowly become activated by the drums and the singing. The event unfolds as a collective activity of all participants, not as one mandated and controlled from the top. Each participant responds to the collective mentality and mood of the whole group but not to a single, directing voice.

This Indian penchant for respectful individualism and equality seems as strong today in Fargo, North Dakota, as when the first explorers wrote about it five centuries ago. Much to the dismay of contemporary bureaucrats and to the shock of the Old World observers, Indian societies operated without strong positions of leadership and coercive political institutions.

Freedom does not have a long pedigree in the Old World. When it appears in the ancient literature of the Mediterranean, freedom usually refers to the freedom of a tribe, a nation, or a city from the domination of another such group, as in the freedom of the Jews from Egyptian bondage or the freedom of the Greek cities from Persian rule. In this sense the word echoes our contemporary notion of national sovereignty, but it resembles only slightly our concept of freedom as personal liberty. Occasionally, this sense of the word appeared in connection with a Roman or Greek slave who was freed, but this was a very specialized use that meant a person became human and was no longer merely the property of someone else.

After the people of the Old World learned to accept the strange animals reported from America and had at least a slight acquaintance with the new plants, they began to examine more closely the people and their culture. By this time the Spanish had virtually decapitated the native societies that they had encountered, and they had then grafted the Spanish monarchy, the Spanish language, and Spanish Catholicism to the native roots of American culture. In contrast, the more marginal areas of America that fell into the hands of the French and British still had flourishing native societies.

The most consistent theme in the descriptions penned about the New World was amazement at the Indians' personal liberty, in particular their freedom from rulers and from social classes

based on ownership of property. For the first time the French
and the British became aware of the possibility of living in social
harmony and prosperity without the rule of a king.

As the first reports of this new place filtered into Europe, they
provoked much philosophical and political writing. Sir Thomas
More incorporated into his 1516 book *Utopia* those characteristics
then being reported by the first travelers to America, especially
in the much-discussed letters of Amerigo Vespucci. More made
his utopia one of equality without money. The following year,
More's brother-in-law John Ratsell set out in search of some such
paradise in America. Although his trip failed, he continued to
advocate the colonization of America in his writings, and his son
did make the trip in 1536 [Brandon, p. 10].

More's work was translated into all the major European languages and has stayed in print until the present day. His thought
carried influence throughout the European continent, and in the
following century, other writers strengthened and developed the
idea of freedom that he described and the ways that the Indians
in America maintained it.

Writing a little later in the sixteenth century, the French essayist
Michel de Montaigne presented a similar description of American
Indian life based primarily on the early reports from Brazil. In
his essay "On Cannibals," Montaigne wrote that they are "still
governed by natural laws and very little corrupted by our own."
He specifically cited their lack of magistrates, forced services,
riches, poverty, and inheritance. As in More's utopia, Brazil
emerged as the ideal place and Indians as having created the
ideal society [Montaigne, pp. 109–10]. Most of these early writings
contained strongly satirical veins—the writers indicated that even
so-called savages lived better than civilized Europeans—but the
satire grew out of the unavoidable truth that the technologically
simple Indians usually lived in more just, equitable, and egalitarian social conditions.

Not until a century after Montaigne did the first French eth-
nography on the North American Indians appear. Louis Armand
de Lom d'Arce, Baron de Lahontan, wrote several short books on
the Huron Indians of Canada based on his stay with them from
1683 to 1694. An adventurer far more than an anthropologist,
Lahontan nevertheless managed to rise above the genre of ad-

venture stories to give the French reader the worldview of the Hurons from inside the Indian mind. By the time of Lahontan's sojourn among the Hurons, they had already survived several decades of sporadic interaction with European explorers and traders, and they had been the subject of numerous commentaries by Jesuit missionaries. From these interactions the Hurons were able to compare their own way of life and the Europeans'. The Indians particularly decried the European obsession with money that compelled European women to sell their bodies to lusty men and compelled men to sell their lives to the armies of greedy men who used them to enslave yet more people. By contrast, the Hurons lived a life of liberty and equality. According to the Hurons, the Europeans lost their freedom in their incessant use of "thine" and "mine."

One of the Hurons explained to Lahontan, "We are born free and united brothers, each as much a great lord as the other, while you are all the slaves of one sole man. I am the master of my body, I dispose of myself, I do what I wish, I am the first and the last of my Nation . . . subject only to the great Spirit" [Brandon, p. 90]. It is difficult to tell where the Huron philosopher speaks and where Lahontan may be promoting his own political philosophy, but still the book rested on a base of solid ethnographic fact: the Hurons lived without social classes, without a government separate from their kinship system, and without private property. To describe this political situation, Lahontan revived the Greek-derived word "anarchy," using it in the literal sense meaning "no ruler." Lahontan found an orderly society, but one lacking a formal government that compelled such order.

After the appearance of Lahontan's *New Voyages to North America* in 1703 in The Hague and his *Curious Dialogues* soon thereafter, Lahontan became an international celebrity feted in all the liberal circles. The playwright Delisle de la Drevetière adapted these ideas to the stage in a play about an American Indian's visit to Paris. Performed in Paris in 1721 as *Arlequin Sauvage*, the play ends with a young Parisian woman named Violette falling in love with the Indian and fleeing with him to live in the liberty of America beyond law and money.

As usually happens in the theatrical world, this success initiated dozens of imitations, and there soon followed a spate of plays, farces, burlesques, and operas on the wonderful life of liberty among the Indians of America. Impresarios brought over Indians in droves to tour the European capitals and entertain at parties with their tales of liberty and freedom in the American paradise. Plays such as *Indes Galantes* and *Le Nouveau Monde* followed in the 1730s. The original play *Arlequin Sauvage* had a major impact on a young man named Jean Jacques Rousseau, who set about in 1742 to write an operetta on the discovery of the New World featuring Christopher Columbus's arrival with a sword while singing to the Indians the refrain "Lose your liberty!" [Brandon, p. 104]. This contrast between the liberty of the Indians and the virtual enslavement of the Europeans became a lifelong concern for Rousseau and eventually led to publication of his best-known work, *Discourse on the Origins of Inequality*, in 1754.

Despite the excessive literary commercialization of the notion of American liberty, a number of good ethnographic studies of the Indians also appeared during this period. The social descriptions of Lahontan found subsequent corroboration in the more ethnographic but less dramatic writings of the Jesuit Father Joseph François Lafitau, who published in 1724 *Customs of the American Savages Compared with Those of Earliest Times*, describing the Mohawks. The virtues of Indian society so impressed Lafitau that he saw in it a reflection of ancient Greek society. He intimated that the Indians actually might be descendants of refugees from the Trojan wars who managed to transfer their Greek ideals to America.

During this era the thinkers of Europe forged the ideas that became known as the European Enlightenment, and much of its light came from the torch of Indian liberty that still burned brightly in the brief interregnum between their first contact with the Europeans and their decimation by the Europeans. The Indian, particularly the Huron, became the "noble savage," the man of liberty living in the "natural state." While a few Europeans chose the path of Violette and left the corrupt world of Europe for America, others began working on ideas and plans to change Europe by incorporating some of the ideas of liberty into their own world. Almost all of the plans involved revolutionary changes to overthrow the monarchy, the aristocracy, or the church, and in some cases even to abolish money and private property.

The greatest political radical to follow the example of the Indians was probably Thomas Paine (1737–1809), the English Quaker and former craftsman who arrived in Philadelphia to visit Benjamin Franklin just in time for Christmas of 1774. Because the Quakerism of his family restricted his study of Latin, the language of learning, Paine was not an intellectual trained in philosophy. He left school at age thirteen to become an apprentice staymaker. He earned his education in life, something that many people have attempted and few have accomplished. His experiences made him a radical proponent of democracy.

After arriving in America he developed a sharp interest in the Indians, who seemed to be living in the natural state so alien to the urban and supposedly civilized life he encountered around himself. When the American Revolution started, Paine served as secretary to the commissioners sent to negotiate with the Iroquois at the town of Easton near Philadelphia on the Delaware River in January 1777 [Johansen, p. 116]. Through this and subsequent encounters with the Indians, Paine sought to learn their language, and throughout the remainder of his political and writing career he used the Indians as models of how society might be organized.

In his writings, Paine castigated Britain for her abusive treatment of the Indians, and he became the first American to call for the abolition of slavery. He refined his knowledge and opinions in order to disseminate them to the world in eloquent works bearing such simple titles as *Common Sense*, which he issued in January 1776 as the first call for American independence. Subsequently he became the first to propose the name "United States of America" for the emerging nation. After the revolutionary victory in America, he returned to Europe in 1787 to carry the Indian spark of liberty. The French made him an honorary French citizen, and they offered him a seat in the National Assembly in order to help draft a just constitution for their nation. He fought hard for the French Revolution, but despite his belief in revolutionary democracy, he abhorred terrorism, including the French reign of terror. Despite these excesses of the French, Paine laid out his logical defense of revolution in *The Rights of Man* in 1792, and then turned his attention to the role of religion by writing the book that gave its name to the whole Enlightenment, *The Age of Reason* (1794–95).

After this life of activism and writing, Paine wrote *Agrarian Justice* (1797), in which he asked a question that still haunts our own time: can civilized society ever cure the poverty it has created? He was not entirely optimistic that it could. He returned once again to the Iroquois, among whom he had learned democracy, when he wrote, "The fact is, that the condition of millions, in every country in Europe, is far worse than if they had been born before civilization began, or had been born among the Indians of North-America at the present day" [Paine, p. 338]. Unfortunately, however, Paine concluded that "it is always possible to go from the natural to the civilized state, but it is never possible to go from the civilized to the natural state" [Paine, p. 337].

When the French so ardently embraced Napoleon as emperor, Paine felt that they had betrayed everything he had been preaching, and he left France in disgust in 1802 to return to America, which still struggled with the implementation of liberty. He found the citizens of America now more complacent. Following their revolution they seemed intent on settling down, making money, and enjoying the pursuit of happiness. They showed no tolerant mood for an aging radical who held up savage Indians to them as paragons of the proper human values.

By the time Paine died, the Indians had been permanently enshrined in European thought as exemplars of liberty. In the next generation, Alexis de Tocqueville, writing in the first volume of *Democracy in America*, repeatedly used phrases such as "equal and free." He said that the ancient European republics never showed more love of independence than did the Indians of North America. He compared the social system and the values of the Indians to those of the ancient European tribes prior to becoming "civilized" and domesticated [Tocqueville, Vol. I, p. 357].

Even in the twentieth century, French anthropologists continued the analysis of liberty and equality among surviving American Indian groups, particularly those in the jungles of South America. Describing it as "society against the state," Pierre Clastres analyzed political institutions in Indian America to determine anew whether society could function without political oppression and coercion. He found that even in societies with chiefs, "the chief's word carries no force of law." He quoted the great cacique, or chief, Alaykin of the Argentine Chaco as saying that "if I were to use orders or force with my comrades, they could turn their backs on me at once." He continued, "I prefer to be loved and not feared by them." Clastres summed up the office of chief by observing that "the chief who tries to act the chief is abandoned" [Clastres, pp. 176, 131].

From the moment the notion of democracy and the noble savage appeared in Europe, some skeptical thinkers rejected it entirely. Thomas Hobbes launched one of the first attacks against this primitivism. Although he had never been to America, he claimed in his *Leviathan* (1651) that the savage people in many places of America led a life that was "solitary, poor, nasty, brutish, and short." He then went on to attack the ideas of liberty. For Hobbes the natural state of man was the horror of "war of all against all," and only through total subjugation of everyone to a ruler could the individual be protected from the perfidy and savagery of others.

In the next century a philosopher as eminent as Voltaire joined Hobbes in belittling the American Indians, but he used Indian characters in several of his works. Even the German philosopher Immanuel Kant attacked the idea of the noble American savage. In his 1772 lectures on philosophical anthropology at the University of Königsberg, Kant proclaimed that the American Indians "are incapable of civilization." He described them as having "no motive force, for they are without affection and passion. They are not drawn to one another by love, and are thus unfruitful. They hardly speak at all, never caress one another, care about nothing, and are lazy." In a note in his lecture he foreshadowed two long centuries of racist thought in Germany when he wrote that the Indians "are incapable of governing themselves" and are "destined for extermination" [Commager, p. 89].

As the eighteenth century closed in the bloodshed of the French Revolution, Europeans momentarily tired of constant political debate and the question of the natural social or political state of man. They turned away from the American Indian and let their fantasies flow to the South Pacific, where they envisioned a paradise of sensuality. Unlike the Indians who had suffered no rulers, many of the island people of Polynesia had rulers, and yet they seemed to be happy and to have found sexual, if not political, liberation. The notion of the noble savage took a new turn away from politics and into a frivolous image that still persists in some writings today.

Egalitarian democracy and liberty as we know them today owe little to Europe. They are not Greco-Roman derivatives somehow revived by the French in the eighteenth century. They entered modern western thought as American Indian notions translated into European language and culture.

In language, custom, religion, and written law, the Spaniards descended directly from ancient Rome, yet they brought nothing resembling a democratic tradition with them to America. The French and Dutch who settled parts of North America also settled many other parts of the world that did not become democratic. Democracy did not spring up on French-speaking Haiti any more than in South Africa, where the British and Dutch settled about the same time that they settled in North America.

Even the Netherlands and Britain, the two showcases for European democracy, had difficulty grafting democracy onto monarchical and aristocratic systems soaked in the strong traditions of class privilege. During the reign of George III of Great Britain, while the United States was fighting for its independence, only one person in twenty could vote in England. In all of Scotland, three thousand men could vote, and in Ireland no Catholic could hold office or vote [Commager, pp. 146–48]. In their centuries of struggle to suppress the Irish, the British possibly encumbered their own democratic development.

American anglophiles occasionally point to the signing of the Magna Carta by King John on the battlefield of Runnymede in 1215 as the start of civil liberties and democracy in the English-speaking world. This document, however, merely moved slightly away from monarchy and toward oligarchy by increasing the power of the aristocracy. It continued the traditional European vacillation between government by a single strong ruler and by an oligarchic class. An oligarchy is not an incipient democracy, and a step away from monarchy does not necessarily mean a step toward democracy. In the same tradition, the election of the pope by a college of cardinals did not make the Vatican into a democratic institution, nor did the Holy Roman Empire become a democracy merely because a congress of aristocrats elected the emperor.

When the Dutch built colonies in America, power in their homeland rested securely in the hands of the aristocracy and the burghers, who composed only a quarter of the population. A city such as Amsterdam fell under the rule of a council of thirty-six men, none of whom was elected; instead each council member inherited his office and held it until death [Commager, p. 153].

Henry Steele Commager wrote that during the Enlightenment "Europe was ruled by the wellborn, the rich, the privileged, by those who held their places by divine favor, inheritance, prescription, or purchase" [Commager, p. 154]. The philosophers and thinkers of the Enlightenment became quite complacent and self-congratulatory because the "enlightened despots" such as Catherine of Russia and Frederick of Prussia read widely and showed literary inclinations. Too many philosophers became court pets and because of that believed that Europe was moving toward enlightened democracy. As Commager explained it, Europe only imagined the Enlightenment, but America enacted it. This Enlightenment grew as much from its roots in Indian culture as from any other source.

When Americans try to trace their democratic heritage back through the writings of French and English political thinkers of the Enlightenment, they often forget that these people's thoughts were heavily shaped by the democratic traditions and the state of nature of the American Indians. The concept of the "noble savage" derived largely from writings about the American Indians, and even though the picture grew romanticized and distorted, the writers were only romanticizing and distorting something that really did exist. The Indians did live in a fairly democratic condition, they were egalitarian, and they did live in greater harmony with nature.

The modern notions of democracy based on egalitarian principles and a federated government of overlapping powers arose from the unique blend of European and Indian political ideas and institutions along the Atlantic coast between 1607 and 1776. Modern democracy as we know it today is as much the legacy of the American Indians, particularly the Iroquois and the Algonquians, as it is of the British settlers, of French political theory, or of all the failed efforts of the Greeks and Romans.

The American Revolution did not stop with the thirteen Atlantic colonies; it soon spread around the world. As Thomas Paine wrote in *The Rights of Man,* "from a small spark, kindled in America, a flame has arisen, not to be extinguished." He went on to say that the flame "winds its progress from nation to nation, and conquers by silent operation" [Paine, p. 223].

Although today the notion of the noble savage usually reaps only scorn and historical footnotes as a quaint idea of a less-informed era, the idea had ramifications of great width and magnitude. The noble savage represented a new ideal of human political relations that mutated into the hundreds of political theories that have swept the world in the past five hundred years. The discovery of new forms of political life in America freed the imaginations of Old World thinkers to envision utopias, socialism, communism, anarchism, and dozens of other social forms. Scarcely any political theory or movement of the last three centuries has not shown the impact of this great political awakening that the Indians provoked among the Europeans.

The descriptions of the Baron de Lahontan and other New World travelers of the so-called anarchy among the American Indians contributed to several different brands of anarchistic theory in the nineteenth century. Today, anarchism is often equated with terrorism and nihilism, which denies any values, but early anarchism lacked both of these qualities. Pierre Joseph Proudhon (1809–1865), the father of modern anarchistic theory, stressed the notion of "mutualism" in a society based on cooperation without the use of coercion from any quarter. This was to be brought about peacefully through workers helping one another in labor associations.

From these simple ideas about the noble savage, there followed a wild array of theories as varied and exotic as the different types of birds in the Amazon. Michael Bakunin developed anarchist collectivism. Peter Kropotkin became associated with the ideas of anarchist communism that achieved popularity in Spain, while in France anarcho-syndicalism helped inspire the work of Georges Sorel. Pacifist anarchism developed around the ideas of the Russian writer Leo Tolstoy and the Dutch political philosopher Domela Nieuwenhuis.

In one of its mildest expressions, these ideas of pacific anarchism showed up in America in the writings of Henry David Thoreau (1817–1862). Worshiping the New England countryside by then denuded of its aboriginal Indian inhabitants, Thoreau withdrew from society in order to practice his individualistic anarchism. In 1849 these ideas of the individual's right to refuse cooperation with the state received its highest expression in his essay "Civil Disobedience." In the twentieth century the ideas of Thoreau came to play almost as important a role in world politics as did the many revolutionary theories that developed from more activist brands of anarchism. In 1907 Thoreau's essay helped Gandhi to select the appropriate means of struggle for Indian independence from Britain. Rather than launch a war of liberation, he launched a peaceful movement of civil disobedience. This movement eventually liberated Pakistan and India, and in so doing, sealed the fate of colonialism everywhere in the world. The peaceful movements of Gandhi did more to bring independence than did all the twentieth-century wars of independence.

Thoreau and Gandhi together inspired many different versions of their struggle, one of the most notable being that of the civil rights movement in the United States. Opting for the same peaceful struggle and for civil disobedience, the movement under Martin Luther King, Jr., ended virtually all legal forms of racism in the United States.

Like the American plants that spread all over the world and changed forever the economic, social, and demographic patterns of the world, the Indian love of liberty, freedom, and individuality have also spread. Even though the Indians never had a monopoly on these values, they did achieve the highest cultural development of them. Thus, today in the ordered anarchy of a powwow in North Dakota these same values are articulated even better and more eloquently than in the writings of Paine, Rousseau, Thoreau, and Gandhi.

THE FOUNDING INDIAN FATHERS

Every day of the school year, troops of children march across the lawn of the United States Capitol perched atop the District of Columbia's highest elevation. The building dominates the Washington skyline, a model of classical symmetry and precision. Two giant wings of precisely equal proportion reach out from a Roman dome that surveys the city of Washington. If reduced to a ruin, the forest of Greek columns decorating the building would appear to be as much at home in Rome or Naples as in Athens or Corinth. The building revels in its Old World heritage.

Indian schoolchildren walking through the halls of Congress would rarely see a hint that the building sits in America overlooking the Potomac River and not along the shores of the Mediterranean Sea. The building copies European, primarily classical, styles, and its halls proudly display pictures, friezes, and busts of famous political thinkers from Hammurabi and Solomon to Rousseau and Voltaire. In the hallways stand statues of American politicians posing in Greek tunics and Roman togas as though they were Roman senators or Athenian orators. Greek busts of the vice-presidents of the United States line the halls of the Senate, lending them the aura of a classical cemetery.

The children pass under doorways that bear weighty engravings and quotations from European documents such as the Magna

Carta interspersed with quotes from the United States Declaration of Independence or Constitution. The building and its appointments proudly proclaim their part in the great march of European progress and civilization. They portray the blessed dove of democracy hatching in Athens and then taking wing for a torturous flight of two millennia, pausing only momentarily over Republican Rome, the field of Runnymede, and the desk of Voltaire before finally alighting to rest permanently and securely in the virgin land of America.

A child standing squarely in the middle of the Capitol beneath the great dome sees a painted band circling the upper wall representing the history of America. In that work, the Indians appear as just one more dangerous obstacle, like the wild animals, the Appalachian Mountains, the Mississippi River, and the western deserts, that blocked the progress of European civilization and technology in the white man's march across America. The most peaceful picture with an Indian theme in the rotunda shows the baptism of Pocahontas, daughter of the Indian leader Powhatan. Surrounded by Europeans and dressed in English clothes, she symbolically renounces the savage life of the Indians for the civilization of the British.

The lesson in this august setting presents itself forcefully on every visitor. The United States government derives from European precedents, and the Americans gave civilization to the Indians. Nothing in the Capitol hints that contemporary Americans owe the slightest debt to the Indians for teaching us about democratic institutions.

Despite these civic myths surrounding the creation of American government, America's settlers from Europe knew little of democracy. The English came from a nation ruled by monarchs who claimed that God conferred their right to rule and even allowed them to wage wars of extinction against the Irish. Colonists also fled to America from France, which was wandering aimlessly through history under the extravagances of a succession of kings named Louis, most of whom pursued debauched and extravagant reigns that oppressed, exploited, and at times even starved their subjects.

Despite the ideal government sketched by Plato in The Republic, and the different constitutions analyzed by Aristotle in his Politics, the Old World offered America few democratic models for government. Democratic government had no fortress in the Old World. Despite the democratic rhetoric that came into fashion in eighteenth-century Europe, no such systems existed there at that time. The monarchy and the aristocracy of England were engaged in a protracted struggle that would eventually lead to the supremacy of Parliament (and a closely limited electoral franchise until the reforms of the nineteenth century). France had not yet begun its experiments with participatory democracy. The Founding Fathers of the United States judiciously assembled bits and pieces of many different systems to invent a completely new one. In fashioning the new system, they even borrowed some distinctive elements from the American Indians.

The Founding Fathers faced a major problem when it came time to invent the United States. They represented, under the Articles of Confederation, thirteen separate and sovereign states. How could one country be made from all thirteen without each one yielding its own power?

Reportedly, the first person to propose a union of all the colonies and to propose a federal model for it was the Iroquois chief Canassatego, speaking at an Indian-British assembly in Pennsylvania in July 1744. He complained that the Indians found it difficult to deal with so many different colonial administrations, each with its own policy. It would make life easier for everyone involved if the colonists could have a union which allowed them to speak with one voice. He not only proposed that the colonies unify themselves, but told them how they might do it. He suggested that they do as his people had done and form a union like the League of the Iroquois [Johansen, pp. 12, 61].

Hiawatha and Deganwidah founded the League of the Iroquois sometime between A.D. 1000 and 1450 under a constitution they called the *Kaianerekowa* or Great Law of Peace. When the Europeans arrived in America, the league constituted the most extensive and important political unit north of the Aztec civilization. From earliest contact the Iroquois intrigued the Europeans, and they were the subject of many amazed reports. Benjamin Franklin, however, seems to have been the first to take their system as a potentially important model by which the settlers might be able to fashion a new government.

Benjamin Franklin first became acquainted with the operation of Indian political organization in his capacity as official printer for the colony of Pennsylvania. His job included publication of the records and speeches of the various Indian assemblies and treaty negotiations, but following his instinctive curiosity, he broadened this into a study of Indian culture and institutions. Because of his expertise and interest in Indian matters, the colonial government of Pennsylvania offered him his first diplomatic assignment as their Indian commissioner. He held this post during the 1750s and became intimately familiar with the intricacies of Indian political culture and in particular with the League of the Iroquois. After this taste of Indian diplomacy, Franklin became a lifelong champion of the Indian political structure and advocated its use by the Americans. During this time he also refined his political techniques of persuasion, compromise, and slow consensus building that proved so important to his later negotiations as the ambassador to France and as a delegate to the Constitutional Convention.

Echoing the original proposal of Canassatego, Franklin advocated that the new American government incorporate many of the same features as the government of the Iroquois [Wilson, p. 46]. Speaking to the Albany Congress in 1754, Franklin called on the delegates of the various English colonies to unite and emulate the Iroquois League, a call that was not heeded until the Constitution was written three decades later [Hecht, p. 71]. Even though the Founding Fathers finally adopted some of the essential features of the Iroquois League, they never followed it in quite the detail advocated by Franklin.

The Iroquois League united five principal Indian nations—the Mohawk, Onondaga, Seneca, Oneida, and Cayuga. Each of these nations had a council composed of delegates called sachems who were elected by the tribes of that nation. The Seneca Nation elected eight sachems to its council, the Mohawk and Oneida nations each had councils of nine sachems, the Cayuga Nation had a council of ten, and the Onondaga Nation had a council of fourteen. Each of these nations governed its own territory, and its own council met to decide the issues of public policy for each one. But these councils exercised jurisdiction over the internal concerns of that one nation only; in this regard they exercised powers somewhat like the individual governments of the colonies.

In addition to the individual councils of each separate nation, the sachems formed a grand Council of the League in which all fifty sachems of the six nations sat together to discuss issues of common concern. The sachems represented their individual nations, but at the same time they represented the whole League of the Iroquois, thereby making the decisions of the council the law for all five nations. In this council each sachem had equal authority and privileges, with his power dependent on his oratorical power to persuade. The council met in the autumn of at least one year in five in a longhouse in the Onondaga Nation; if needed they could be called into session at other times as well. Their power extended to all matters of common concern among the member nations. In the words of Lewis Henry Morgan, America's first modern anthropologist, the council "declared war and made peace, sent and received embassies, entered into treaties of alliance, regulated the affairs of subjugated nations, received new members into the League, extended its protection over feeble tribes, in a word, took all needful measures to promote their prosperity, and enlarge their dominion" [Morgan, pp. 66–67].

Through this government the nations of the Iroquois controlled territory from New England to the Mississippi River, and they built a league that endured for centuries. Unlike European governments, the league blended the sovereignty of several nations into one government. This model of several sovereign units united into one government presented precisely the solution to the problem confronting the writers of the United States Constitution. Today we call this a "federal" system in which each state retains power over internal affairs and the national government regulates affairs common to all. Henry Steele Commager later wrote of this crucial time that even "if Americans did not actually invent federalism, they were able to take out an historical patent on it" [Commager, p. 207]. The Indians invented it even though the United States patented it.

Another student of the Iroquois political organization was Charles Thomson, the perpetual secretary of the Continental Congress. He spent so much energy studying the Indians and their way of life that the Delaware Nation adopted him as a full member.

Following Thomas Jefferson's request, Thomson wrote at length on Indian social and political institutions for inclusion in an appendix to Jefferson's *Notes on the State of Virginia*. According to his description of Indian political tradition, each Indian town built a council house for making local decisions and for electing delegates to the tribal council. The tribal council in turn elected delegates to the national council [Thomson, p. 203]. Even though Thomson wrote this several years before the Constitutional Convention, this description reads like a blueprint for the United States Constitution, especially when we remember that the Constitution allowed the state legislatures (rather than the general populace) to elect senators. Thomson stresses that the sachems or political leaders do not acquire their positions by heredity but by election, and he adds that because outsiders can be naturalized into the Indian nation, even they can be elected to such offices.

The Americans followed the model of the Iroquois League not only in broad outline but also in many of the specific provisions of their *Kaianerekowa*. According to the *Kaianerekowa*, the sachems were not chiefs, a position frequently associated with leadership in war. As a lawmaker, the sachem could never go to war in his official capacity as a sachem. "If disposed to take the warpath, he laid aside his civil office, for the time being, and became a common warrior" [Morgan, p. 72]. This followed the tradition in many Indian tribes that relied upon separate leaders for peace and for war. The colonists followed this model too in eventually separating civilian authorities from military ones. Members of Congress, judges, and other officials could not also act as military leaders without giving up their elected office; similarly, military leaders could not be elected to political office without first resigning their military position. This contrasted with British traditions; church and military leaders frequently served as members of the House of Lords and frequently played major political roles in the House of Commons as well. Similarly, this inability to separate the civil government and the military has doomed many of the imitators of American democracy, particularly in Africa and Latin America.

If the conduct of any sachem appeared improper to the populace or if he lost the confidence of his electorate, the women of his clan impeached him and expelled him by official action, whereupon the women then choose a new sachem [Goldenweiser, p. 570]. This concept of impeachment ran counter to European tradition, in which the monarch ruled until death, even if he became insane or incapacitated, as in the case of George III. The Americans followed the Iroquois precedent of always providing for ways to remove leaders when necessary, but the Founding Fathers saw no reason to follow the example of the Iroquois in granting women the right to vote or any other major role in the political structure.

One of the most important characteristics of the Iroquois League permitted it to expand as needed; the council could vote to admit new members. This proved to be an important feature of the system after the Tuscarora Indians of North Carolina faced attack in 1712 by the army of Colonel John Barnwell and again in 1713 by the army of Colonel James Moore. Having thoroughly defeated the Tuscaroras, the Carolina colonists demanded reparations from the Indians to pay the colonists' expenses incurred in the war. Because the Indians had no money to pay, the colonists seized four hundred of them and sold them into slavery at the rate of ten pounds sterling apiece. The surviving Tuscaroras fled North Carolina to seek refuge among the Iroquois. In 1714 the Tuscaroras applied for formal membership in the league, and the Iroquois admitted them in 1722 as the Sixth Nation [Waldman, p. 104]. Similarly the league later incorporated other decimated groups such as the Erie, but the league did not allow for an entity such as a colony, which had played such an important part in European governments since the times of the ancient Greeks.

In a radical break with Old World tradition, the emerging government of the United States emulated this Iroquois tradition of admitting new states as members rather than keeping them as colonies. The west became a series of territories and then states, but the United States treated each new territory as a future partner rather than as a colony. The new government codified this Indian practice into American law through the Congressional Resolution of 1780, the Land Ordinances of 1784 and 1785, and the Northwest Ordinance, together with similar provisions written directly into the Constitution. No direct proof links these laws with the Iroquois, but it seems likely to be more than mere coincidence that both the Iroquois and the United States governments enacted such similar procedures.

Although the Iroquois recognized no supreme leader in their system analogous to the president of the United States, the framers of the Constitution deliberately or inadvertently imitated the Great Council in establishing the electoral college system to select a president. Each state legislature selected a group of electors equal in number to that state's combined total of senators and representatives. Like the sachems, each elector then had one vote in the electoral college.

In the two centuries since the Constitution went into effect, some aspects of the system have changed. The voters rather than the state legislatures now elect both the electoral college and the senators through popular vote, but the system preserves the general features of the League of the Iroquois.

Upon election to the council, the new sachem "lost" his name and thenceforth other sachems called him by the title of his office. In much the same way, proceedings of the United States Senate do not permit the use of names such as "Senator Kennedy" or "Rudy Boschwitz." Instead the senators must be addressed by their office title as "the Senior Senator from Massachusetts" or "the Junior Senator from Minnesota." Other titles such as "Majority Leader," "Mr. Chairman," or "Mr. President" may be used, but all personal names remain strictly taboo.

Another imitation of the Iroquois came in the simple practice of allowing only one person to speak at a time in political meetings. This contrasts with the British tradition of noisy interruptions of one another as the members of Parliament shout out agreement or disagreement with the speaker. Europeans were accustomed to shouting down any speaker who displeased them; in some cases they might even stone him or inflict worse damage.

The Iroquois permitted no interruptions or shouting. They even imposed a short period of silence at the end of each oration in case the speaker had forgotten some point or wished to elaborate or change something he had said [Johansen, p. 87]. Even though the American Congress and legislatures did not adopt the practice of silence at the end, they did allow speakers "to revise and extend" the written record after speaking.

The purpose of debate in Indian councils was to persuade and educate, not to confront. Unlike European parliaments, where opposing factions battle out an issue in the public arena, the council of the Indians sought to reach an agreement through compromise. This important difference in nuance led Bruce Burton to observe in his study of American law that "American democracy owes its distinctive character of debate and compromise to the principles and structures of American Indian civil government" [Burton, p. 5]. Still today, this difference separates the operation of the United States Congress and the state legislatures from their European counterparts. American legislative bodies are composed primarily of individuals forming shifting factions from one issue to another, whereas the legislative bodies of Europe operate through opposing political parties that control the votes of individual representatives.

In keeping with Iroquois tradition, Franklin proposed that since the sachems did not own land or receive any financial compensation for their work, the officials of the United States should not be paid. They should perform their work as a sacred trust freely given to the communal welfare. Even though the Founding Fathers did not incorporate this, they did work to prevent property qualifications for holding office and for exercising the right to vote. They also tended to limit salaries paid to officeholders to a minimum to cover basic expenses of life rather than making public office a sinecure or a route to wealth.

In his democratic zeal to imitate the system of the Indians, Franklin even proposed that military officers should be elected by the men whom they ordered into battle. The Indians routinely fought this way, and Franklin organized such a militia himself in 1747 to protect Philadelphia from harassment by French and Dutch pirates. Even though the American army did not adopt the practice of electing officers, it gradually abandoned the European practice of allowing the purchase of commissions by the wealthy. The American system did allow for mobility within the ranks and prevented the officer corps of the army from resembling too closely an aristocratic class as in Europe or an oligarchy as in many Latin American nations.

The League of the Iroquois operated with only a single chamber in its council. Franklin became an ardent supporter of this unicameral organization, and he even wanted to use the English translation of the Iroquois term meaning "grand council" rather than the Latinism "congress." The United States government relied on only a single chamber during the years of the Continental Congress, and some states, such as Pennsylvania and Vermont, reduced their state legislatures to unicameral bodies for a while. The unicameral congress and legislature, however, did not endure, and today only Nebraska has a unicameral legislature, instituted to save money and not to emulate the Iroquois.

In addition to Benjamin Franklin, Thomas Paine, and Charles Thomson, many of the Founding Fathers of American federalism had worked closely with the Indian political institutions. George Washington had extensive contacts with the Indians in his surveying expeditions into the western part of Virginia and fought with Indians and against Indians in the French and Indian War. Washington showed a greater interest in land speculation and making money than in observing the political life of the Indians. Thomas Jefferson, author of the Declaration of Independence, also lived close to the frontier, and he himself was the son of a pioneer. He studied and wrote numerous articles and essays on the Indians, leading a later historian to call Jefferson "the most enlightened of amateur ethnologists" [Commager, p. 179]. In his recommendations for the University of Virginia, he became the first person to propose a systematic ethnological study of the Indians in order "to collect their traditions, laws, customs, languages and other circumstances" [Jefferson, p. 151].

Because of men such as Thomas Paine, Benjamin Franklin, Charles Thomson, and Thomas Jefferson, we today know a great deal about the League of the Iroquois and some of the other Indian groups of the eastern United States. Subsequent years of ethnological research into the political organizations of the New World have shown that the League of the Iroquois seems representative of political institutions throughout all of America north of Mexico and much of Central and South America as well. Councils chosen by the clans, tribes, or villages governed most Indian nations.

From Hollywood films and adventure novels Americans often conclude that strong chiefs usually commanded the Indian tribes. More often, however, as in the case of the Iroquois, a council ruled, and any person called the "head" of the tribe usually occupied a largely honorary position of respect rather than power. Chiefs mostly played ceremonial and religious roles rather than political or economic ones. Unlike the words "caucus" and "powwow," which are Indian-derived and indicative of Indian political traditions, the word "chief" is an English word of French origin that British officials tried to force onto Indian tribes in order that they might have someone with whom to trade and sign treaties.

In Massachusetts the British tried to make one leader into King Philip. The British imputed monarchy to the Indian system when no such institution existed. Thus while the English settlers learned from the Indians how to speak and act in group councils, they simultaneously pushed the Indians toward a monarchical and thus less democratic system.

We see the same collective system in the early 1500s in the pueblos of the southwest when one of Francisco Coronado's soldiers wrote that the Zuni had no chiefs "but are ruled by a council of the oldest men" whom they called *papas*. The Zuni word *papa* means "elder brother," and each clan probably elected its *papa* the way the Iroquois clans elected their sachems.

Even the Aztecs' government conformed to this pattern. They divided themselves into twenty *calpulli* or corporate clans, each of which owned property in common. Each *calpulli* elected a number of administrative officers to oversee the administration of property and law within its clan, and they elected a *tlatoani*, literally a "speaker," who functioned as the representative of the *calpulli* to the outside world. All the *tlatoani* met together to form the supreme council of the nation, and they elected the supreme speaker, or *huey-tlatoani*, an office with life tenure. By the time the Spanish arrived, this highest office of the nation had been reserved for a single family, but the council decided who within that family would have the office. The Spanish assumed that the Aztec system was like their own system or like that of their neighbors the Moors; they translated *huey-tlatoani* as "emperor" and called the *tlatoani* the "nobles" of the empire. Moctezuma, the Aztec leader captured by Hernando Cortés, held office as the supreme speaker of the Aztec nation, not as its emperor.

This Aztec system was no more of a democracy or a federal union because of these councils than was the Holy Roman Empire, which also had a council to elect its emperor from one family. Still, in the Aztec system we can see the outlines of a political format common throughout the Americas and in many ways closer to our democratic system in the United States today than to the systems of Europe of that time. The difference in the Aztec system and a European monarchy appeared most clearly when the Aztec people removed Moctezuma from office after the Spaniards captured him. The people even stoned him when he tried to persuade them to acquiesce to the Spanish. The Spaniards had expected the people to revere and obey their "emperor" no matter what, but they assumed erroneously that Moctezuma held the same power over the Aztec people that the Spanish king held over themselves.

The depth of democratic roots among North American Indian groups shows clearly in the detailed study of the Yaqui by historian Evelyn Hu-DeHart. Living in the present-day states of Sonora and Sinaloa of northwestern Mexico just south of the Apaches of Arizona, the Yaquis coaxed a livelihood from this desert setting through hunting and simple agriculture. In July 1739 the Yaquis sent two emissaries named Muni and Bernabe to Mexico City for a rare audience with the Spanish viceroy to plead for free elections of their own government administrators in place of the Jesuits appointed over them. After 1740 the government allowed the Yaquis to elect their own captain general as head of their tribe, but the government still sought to exercise control over the Yaquis through clerical and civilian administrators [Hu-DeHart, p. 17]. Thus in the wilds of Mexico a full generation before the Revolution in the English colonies of North America, we see evidence of the Indians demanding the franchise and free elections in order to maintain their traditional political values.

In almost every North American tribe, clan, or nation for which we have detailed political information, the supreme authority rested in a group rather than in an individual. It took many generations of close interaction between colonists and Indians before the principles of group decision-making replaced the European traditions of relying on a single supreme authority. The importance of these Indian councils and groups shows clearly in the English lack of words to explain such a process.

One of the most important political institutions borrowed from the Indians was the caucus. Even though the word appears to be proper Latin and some law students with a semester of Latin occasionally decline the plural as *cauci*, the word comes from the Algonquian languages. The caucus permits informal discussion of an issue without necessitating a yea or nay vote on any particular question. This agreed with the traditional Indian way of talking through an issue or of making a powwow; it made political decisions less divisive and combative. The caucus became a mainstay of American democracy both in the Congress and in political and community groups all over the country. The caucus evolved into such an important aspect of American politics that the political parties adopted it to nominate their presidential candidates. In time this evolved into the political convention, which still functions as an important part of contemporary American politics but is largely absent from European politics.

Not all the Founding Fathers showed interest in Indian political traditions. They turned instead toward models such as the British Parliament and some of the Greek and Italian city-states. Many of them had been deeply trained in classic literature, in ways that Franklin and Paine had not been trained, and they sought to incorporate the classic notions of democracy and republicanism into the new nation.

Often this proved to be a tricky undertaking, for the ancient Greeks observed democracy far more in the breach than in its enactment. The Greeks who rhapsodized about democracy in their rhetoric rarely created democratic institutions. A few cities such as Athens occasionally attempted a system vaguely akin to democracy for a few years. These cities functioned as slave societies and were certainly not egalitarian or democratic in the Indian sense. Most of the respected political thinkers of Greece despised democracy both theoretically and in practice. The people of Athens executed Socrates during one of their democratic eras because he had conspired with the oligarchs to destroy democracy. On the other hand, Plato favored rule by a philosopher-king and even went to Syracuse to help the tyrant Dionysius rule.

In the United States, the southerners identified much more closely with the ideals of Greek democracy based on massive slavery than with Iroquois democracy, which did not permit slavery. As historian Vernon Parrington wrote, the "dream of a Greek civilization based on black slavery was discovered in the bottom of the cup of southern romanticism" [Parrington, p. 130].

Carolinians, Georgians, and Virginians identified so closely with the so-called democracies of Greece that they considered the south to be a virtual reincarnation or at least renaissance of Greek life. By the beginning of the nineteenth century, southerners had created a virtual Greek cult as an intellectual bulwark to protect their way of life. European romantics such as Lord Byron and John Keats flirted with Greek aesthetics, but the Europeans quickly dropped them in favor of a more personal form of romanticism.

The American south, however, embraced everything Greek. The southern gentleman with his leisurely life of relaxation in the study, friendly conversation in the parlor, fine meals in the dining room, courting in the ballroom, and hunting in the forest identified closely with the good life of Greek literature. At least a passing acquaintance with the Greek and Latin languages became the true mark of a gentleman in the south, and the Greek ideal of a sound mind in a sound body became the creed of the southern leisure class. Southerners wrote poems in mock-Greek style and wrote letters in a classical form. In their excess they even gave their house slaves, horses, and hunting dogs names such as Cicero, Athena, Cato, Pericles, Homer, Apollo, and Nero.

They adorned their plantations with Greek names, and even built their homes in the style of Greek temples. Greek architecture prevailed so widely in the South that today the stereotyped image of a plantation house includes Corinthian columns in Greek Revival style. In their gardens they built gazebos that were styled after Greek shrines, and they set Greek statues out among the magnolia trees and the palms. Even the churches of the south added porticos and rows of columns to their fronts, topped off by very un-Greek steeples.

In making itself over in the Greek image, America neglected a major part of its democratic roots in the long house of the Iroquois and the humble caucus of the Algonquians in favor of the ostentatious props and models looted from the classical Mediterranean world. For almost the whole first century of American independence this Greek architecture and Greek oratory helped to disguise the fact that the nation was based on slavery, an institution that could never be compatible with democracy no matter how much that architectural and verbal edifice tried to cover it.

Prior to this Greek cult, most government buildings in America had been built in a very simple style, as in the state capitol of Massachusetts, Independence Hall in Philadelphia, or the government buildings of colonial Williamsburg. But with the rise of the Greek cult in the south, government architects moved away from the simple Federal style to make public buildings appear Greek. At the height of this classical obsession the United States government began work on a new Capitol. The Senate chamber took the form of a small Greek amphitheater covered in excessive classical ornaments, while the House of Representatives crowned itself with a large clock encased in a sculpture of Clio, the muse of history, riding in her winged chariot and recording the historic events below her.

Although the Greek cult spread out of the south, New Englanders never embraced it very fondly. For them mystic philosophies such as Transcendentalism, often accompanied by ideas of liberty and abolition of slavery, seemed far more alluring. For them the existence of slavery at the foundations of democracy bastardized the whole system.

Even in the south the Greek cult did not reign as the only intellectual and social fashion. In stark contrast to this indulgence of the rich, the black population and the poor whites embraced a strict form of Old Testament fundamentalism closely associated with Moses, the liberator of the slaves, and of New Testament salvation focused on a very personal savior and protector.

Meanwhile in the west the process of learning democracy through experience of the frontier and Indians continued without regard to the supposed classical models. Even after the founding of the United States, the Indians continued to play a significant role in the evolution of democracy because of their sustained interactions with Americans on the frontier. The frontiersmen constantly reinvented democracy and channeled it into the eastern establishment of the United States.

Time and again the people of the frontier rebelled against the entrenched and conservative values of an ever more staid coastal elite. As the frontier gradually moved westward, the settlements on the edge sent such rebels as Henry Clay, Andrew Jackson, David Crockett, and Abraham Lincoln back to reinvest the spirit of democracy into the political institutions of the east. Some of these men, such as Sam Houston, lived for long periods with Indians. Houston spent so much time with the Cherokee that they adopted him into their nation about 1829. The influence of the Cherokees stayed with him throughout his tenure as president of Texas from 1836 to 1838 and again from 1841 to 1844. Throughout his life he maintained close working relations with a variety of Indian nations and a strong commitment to liberty.

Even Alexis de Tocqueville, who denigrated the achievements of the Indians, noticed that the settlers on the frontier "mix the ideas and customs of savage life with the civilization of their fathers." In general he found this reprehensible, for it made their "passions more intense" and "their religious morality less authoritative" [Tocqueville, Vol. I, p. 334], but these traits certainly may be interpreted by others as among the virtues of a democratic people.

Most democratic and egalitarian reforms of the past two hundred years in America originated on the frontier and not in the settled cities of the east. The frontier states dropped property and religious requirements for voters. They extended the franchise to women, and in 1916 Montana elected Jeannette Rankin as the first woman in Congress four years before the Nineteenth Amendment to the Constitution gave women the right to vote. The western states started the public election of senators in place of selection by the legislature. They also pioneered the use of primary elections and electoral recalls of unpopular officers. Even today they have more elective offices, such as judges; such offices in the east are usually filled by appointment by the governor or the legislature. This strong bias toward the electoral process and equal votes for all has been reinforced repeatedly by the people who have had the closest and the longest connections with the Indians on the frontier.

****

The final extension of the federal principles used in the Iroquois Nation and later in the formation of the United States came in 1918 with establishment of the League of Nations. The framers of this new league also chose the Iroquois federal system of allowing each member an equal voice no matter how small or large a country he represented. The same principle underlay creation of the General Assembly of the United Nations a generation later. By ironic coincidence, the founders of this international body located it in New York in the very territory that once belonged to the League of the Iroquois. In one respect the United Nations was an international version of that Indian league.

Washington, D.C., has never recognized the role of the Indians in the writing of the United States Constitution or in the creation of political institutions that seem so uniquely American. But an inadvertent memorial does exist. An older woman from Israel pointed this out to me one spring day as I cut across the lawn of the United States Capitol, where I then worked for Senator John Glenn. She stopped me, and in a husky voice asked me who was the Indian woman atop the Capitol dome. Suddenly looking at it through her eyes, I too saw the figure as an Indian even though I knew that it was not.

When the United States government embarked on an expansion of the Capitol in the middle of the nineteenth century, the architects proposed to cap the dome with a symbol of freedom. They chose for this a nineteen-foot bronze statue of a Roman woman who would stand on the pinnacle of the Capitol. Sculptor Thomas Crawford crowned the woman with a Phrygian cap, which in Roman history had been the sign of the freed slave. At that time Jefferson Davis, the future president of the Confederate States of America, still served as the secretary of war for the United States, and he objected strongly to what he interpreted as an antisouthern and antislavery symbol. He compelled Crawford to cap her with something less antagonistic to southern politicians. Crawford designed a helmet covered with a crown of feathers, but in putting this headdress on the figure, her whole appearance changed. Now instead of looking like a classical Greek or Roman, she looked like an Indian.

She still stands today on the pseudoclassical Capitol overlooking the city of Washington. The Washington Monument rises to the same height, but no other building has been allowed to rise higher than she. Even though no one intended her to be an Indian, she now reigns as the nearest thing to a monument that Washington ever built to honor the Indians who contributed to the building of a federal union based on democracy.

▲ ▲ ⑨ ▲ ▲
RED STICKS
AND REVOLUTION

One warm January afternoon, I was driving a Land Rover with some of my students over a virtually impassable road in Guatemala's northeastern province of Petén. We had just entered Guatemala that day from Carmen Viejo del Benque in Belize, where we had spent the previous night in very commodious huts along the Mopán River just below the fortified Mayan ruins of Xunantunich. We were exploring the ruins but also visiting various contemporary villages of Kekchi and Mopán Maya. Now we were on the way to the unique city called Flores.

Flores sits on an island in the middle of Lake Petén-Itzá, and its roughly two thousand inhabitants go to the mainland by boat or by a thin causeway about a mile in length. Foreigners sometimes visit the city because it is only an hour's drive from Tikal, the classical Maya site that flourished from A.D. 300 to 900, and which is in the middle of the jungle, surrounded by spider monkeys, parrots, jaguars, oscillated turkeys, and the poisonous fer-de-lance known locally as *barba amarilla,* "yellow beard."

Lake Petén-Itzá had another significance for us, however, because on its shore stood Tayasal, the last American Indian city to fall to the Europeans. Mayan refugees from the Yucatecan city of Chichén Itzá founded Tayasal long after Tikal had been abandoned. Protected by the remote location and the thick jungle of Petén, it did not succumb to the Spanish rule until 1697, when the army of Martín de Ursua conquered it before founding the modern city of Flores in 1700.

On the day of our visit, we pushed hard to reach Flores before nightfall to avoid trouble from either the guerrillas or the anti-guerrilla army units. Not long after crossing the border into Guatemala we had passed the army camp, which displayed menacing hand-painted signs proclaiming that therein was the best army in Central America and threatening death to all guerrillas. To stress the point for even the illiterate, the signs exhibited graphic pictures of the fierce soldiers attacking the guerrillas. Because of the tense situation, we had been forbidden to bring in a Land Rover, which could easily have been seized by the guerrillas, but through negotiations at the border, we had managed to slip it into the country. Several weeks later that deed caused me to be detained by Belizean soldiers when I was back in Belize, but on this first night in Guatemala, I thought only of getting our group to the safety of Flores before dark.

Still several hours away from our goal, we came upon an Indian village, but because of the late hour, I had no intention of stopping. Even before the Land Rover crossed into the village, I smelled the evening fires mixed with the thicker odor of animal manure. Like most of the villages we had seen on the road that day, it was liberally sprinkled with small blotches of paint in the official colors of the army unit stationed in the district. Their sign appeared on every signpost, house, or utility pole in the area. As I drove slowly through the ruts in the road, swerving to avoid gaping holes, small children, and pigs, we suddenly descended on the main plaza, which offered nothing more than an open field of hardened mud surrounded by rambling single-story houses. On the edge of the plaza, I suddenly had to stomp on the brakes to avoid crashing into an army blockade. The soldiers rushed over and motioned with guns for me to pull in behind three other vehicles. Unlike those at other blockades we had passed through, these soldiers showed no intention of letting any of us pass. We sat in silence. Feeling cramped inside the Land Rover, the students and I got out to stretch, but two young soldiers excitedly motioned us back inside by threatening jabs in our direction with their automatic rifles. Even though we could not pass, the soldiers seemed only marginally concerned with us.

Aside from a few guards, most of the soldiers ran around the village rounding up all the Indian men and bringing them into the plaza.

Once the men of the village had assembled, the soldiers stood around them in an armed circle ordering the Indians to stand in straight lines at attention. While several soldiers strolled menacingly through the ranks of Indians, the commanding officer harangued the group. Although we heard his angry shouts and saw his flailing arms, the distance and the wind prevented our understanding what he was saying. After nearly half an hour the commandant ordered the Indians into two long lines facing one another for a series of military drills that involved pointing rifles at one another point-blank and pretending to shoot.

Satisfied that they had mastered this exercise, the commandant marched his Indian civilians toward our blockaded caravan of three pathetic vehicles. Under the watchful guidance of the soldiers, who barked orders continuously, the Indians ordered all of us from our vehicles. Slowly, they searched each vehicle in turn. They went through our duffel bags and knapsacks as well as the assorted collection of foods we carried. They pulled and pushed on every gear and lever, managing to damage the four-wheel-drive mechanism of our Land Rover. After deciding that the car contained nothing of interest for them, they separated us from one another and searched us in the same way.

Only after this exhausting search did they interrogate us, with blistering speed:

Who are you?

What are you doing in this guerrilla zone?

Why are you so far from the main highway?

Where are you going?

Where are you coming from?

Do you have any weapons?

Finally accepting that we posed no threat, the soldiers barked at us for being on the highway so late and warned us that even though they were allowing us to pass, we might not be so lucky up ahead when we ran into another unit.

By the time they released us it was nearly dark. Before we reached Flores that night, three more army units stopped us along the road, and each time the soldiers badgered us with increasingly belligerent questions as the night grew later and we therefore increasingly provoked suspicions. In this way we unexpectedly came to experience the *Fusiles y Frijoles* or "Guns and Beans" campaign of the Guatemalan army to pacify the Indians when practical and to kill them otherwise. What we had witnessed that evening had been one of the peaceful efforts by the army to lecture the Indians on resistance to the guerrillas, to instill a fear of the military, and to teach them how to protect their village against the rebels.

Ironically we had come to Petén to visit the site where the Indians had surrendered their last city holdout nearly three hundred years ago; yet, continuing Indian skirmishes delayed us in route. In the past decade, several hundred thousand Indian men, women, and children have been killed in skirmishes, raids, retaliatory maneuvers, and acts of sheer terrorism against them. Almost all of these Indians have been part of the approximately two million Maya living in the area. The Indians usually resist in a fairly passive way; yet they continue the struggle and use violence when all else fails them.

The history of America is the history of constant resistance and periodic armed revolution against the Old World forms of tyranny. No matter how many times the Indians lost, and no matter how many tribes were permanently obliterated, other Indians continued the struggle. The perpetual Indian wars of the last half millennium have taken many ideological and tactical forms, but they have always focused on the basic issues of land, food, and human rights.

Today the Indian problems of governments in Guatemala, Peru, and Nicaragua seem to be quite different from the Indian problems of the U.S. government. Yet, only a historically short time has passed since the Indians of the United States rose up in a series of wars much like those being fought by remote Indian groups in Latin America in the twentieth century.

During the nineteenth century, the Indians frequently initiated campaigns of resistance that rejected many of the white influences, including Christianity, while opposing the new settlers. One of the most important such movements started among the Creek or Muskogee Indians of the southeastern United States. They lived in approximately a hundred autonomous towns called *talwa*, but they organized themselves into a loose confederacy. Like the Iroquois, they had matrilineal clans, and their political organization centered around elected councils. Perhaps because of their proximity to Mexico, they had large mound pyramids in their territory, showed similarities in art, and they played ball games similar to those of the Maya and Aztecs.

Like other "civilized" Indian nations, the Creeks had slowly adopted many traits of European life in the three hundred years of contact beginning with the visit of Hernando de Soto in 1540. They still grew their native crops and wore buckskins, but they also used cotton clothing spun by the Creek women on spinning wheels. They cultivated wheat to make white bread, and they allowed schools and Christian churches in their communities. In 1720 a woman of the Wind Clan married a French army officer, and thus began the development of a native aristocracy of mixed bloods who sent their children to France and Britain for education.

During the first three hundred years of contact, the Creek leaders played a systematic policy of neutrality toward the Spanish who occupied Florida to their south, the French who occupied Louisiana to their west, and to the British who had already pushed them out of South Carolina and Georgia to their east. The Creek Nation traded extensively with Jamaica and the Bahamas as well as with the Spanish in Pensacola, the French in New Orleans, and the British in Savannah and Charleston.

Even though the aristocratic clan members spoke English, French, and Spanish, and were often literate in classical Greek and Latin as well, many of them claimed they could barely speak their own Muskogean language. The Creek leader Alexander Mc-Gillivray, who was part French and part Scotch as well as Creek, preferred speaking to his people through interpreters as though he could not speak his native language. Under McGillivray, the highest military office of the Creek Confederacy, called the *tustenegee*, was offered to a French officer, LeClerc Milfort, in an effort to modernize the Indian army between 1776 and 1796. Milfort then married McGillivray's sister Jeanette to secure a permanent place in Creek society. The Indian elite lived in houses modeled after the plantations of whites, and some of them owned slaves. Because their European educations often surpassed those of the nearly illiterate white colonists, great resentments arose between the two groups.

McGillivray fought hard to hold back the whites and to unify all of the Creeks and other southern Indians in a single confederacy. To do this he played the Spanish, British, and Americans against one another much as a modern Third World country might play off the United States and the Soviet Union. In 1778 he was made a colonel by the British, and then in 1784 the Spanish signed a treaty giving him a monthly salary and granting him a monopoly in Spanish trade. In 1790 with the Treaty of New York, George Washington raised him in rank to brigadier general and gave him a secret annuity of $1,200. The Spanish raised this sum to $3,500 in 1792 and recognized him as superintendent general of the Creeks and Seminoles. The Spanish also recognized him by treaty as the emperor of the Creeks, a title that the British later accepted as well. McGillivray sought some guarantee of Creek sovereignty, but his nation had to accept an inferior position as a protectorate destined to become a white territory and eventually a state of the United States [Spicer, p. 24].

The unity of the Creek Nation dissolved after the Revolution and the death in 1793 of Alexander McGillivray, its last leader. LeClerc Milfort returned to Paris in 1802 to agitate for the Creeks from the court of Napoleon, but aid never came. Alexander McGillivray's children refused to return from Europe, and no new leader arose.

In 1812 when a new war broke out between Britain and the United States, two of McGillivray's nephews announced that the time had come to purge their nation of the settlers. The eldest discarded his European name to take on a Muskogean name that meant Red Eagle in English, red being the Creek color of war. Red Eagle apparently adopted some of the ideology of the Shawnee prophet Tecumseh when he launched a movement to purify the Creek Nation by driving out many of the evil European influences. As precursors of the red revolutionary movements in Europe later in the century, Red Eagle's followers took the name of Red Sticks (also called Baton Rouge in French) because they painted their ceremonial war clubs red. They hoped to return to the traditional Indian language, religion, culture, and way of life.

The reformists advocated a return to the sacred ceremonies of their people and to honoring the Master of Breath as the power in their universe. They emphasized the ritual importance of tobacco and of taking the traditional Black Drink, a concoction made from *Ilex cassine*, but they rigorously abstained from all alcohol, something which had been introduced and promoted by the settlers. The Red Sticks banned the use of European guns for hunting, since they were used mostly for the commercial hunting of skins and pelts and had thereby destroyed the native food supply. With simple yet astute ecological reasoning they asserted that the bow and arrow sufficed to feed the people without depleting the forests and destroying the game. Abjuring the use of guns would also pull the Indians out of the enslaving commercial trade that kept them in debt to the traders for ammunition and thus forced them to travel ever farther in search of ever more game with which to pay the debts. Some of the stricter Red Sticks harangued their fellow Indians to return to eating venison instead of beef and to native turkeys in place of European chickens as a way to save their forest homeland from becoming open pastures.

The movement identified European culture as the enemy, but it was not a racist movement against white people. Red Eagle and most of his brothers themselves had white blood, since their mother, Sehoy, had had several white husbands. Many of the Creeks sprang from mixed Indian-Scottish or Indian-African ancestry after extensive intermarriage with traders and escaped slaves. The Creeks, however, insisted that any child born of a Creek mother was Creek no matter if the father was French, African, or Scottish. Their revitalization movement emphasized cultural purity and adherence to a way of life but had nothing to do with blood lines, race, or genes. They freely admitted both whites and blacks who wanted to join them; one of the main war leaders and interpreters for the Creek Nation was a West African who escaped from slavery and became known among the Creeks as Souanakke Tustenukke and among the whites as the Prophet Abraham.

This mixture of Indians and blacks provoked fear among the white settlers, who had so recently been terrorized by the gruesome and successful slave revolts in Haiti and the ensuing massacre of the whites. The whites and their Indian allies began raiding and harassing the Creeks. The anti-Creek forces gathered their families and slaves together for safety and to plan a campaign from Fort Mims on Lake Tonsas in what is now Alabama. On August 30, 1813, some of the Red Sticks attacked the poorly guarded fort, and in the ensuing battle killed the 170 soldiers and their white commander, Major Beasley, and his mixed-blood second-in-command, Captain Dixon Bailey. The Red Sticks mostly relied on the traditional Indian weapons of bows and arrows and tomahawks. When they set the fort afire with flaming arrows, approximately a hundred civilians perished, some of whom were white but most of whom were Indians and mixed-bloods who owned slaves and thus did not support the Red Stick revolution. To terrorize others who might try to invade Creek territory, the Red Stick soldiers scalped the dead and burned the fort to the ground. The Red Sticks killed the slaves who fought, but they spared the ones who did not. Labeled as one of the worst massacres of North American history, the tragedy torched the rage of the whole nation. The United States seemed in no mood to tolerate such incidents on its borders, especially when it was already fighting another war with Britain and Canada. In response, Andrew Jackson organized a Tennessee army to march against the Creek Nation. Meanwhile, the Creeks made hasty alliances with Spain to supply arms and ammunition through Pensacola in Spanish Florida.

Despite the arms from Spain and the support of the French, the Creeks lost the war, and Andrew Jackson ravaged their country during the winter of 1813–1814, killing Indians, blacks, and mixed-bloods indiscriminately. He finally crushed the Red Sticks at the Massacre of Tohopeka or Horseshoe Bend beside the Tallaposa River in Alabama on March 27, 1814. To count the dead Indians, the whites cut off their noses and accumulated a pile of 557 noses. They then skinned the bodies in order to tan the Indian hides and make souvenirs such as bridle reins. When the whites finished mutilating the Creeks, they allowed their own Indian allies to scalp the dead [Halbert and Ball, p. 276].

The ensuing Treaty of Fort Jackson of August 9, 1814, opened the Creeks' entire nation up to settlement and stripped them of most of their territory as the cost of the war. In that same year,

Britain officially recognized the Indians as a nation and not merely a tribe and vowed to protect their rights. The United States signed the Treaty of Ghent ending the war of 1812 with Britain, and Article Nine specified that all lands belonging to Indians allied with Britain must be returned to their Indian owners, but the United States stubbornly ignored this provision.

Andrew Jackson never overcame his hatred for the Creeks, and when he became president he persuaded Congress to pass the Indian Removal Act of 1830 and forced the surviving Creeks to abandon their lands east of the Mississippi River by the Treaty of Cusseta, which the Creeks signed under duress. Now they were to be sent to Indian Territory, where they might form another buffer state separating the United States from the Mexican territories. The American army together with their Cherokee allies invaded the Creek Nation and forced the remnants of the Creeks into detention camps. Settlers claimed many of the Indians as slaves to work the newly established cotton plantations. Soldiers chained the remaining Creek men one to another in a long chain gang, and the women and children followed them as they blazed the path that soon became known to the world as the Trail of Tears. In the decade ahead, many more Indian nations had to follow the same route.

Some of the Creeks sailed for the Bahamas and the safety of the Union Jack, while others headed south for Cuba and protection under the Spanish. A few of the Creeks and the former slaves with whom they had intermarried continued to fight from the swamps under Osceola, one of Red Eagle's lieutenants. Their struggle combined elements of both a slave rebellion and a war of resistance against the invaders. Known as the Seminoles from the Spanish word *cimarrones*, meaning savages, they and the slaves who joined them fought a long hard war until the whites captured Osceola and imprisoned him in Charleston, South Carolina, where he died in 1838.

Repeatedly throughout the nineteenth century, other Indian groups rose up to pursue the quixotic quest of the Red Sticks for an autonomous Indian culture, preaching the pan-Indian doctrine of unity. A succession of prophets in various tribes appeared to announce a new ritual, a sacred object, or some new magic that was guaranteed to rid the Indians of their increasing oppression and free them from the twin threats of ethnocide and genocide. The Ghost Dance movement arose in the western United States and culminated in the unprovoked slaughter of three hundred Sioux men, women, and children at the Massacre of Wounded Knee in 1890.

Soon after the Red Stick revolt of the Creeks, the Yaquis rose up demanding that the newly independent nation of Mexico restore some of the rights of the Indians, since the Indians had helped secure Mexican independence by fighting against the Spanish. From 1826 until his execution in 1833, the Yaqui Juan de la Cruz Banderas led his nation in a war against Mexico. In a campaign to return to the golden era of Indian society, Banderas claimed that the Indian Virgin of Guadalupe had told him to restore the empire of Moctezuma. Just as they had asked the viceroy in 1739, once again they sought their traditional rights to free elections and self-government, including the right to elect their own mayors of their communities and governors of their small nation [Hu-DeHart, p. 37]. This war lasted intermittently until 1908, when the Mexicans imposed the final solution of deporting the Yaquis to work to death as virtual slave laborers on the sisal plantations of the Yucatan. The United States government assisted by deporting back to Mexico all Yaquis who sought asylum in the Territory of Arizona.

At this time the Yucatan needed laborers because it was just recovering from its own long wars with the Maya. In a revival of Mayan religion with some Christian overtones starting as early as 1847, the Indian peasants followed the "talking cross" in hopes of freeing themselves from white domination. They fought for years, retreating into the most remote parts of Mexico and Belize under dogged pursuit by the Mexican army. Eventually they lost, but they helped pave the way for a larger uprising in the twentieth century that became the Mexican Revolution.

Today these Indian revolts rarely receive attention as political movements. Instead they are dismissed under the general term of "uprisings," as though the Indian were much too primitive to have a high degree of social consciousness or any notion of political ideology. Even partisans of the Indian movements tend to glorify these efforts as the last desperate acts of a people yearning to be free but lacking an understanding of the political realities around them. Often these Indians had well-developed ideologies, but they framed them in religious terms and in the imagery of nature rather than in the political vocabulary of Europeans. Today, it is sometimes difficult for us to accept the Master of Breath as anything more than the naive formulation of a benighted people, but such terms merely represented political, ecological, and religious concepts that seem to have little place in our modern world. Far more than quixotic surges of a doomed race, these wars were portents of the liberation movements that would sweep the world in the twentieth century when other colonized people in Africa and Asia would rise up more successfully against the imperial powers controlling them. The repeated failures of the Indian movements during the nineteenth century prepared the way for the successes of other peoples in the twentieth century.

During the nineteenth century, many books dealt with the political institutions of the native Americans. Once the Europeans abandoned the eighteenth-century notions of the noble savage, they began to examine Indian institutions more closely and objectively. LeClerc Milfort wrote a description of the southeastern Indians, which he published in Paris in 1802 as Gen. *Milfort's Creek Indians*. This went beyond the usual adventure story of captives held by the Indians to explain something of Indian political and cultural institutions. More scholarly works followed, such as those of Thomas Jefferson and most particularly Lewis Henry Morgan's *League of the Iroquois* in 1851.

Karl Marx, in particular, developed a fascination with the political activities and economic lives of the Indians. From his reading of Lewis Henry Morgan, Marx sharpened his appreciation of the delicacy and sophistication of Indian political institutions, particularly as evidenced in the League of the Iroquois. At the time of his death in 1883, Karl Marx was in the midst of an extensive study of the American Indians; he had filled several notebooks with material on them in 1880 and 1881. Friedrich Engels, as the collaborator and literary executor of Marx's estate, assembled and rewrote this material to form *The Origin of the Family, Private Property, and the State*, published in 1884 with the subtitle *In the Light of the Researches of Lewis H. Morgan*.

The book is a paean to Morgan's work among the Iroquois and to the American Indians themselves. Engels wrote joyfully in the preface to the first edition that "in the kinship groups of the North American Indians he has found the key to the hitherto insoluble riddles of earliest Greek, Roman, and German history" [Engels, p. 6]. Using Marx's notebooks, which draw from Morgan as well as from missionaries and other writers who dealt with the Iroquois, Engels describes in minute detail the organization of the Iroquois Confederacy, the tribes, the clans, and the various offices and sachems. He concludes that aside from the classical civilizations of Peru and Mexico, the "Iroquois confederacy represents the most advanced social organization achieved by any Indians," and he reduces their organization to ten basic principles, which he discusses in detail. Engels calls this "a wonderful constitution" under which there are "no soldiers, no gendarmes or police, no nobles, king, regents, prefects, or judges, no prisons, no lawsuits—and everything takes its orderly course" [Engels, pp. 84*ff*].

The kinship states of the Indians became in Marxist thought exemplars of primitive communism. Living as they did without the "state" or private ownership of property, the Indians knew neither exploitation nor social class. As Engels described life among the Iroquois, there "cannot be any poor or needy—the communal household and the gens know their responsibilities towards the old, the sick, and those disabled in war." They became in Marxist theory the ideal to which industrial communism would return once the workers smashed private property, classes, and the state. The final communist society would be an industrialized version of the Iroquois social system in which "all are free and equal—the women included" [Engels, p. 87].

This image of a utopian future offered inspiration to generations of revolutionaries and reformers, but the image quickly lost any connection with the Iroquois or any other Indian group. Marx and Engels translated the Iroquois image into a European one that fit their own materialist theories. Subsequent political theorists and activists cut from these ideas their own African and Asian ideologies, but the Indians were dropped from the theories and future generations pushed them once again into the nether regions of world consciousness.

By the twentieth century it appeared that the Indians had finally been crushed in America. In Minnesota in 1862 the United States army defeated the Dakota Indians, and on the day after Christmas of that year, the military hanged thirty eight Dakotas in Mankota, Minnesota, in the largest mass public execution in the history of the United States. The cavalry easily crushed the last uprisings in the United States, and despite General George Custer's defeat at the Battle of Little Big Horn in 1876 the whites' victory in the United States seemed assured. The Maya rebellion in the Yucatan had apparently failed, and the Indians in South America seemed to have accepted the fact that liberation from Spain did not change their subservient position in the hierarchy of their new countries that claimed to be democratic republics.

In 1911 the United States grew confident enough of its permanent defeat of the Indian nations that an Indian named Ishi went on display at the museum of the University of California as the last Stone Age Indian in America. He had been born to a small group of Yahi Indians who had been steadily hunted to extinction, leaving him as the sole survivor, who was finally captured and lived out his last five years at the museum.

In this context, the world was shocked during that same year of 1911 by the greatest uprising of Indians ever, and the Indians scored their first major victory against the whites in over four hundred years of intermittent struggle. That victory came in one of the American backwaters, in the south of Mexico, where the Indians rose up under the mestizo Emiliano Zapata (1877?-1919), and in a long decade of bloody war they destroyed the power of the haciendas and overthrew the urban white elite that controlled banking, newspapers, businesses, churches, and the land. In the protracted struggle a million Mexicans died.

Zapata led a movement different from any other in history. Unlike so many of the Indian uprisings of the previous century, Zapata's was not a religious movement. The followers of Zapata fought an openly political and economic campaign, as proclaimed in their simple motto, "Land and Liberty." Zapata issued his statement of purpose, called the Plan of Ayala, on November 25, 1911, telling the world that "we are partisans of principles and not of men" [Riding, p. 61]. His group did not fight merely to oust the old dictator in favor of a new one or to replace one *caudillo* with another; nor was it merely a race or ethnic war against the whites. The Indians sought to destroy the cruel and oppressive system of dictators and the white oligarchy that kept the Indians enslaved as peons on large haciendas and ranches. To emphasize their adherence to traditional values, the Indian soldiers of Zapata wore the loose white cotton pants and wide sombrero that Indian peasants had worn for centuries instead of the khaki uniforms and helmets of European soldiers. As the Indian army moved through the south, fighting with their poor and simple weapons, they seized the large estates and divided the land among the Indian peasants. Zapata's followers created peasant banks and schools and empowered local councils [Galeano, p. 138]. Their struggle was a true revolution that actually redistributed the whole bases of private property and sought to build an entirely new social order. In this it showed a far more radical bent than did the earlier French and American revolutions.

The Indians under Zapata inspired other groups in the north to rise up, but there most of the Indian tribes had been destroyed in a series of nineteenth-century wars. The remnants had been incorporated into mestizo society, and were organized into rival gangs and private armies rather than into traditional clan and tribal units. The leader of one such group was a mestizo who was named Doroteo Arango (1877–1923) but preferred the more exciting alias Pancho Villa. He led a war in the north much like that of Zapata in the south. The turning point for Villa's campaigns came in 1914 when he fought a battle to take Zacatecas on the site of La Bufa, the first Mexican silver mine, which had begun the painful centuries of forced Indian labor.

This Indian revolution was uniquely American. The political activists of Europe had claimed revolution as the exclusive domain of the urban workers, of the proletariat. Since 1848 in Europe one wave after another of workers' movements had tried to overthrow governments through armed struggle or through ballots, but they all failed. Communists and socialists seemed to be the vanguard of the future, but they had great trouble enacting that future.

Zapata knew, however, that the working classes of the cities had long since been absorbed by urban life; they offered little hope of a true revolution. For Zapata, the potential for revolution lay in the rural Indians, the *campesinos*, or peasants. Consequently, Zapata made no effort to organize the workers but stuck to a peasant revolution. Even though his forces took Mexico City, they did not plunder it or occupy it for long. He and his men returned to their homes, where he kept his headquarters in the small town of Tlaltizapán near Yautepec. In his campaign, Zapata emphasized cultural and ethnic ties uniting his people in their struggle for a generalized justice rather than the specific agenda of one political ideology.

The rest of the world did not know what to make of this revolution in Mexico. It was the first of the twentieth century's great revolutions, but because the "civilized" world was busy fighting World War I, they had little attention to spare for this remote corner of the earth. The subsequent Russian Revolution, which was urban, Marxist, and working-class in orientation as well as much closer to the Europeans, seemed easier to understand, and many people then dismissed the Mexican Revolution as an eccentric anomaly in a barbaric land.

Zapata never sought public office for himself; he let the city people enjoy that. The presidency of the nation fell into the hands of Venustiano Carranza, while Zapata continued living his quiet life on his ranch. Zapata watched the government carefully, and when it appeared that Carranza might not legalize the land redistribution and reform already enacted by the Indians, Zapata rose up again and denounced the president in very undiplomatic terms. Zapata accused Carranza of having betrayed the revolution and of having fought merely for "riches, honors, businesses, banquets, sumptuous feasts, bacchanals, and orgies" [Harris, p. 281]. Carranza could not let such an insult to his macho honor pass unanswered, but he also knew that he could never defeat Zapata's Indian army in battle. Carranza therefore laid a trap for Zapata, and on April 10, 1919, Carranza's military supporters assassinated Zapata after luring him to a secret meeting with a man pretending to be his ally. The Indians had won the war, but with the assassination of Zapata, they began to lose the peace into the hands of a new mestizo and white elite that was shrewd enough to run a whole country. The new leaders institutionalized the revolution, made the Indian into a glorious symbol of the new Mexico, and relegated Cortés to the status of a hunchbacked demon. They redistributed land, and in time they nationalized the oil industry. But the Indian revolution made a country that was to be ruled by others.

The impact of this Indian revolution was not entirely lost. Thus, when Joseph Stalin exiled fellow revolutionary Leon Trotsky in 1929, it was to Mexico, home of the first revolution, that Trotsky retreated. In subsequent decades other revolutionaries from the undeveloped world have also looked to the Zapata revolution for guidance in peasant warfare.

Zapata and the success of the Indian revolution in overthrowing the old established order in Mexico inspired other Indian groups throughout the Americas. The next notable success did not come until a generation later in distant Bolivia. As early as May 1945, the natives of Bolivia formed an Indian assembly. Rejecting the name "Indian" or "Indio" as insulting and degrading, they formed a National Federation of Peasants and from that time demanded to be called "peasants" or *campesinos*. The government met their demands to restore to the Indian communities their ancient land rights, and for the first time the government allowed the Indians in the mines such as Potosí to unionize [Arnade, p. 188]. They even recognized the Indian marriages outside of the Catholic church as legal and binding.

Despite the concessions and even the genuine support of the Bolivian government for the reforms, the oligarchic families refused to turn over their land and instead lynched the president and his aides in 1946. The oligarchy began a repressive era, trying to wipe out the gains of the Indian peasants and miners and return them to feudal servitude. Even though Indians, who composed about two-thirds of the total population, still could not vote, the next election saw a moderate victory against the oligarchs. The small middle class of mestizo merchants and teachers had voted against the oligarchy, but rather than surrender any power at all, the oligarchs used the army to stage a coup and to rule through a junta. Finally unable to find any peaceful alternative and being persecuted unmercifully, the Indians ignited a Zapata-style revolution in the remote parts of the Indian heartland in agricultural areas. The Quechua Indians of Cochabamba rose against the hacienda system that kept them as virtual slaves. Other groups spontaneously followed around the nation, including the Indian miners of Potosí. They killed off rich families and appropriated the land for themselves. Armed with machetes and knives, they paralyzed all transportation, closed down newspapers, burned out exploitive merchants, and attacked any oligarchs or soldiers who stood against them.

Like the followers of Zapata, the Indians lacked such basic skills as literacy that would have allowed them to make a government and control the country. They were forced to rely on the middle class and urban whites, mestizos, and *cholos*, as they contemptuously called Hispanicized Indians, to make the new government. The government came under the leadership of Victor Paz Estenssoro, who had been forced into exile by the oligarchs. His Revolutionary National Movement (MNR) party unified a leftist coalition of xenophobic elements who preached anti-imperialism, anticommunism, and antifascism, but lacked a clear ideology of its own. This strange combination of Trotskyites and extreme nationalists legalized the Indian seizure of the land and mines. They organized a new government in La Paz, and in their first acts proclaimed universal adult suffrage, broke the power of the army, and closed down the military academy. They redistributed land, nationalized the mines and other large companies, limited the amount of land one person could own, ended all forms of the Indian servitude known as *pongueaje*, reestablished communal Indian lands, and created various types of mining and production cooperatives owned and operated by the workers.

The fate of the Indian revolution in Bolivia somewhat paralleled that of the Indian revolution in Mexico. The Indians had destroyed the old, but they lacked the education and resources to take over the country and run it. By virtually any standard, the revolution failed. Politically, even though Paz Estenssoro has been the most important politician of the era and was reelected president in 1985, the nation has had a series of right- and left-wing governments and four coups since the revolution, and there have been over a dozen attempted coups and revolutions. Economically, the oligarchs were crushed, but the country has deteriorated; it has had the worst inflation rate in the world and the lowest standard of living in South America. Soldiers seized power from time to time, but they rarely even controlled the cities for short periods before being ousted. The national government has even been seized by a combination of narcotics traffickers and the military, but even they could not control the nation and surrendered the government in humiliation.

Despite all this apparent failure of the Indian revolution in Bolivia, one might argue that unlike the Mexican Indians, who surrendered power to the urban elite, the Indians of Bolivia continued to resist every source of political, economic, or military domination. If the government does something harmful to the people, demonstrators immediately take to the streets. Peasants who are too poor to pay a single dollar for a bus ticket will march a hundred miles to protest. Miners bomb government offices with dynamite stolen from their jobs. If the army tries to occupy a town, the peasant women with their children strapped to their backs sit down in front of the tanks. Such scenes breed frequent violence as soldiers shoot miners and peasants kill politicians. Despite all that, there has been less killing than in Argentina, Peru, Guatemala, Nicaragua, Colombia, El Salvador, or Haiti. Bolivia has suffered no tyrants as in Paraguay, no long military rule as in Chile and Brazil. The Indians of Bolivia live in desperate poverty, but they did break the bonds of servitude that enslaved them for four and a half centuries. They chose and maintained their impoverished and insecure liberty in place of their impoverished but secure slavery. In this regard theirs takes honor of place as the first Indian revolution that worked.

In Cuba the revolutionary movement of Fidel Castro also borrowed some of the peasant strategy of Zapata and Mao, but by and large it operated as a Soviet-style revolution dependent on urban intellectuals such as Castro himself and aides such as Ernesto "Che" Guevara of Argentina. Cuba, being one of the least Indian nations of America, afterward found it very difficult to connect with the revolutionary movements among Indians in countries such as Guatemala or Bolivia.

After the success of Castro's revolution in Cuba, Guevara served for a while in the new cabinet, but then left Cuba in 1965 to extend the Cuban-style revolution to Bolivia, which seemed to him so ripe for yet another revolution. Che Guevara hoped to reignite and then control the forceful power of the Indians as rebels in a revolt that would spread through the Andes and throughout Latin America. The Indians ignored Che, in large part because they could not understand him. He spoke Spanish and they spoke Quechua. He came from a rich Spanish-Irish family and had been educated in the university. He came there from the big city of Havana to enlighten the Indians in their benighted peasant world, and to them he was just one more white foreigner trying to tell them what to believe and what to do. After two years he had not recruited a single peasant to his cause, and in 1967 the notoriously weak and ineffective Bolivian army tracked him down and killed him at Yuro Ravine, claiming he was a CIA agent.

The Cubans had more success among the whites and the mestizos in the Sandinista movement in Nicaragua, which had only a small Indian population. The Indians refused to participate, for they saw the movement as a threat to their Indian identity. Rather than join the revolution, many of them took up arms against it and started their own guerrilla movement, fighting for Indian autonomy within the nation of Nicaragua.

The revolution of Zapata had a profound impact on a young Peruvian, Víctor Raúl Haya de la Torre, who went into exile in Mexico in 1923. Even though he was not an Indian, he became intoxicated with the revolutionary Indian movement of Mexico and even went to live with a group of Mexican Indians for a while as a schoolteacher. The following year he formed the Alianza Popular Revolucionaria Americana (APRA), or Popular Revolutionary American Alliance, which was to be a unified revolutionary movement of Indians and urban workers throughout the Americas. Despite his efforts to make it a pan-American movement and his travels through several Latin American countries attacking the United States and defending the struggle of Sandino in Nicaragua, the movement did not attract much attention. When Haya returned to Peru, he fashioned APRA into a major voice of the left, heavily anti-imperialist and anti-United States. He considered the Indians to be an admirable but essentially passive people whom he would liberate when he achieved his anti-imperialist revolution. His movement preserved some Indian trappings, but it was essentially inspired by European thought. In 1985, Alan Garcia Pérez became the first APRA candidate elected president of Peru, but by this time the party had lost most of its Indian traces and had become just one more leftist party.

The role of the Peruvian Indian in revolution was worked out instead by the dark, partially Indian José Carlos Mariátegui, who came from rural Peru. The communists condemned him because he wrote of the importance of Indians rather than economic classes in his theory. The international communist movement under the control of Moscow preached an orthodoxy based on class and wanted to minimize ethnic or cultural divisions among people as merely artifacts of the oppressive class system. Mariátegui wanted to combine the European ideals of industrial socialism with the rural socialism that had been practiced for centuries by the Incas. The sickly, crippled Mariátegui [Werlich, pp. 178–87] died on April 16, 1930, at the age of thirty-five, but he left a powerful legacy of ideas if not action. Because of his extensive writings on revolution, many political groups, including APRA, claim him as one of the inspiring founding fathers of their movement, but none has done so as enthusiastically as the group called Sendero Luminoso.

Founded as a political party in 1970 by Abimael Guzmán, a mestizo intellectual who spoke Quechua, the group took its name, Sendero Luminoso, or "Shining Path," from Mariátegui's words *"hay que avanzar por el sendero luminoso del socializmo,"* which exhort the people to advance along "the shining path of socialism." The group started as a legal political party in the highland district of Ayacucho, one of the poorest and most Indian parts of Peru. By 1978, however, Guzmán and his students decided that they could never bring about an Indian Peru by the ballot box, and instead moved their support base to mountain villages and declared a guerrilla war of terrorism against the government in 1980. The Sendero Luminoso exploited the ancient Quechua legend that somewhere in one of the mountains lived one of the great Incas, and when the time came he would ride out on a white horse, slay the Spanish, and restore Indian rule in Peru. Combining this Inca mysticism with Maoist theory and practice, the mostly Indian army followed the Zapata guidelines for a peasant revolution against the urban elites that controlled the country. According to Guzmán, his own work represented the fourth stage of revolutionary thought that advanced from Marx, Lenin, and Mao on to Guzmán. In this way, their revolutionary doctrine combined the best of European, Asian, and native American philosophy.

Another revolutionary group in the urban areas of Peru took the name Tupac Amaru, the name of the last rebel Inca who ruled a small area in Vilcabamba but was captured and executed by the Spanish in 1572. The same name was taken by the Indian headman José Gabriel Condorcanqui, who proclaimed an end to the slave labor of the Potosí mines. He led an uprising of the Indians throughout the Andes from as far as what is now Colombia into Bolivia in 1780. Like the North American colonists fighting for their independence against Britain at the same time, Tupac Amaru II wanted independence from Spain and an end to the rule of the Spanish-speaking elite in the Andes. He issued a proclamation accusing the Spanish of having usurped "the sovereignty of my people for three centuries" and of having "treated the natives of this kingdom like beasts" [Picon-Salas, pp. 135–36]. His rebellion also failed, and he too was executed two years later. In keeping with civilized practice, the limbs of Tupac Amaru II and his followers were scattered along the roads while their hands and heads went on public display in town.

The Tupac Amaru movement of the 1980s took its name and inspiration from the Indians, but its membership and tactics differed from those of traditional Indian movements. With alleged support from the Cubans and the Sandinistas of Nicaragua, the Tupac Amaru faction pursued a traditional Soviet-style campaign of urban intellectuals and workers rather than peasants. Nevertheless, the peasants preserved the memories of both the Tupac Amarus as symbols of their own struggle against the whites of the city. The name Tupac Amaru could be found scrawled on walls and other public places throughout Peru as a reminder to the whites of the tremendous potential for revolutionary justice that seethed in the Indian soul of Andean America.

Some of the Indian revolutionaries of America have incorporated Mao's thought into their movements. The modern governments of countries such as Peru and Guatemala also learned a lesson from Mao in how to handle their Indians. Whether they knew it or not, the Indian rebels followed Mao's dictum that the revolutionary should move among the peasants like a fish in the sea. The governments of Guatemala and Peru found that when they could not catch these fish, they would have to drain the sea. They embarked on policies of driving the Indians out of the area. To do this they killed many thousands of the Indians, burned down villages, razed crops, and disrupted the transportation of crops and goods in hopes of striking fear into the rest and forcing them to leave the country and move to squatter camps on the edge of the cities, where they could be more easily watched and controlled. The incident that I encountered in the Guatemalan village en route to Flores arose from just this attempt by the Guatemalan elite to drain the ocean of peasants.

Even though the last Indian city of Tayasal on the banks of Lake Petén-Itzá fell to the European conquerors in 1697 and even though Ishi went on display in 1911 as the last independent Indian in North America, the struggle for Indian rights never stopped. In the process the Indians gave the world generation after generation of revolutionary inspiration. The Iroquois served as a model for primitive communism, and the Europeans looked to the Incas as exemplars of how to manage a socialist economy without private property, money, or markets. But the Indians offered more than inspiration for European thought. They also provided models of action. Many of the earlier efforts such as the Red Stick movement failed, but with the movement of Zapata, the world had its first truly peasant revolution.

Five hundred years after the arrival of Christopher Columbus in the New World, the Indians are everywhere in America the poorest of the poor and the least powerful of all groups. Future generations, however, may look back on the twentieth century as the turning point in the struggle for Indian autonomy and power in the Americas. After four centuries of nearly constant losses, the Indians scored their first tentative victories. In the United States after centuries of losing on the battlefield and being shunned by the courts and government, the Indians started to win their cases in court and found a legal base upon which to protect some of their rights. In countries such as Mexico and Bolivia they won on the battlefield even though they lacked the power to translate that victory into a permanent improvement for them. Who knows what the next half millennium may bring for Indian rights?

⟁ ⟁ 10 ⟁ ⟁

THE INDIAN
HEALER

The midday sun scorched everything it touched one January afternoon at the height of the dry season in Teli, a village of the Dogon tribe in Mali. I was en route to Kani Kombole and passed the heat of the day napping on a wooden platform bed covered with reed mats beneath a thatched roof. I had eaten my fill of chicken and rice with peanuts and chilies, I had consumed endless calabashes of cool, clear water, and I had only sipped politely from the calabash of *kojo*, the bubbling millet beer proffered by the headman. While I slept the children and women kept a watchful distance, but the men had long before retreated to their *toguna*, an open-sided shelter with a thick roof of millet straw insulating it from the strong rays of the sun.

Even though Teli lies only seventy miles from the nearest town with electricity, the lack of roads cuts it off from the world. The path to the closest market town in the Dogon headquarters of Bandiagara leads across a dry plain to Kani Kombole, up a thousand-foot escarpment to the village of Djuigibombo, and then over a mud track, for a total walk of eighteen hard miles. The Dogon living in Teli value few market goods enough to transport them that long way by foot. The villagers grow their own millet, peppers, peanuts, and onions and raise their own goats, pigeons, and chickens. They bring in a little rice and tobacco from the market as well as brightly printed cotton cloth imported from China, and the village headman owned a transistor radio capable of pulling in garbled voices from Bamako.

When I awoke, I noticed the women and children waiting quietly and watching me from a respectful distance. I could tell from the cautious yet persistent way that they stared at me that they wanted something, but I was unsure what. After putting on my shoes and jacket, I rose from the platform bed to leave. Only then did a woman approach me with her baby slung over her hip. The child's right eye was swollen shut beneath a crust of secretions. The child stared distracted into space, not seeming to notice the mother, the flies, or me. The mother pointed to the child's deformed face and chanted: "Chloroquine, chloroquine, chloroquine." She wanted the tablets used to fight malaria and assumed by so many of the natives in the area to be effective against any type of malady. I had left all my chloroquine tablets in another village to which I was soon returning and would not have wanted to give them to a baby anyway. I reached in my pack and fished up two aspirin for her. With exaggerated thanks, the woman popped the two pills into her own mouth and swallowed them dry while the baby remained motionless, staring through the flies. I left the woman and headed across the village toward the men in the *toguna*, not knowing why the woman had taken the pills herself.

Teli, like so many areas of the world, relies almost exclusively on native cures heavily dependent on ritual and religion. The inhabitants supplement these local herbs and plants with a few imported medicines such as aspirin or chloroquine when they can get them and when they have enough extra millet to afford them. Of all the drugs, it puzzled me that the woman would ask for chloroquine in as remote a place as Teli, since most Africans have a natural immunity to malaria, but the drug has an important reputation as a general febrifuge.

Malaria ravages more people than probably any other disease in many of the backwater areas of the world. For most of human history, no effective cure or preventive existed for this Old World disease. For as long as we have had medical records it appears that malaria struck every part of Africa, Europe, and Asia where mosquitoes thrived, but there was none in the Americas. When the Europeans took malaria to America in the hulls of the trade ships, the Indians quickly found that one of their traditional medicines, Peruvian bark, offered relief from the symptoms. This bark produced quinine, the active ingredient in chloroquine.

The introduction of quinine marks the beginning of modern pharmacology. Prior to that time, Old World doctors had various potions, plasters, odd forms of surgery, and leeches with which to treat diseases and control a few of the symptoms. Essentially, however, they had no cures for smallpox, leprosy, tuberculosis, the plague, malaria, or any of the other dreadful diseases that haunted the Old World and killed hundreds of thousands of people in periodic epidemics. Known also as ague or the shakes, malaria, physicians claimed, originated in the bad air of swamps and other lowland areas. Malaria probably killed Alexander the Great and Oliver Cromwell. Prior to the dissemination of quinine, researchers estimate that malaria killed approximately two million people a year throughout the world and infected tens of millions of others [Taylor, p. 75]. But even today in many tropical zones such as West Africa, malaria tortures millions of people too poor to afford the miracle drugs made from quinine.

The Quechua-speaking Incas of the Andes understood well the medicinal properties of many plants growing not only in the Andes but in the Amazon jungle as well. One of these plants was a tree that grew at elevations of three to nine thousand feet and produced the very bitter-tasting Peruvian bark that could cure many ailments, including cramps, chills, and heart-rhythm disorders. The Quechua word quina means "bark," but this particular bark with such miraculous powers deserved the name quina-quina, "bark of barks," and from this came the name "quinine" [Taylor, p. 78].

Europeans did not use the word "quinine" until 1820, when Parisian scientists Joseph Pelletier and Joseph Caventou finally extracted the active ingredient from the bark and named the substance after the original Quechua word. Until that time the bark was known as cinchona, a corruption of the name of the Countess of Chinchona, Francisca Henrique de Ribera, who married a viceroy of Peru and during the early seventeenth century lived with him in Lima, where Indians supposedly cured her malaria with their miracle bark. When the time came to give the plant a scientific name, Carolus Linnaeus assigned it *cinchona* after the countess who had "discovered" it. Even today in some parts of the world people refer to quinine as *chinchonine*, preferring the French rather than the Quechua name.

The bark seems to have been introduced to Europe about 1630 and had already gained mention in a Belgian medical text, *Discours et Avis sur les Flus de Ventre Doloureux* by Herman van der Heyden, by 1643. The new medicine made extensive European settlement of America possible. For example, the 1671 records of Governor Berkley of Virginia show that before the introduction of quinine into Virginia one colonist of every five died within the first year from malaria. After the incorporation of quinine, no one died from malaria [Hallowell, p. 328]. The change was dramatic and simple.

Not until the twentieth-century work of the British physician Sir Ronald Ross was the etiology of the disease unraveled. He discovered that *Anopheles* mosquitoes carry microscopic *Plasmodium* in their bodies that they acquire while drinking the blood of a malaria patient, and they then pass these into the blood of the next victim they bite. The French physician Charles Laveran had already discovered that *Plasmodium* was the source of the disease, but until the researches of Ross, no one knew that the mosquito transmitted it into the human bloodstream. This discovery led to a Nobel Prize in medicine for Ross in 1902, three hundred years after the unknown Quechua Indians had given the cure for the disease to the world, a gift for which they received no recognition.

Until chemists extracted the active ingredient from the bark in the nineteenth century and could then manufacture it in the laboratory, the medicine remained the exclusive domain of the very rich or of those supported by colonizing governments and companies. Once it became readily available, doctors realized that quinine not only cured malaria but also prevented it when taken before infection. Synthetic forms of quinine sold in recent decades as chloroquine and primaquine serve both as prophylaxis and treatment for malaria.

Colonial officials serving throughout the tropics in the nineteenth century took small but regular doses of quinine to ward off malaria. Because of the extreme bitterness of the drug, they mixed it with sugared water before drinking. This daily concoction became the tonic water that continues today as a popular mixer for making alcoholic drinks even where malaria has long been eradicated.

In some parts of the world, tonic water still serves as a medicine, as I found after leaving Teli for Timbuktu, about three hundred miles north of Teli in the Sahara. Today Timbuktu survives as merely a small town of little importance on the edge of the known world. From King Mansa Munsa's fabled Golden City of great wealth connecting the trade routes of the Sahara with those of black Africa, Timbuktu has shrunk to a mud town of fewer than twenty thousand people. Many of the windowless family compounds of mud brick lie abandoned, and each day a little more sand from the desert creeps into the once bustling streets. The sand has already risen about two feet above the old street level, forcing people to step down to pass between the decorated doorposts and enter their houses or into one of the three ancient mosques.

In many regards Timbuktu lies more isolated today than in the past. It once stood proudly as the most northern city on the mighty Niger River, but through the centuries even the river turned its back on the dying city and withdrew from the Sahara. When I visited Timbuktu I approached it from Mopti, its closest neighboring city, 250 miles to the south. The trip required five days and nights on the river to reach the village of Niafunke and then two days over a desert trail marked only by the bones and mummified skins of camels and donkeys. Traveling east from Timbuktu the next town is Gao, also about 250 miles away. I made the trip on an ancient open truck named the Green Elephant, which reached Gao after a drive of two full days over a marked road that is little more than a series of ruts through the desert. During the wet season in Guinea and lower Mali, rains cause the Niger to flood this modest road for most of the year and thus prevent travel between the two cities.

Life in Timbuktu centers on the market much more than on the mosque or the Koranic school. Caravans still bring salt cut into slabs five feet long and eighteen inches wide in the mines of Taudeni, seven hundred kilometers north of Timbuktu in the middle of the Sahara. Although a few small camel caravans still make the trek, today most of the 3.5 million kilograms of salt mined there annually arrives on caravans of dilapidated desert trucks, which have replaced the trains of up to twenty thousand camels that used to carry the trade.

On the western edge of Timbuktu adjacent to the graveyard, townspeople cut series of neatly terraced gardens circling a small but deep well, protected from people and animals by a fence of dried thorn bushes. Here they hand-water rows of lettuce, to-matoes, chilies, onions, okra, corn, beans, and melons for sale in the market. Tuaregs bring in goats and dates from other oases, fishermen cart in piles of smoked fish from the Niger, and from the south come sacks of rice, wheat, millet, and sun-dried peanuts. Only a few goods are imported from far away. Tea arrives in wooden chests shipped from Hong Kong, and instant coffee comes in small cans from the Ivory Coast. In the market women sell calabashes filled with beef fat to flavor the cooking, chopped and dried okra, freshly baked pita bread, small bundles of charcoal, and assorted fresh vegetables. Men sell the salt, dates, hacked pieces of goat and sheep, sandals, and brightly embroidered gal-abias that the men sew in their stalls along the edge of the market. Young boys hawk piles of deep-fried dough balls, and girls balance on their heads large trays stacked with patties of peanut butter rolled in hot chilies.

Timbuktu remains one of the few places in the world where it is impossible to buy cola drinks, chewing gum, or the chocolate candies that always seem to constitute the first assault of con-temporary western influence. With this conspicuous absence of modernization, it surprised me to find that in the midst of all this traditional culture the Arab shopkeepers sold soda bottles with a clear drink called Indian Tonic, featuring the emblem of an American Plains Indian dressed in a full war bonnet. Both the image and the drink seem incongruous in Timbuktu, one of the most traditional places in the world. The drink turned out to be essentially quinine water sold not as a refreshment but as a medical tonic to restore vitality and cure virtually any ailment.

The Indian Tonic of Timbuktu survives as a relic of a long line of now mostly forgotten tonics sold in the nineteenth and early twentieth century as cures for every known or imagined ailment. The medicine show of the last century frequently featured an Indian healer or claimed that the product being sold originated with an Indian medicine man. These medicine men often added ingredients such as distilled alcohol, opium, kola nuts, sugar, or caffeine, which were not Indian in origin but gave an added kick to the medication.

The evolution of quinine from an important medicine into a soft drink was a pattern repeated numerous times by many of the patent medicines made from Indian drugs. Sassafras and sarsaparilla teas used by the Indians, for example, were also mixed with sugar and other spices to which carbonated water was added to make one of the "Indian root beers" that were hawked as cures for numerous pains. Like the quinine tonic, root beer soon became a drink used primarily for refreshment without a medicinal pretext.

Another American relative of the tree that provided quinine also helped cure amoebic dysentery, a lethal intestinal infection, caused by the ingestion of certain amoebas, that produces high fever and bloody diarrhea. Even today it still ranks as one of the world's major killers of young children and if not treated can kill adults as well. The Indians of the Amazon cured this disease with medicine made from roots of three-to-four-year-old *Cephalaelis ipecacuanha* and *C. acuminaia* plants. The Indians made a medicine that they called *ipecac*. One of the properties of this medicine was that in certain doses it caused the patient to vomit. In this capacity as an emetic, the Indians used it both to expel unwanted substances such as poisons and as a way of ritually purifying the body. Poison clinics throughout the world still use ipecac for the same purposes when children or adults have ingested too much of a toxic substance and need to expel it.

Its most important use, however, came as a cure for the much more common amoebic dysentery. Ipecac killed and expelled the harmful amoebas and allowed the patient to recover. It was introduced to France in 1688 by a Dutch doctor named, inappropriately enough, Schweitzer, which means "the Swiss" in German. He changed his name to Jean Adrien Helvetius, which means "the Swiss" in Latin, and with this Latin name sounded much more professional and credible. His new medicine became the rage of France when it supposedly cured the dysentery of the dauphin, son of Louis XIV. This made the quack Helvetius into a respected pharmacist, and he sired a prosperous family that included his grandson Claude Arien Helvetius (1715–1771), who became a famous philosopher of the Enlightenment and the author of De l'Espirit (1758), in which he expounds on the themes of sensualism or sensationalism. The prosperity and education of this family, however, derived directly from the introduction of the Amazonian cure ipecac to the world.

The Indian discovery of drug cures for a wide range of diseases did not spring merely from the fortuitous circumstance that America was blessed by nature with more drugs to be discovered. Quinine and ipecac happen to come from plants that grew only in America, but the cure of scurvy illustrates the general superiority of Indian medical knowledge and pharmacology. The Old World abounded in plants which could easily have cured this disease, but western science ignored them until the Indians demonstrated their utility.

The cure for scurvy first came to European attention in a dramatic incident during the second of three voyages to Canada made by the French explorer Jacques Cartier (1491–1557) for Francis I. In November 1535, after visiting the Huron town of Hochelaga, which later became the site of Montreal, Cartier's ships, the Grande Hermyne, the Petite Hermyne, and the Emerillon, became frozen in the St. Lawrence River. Cartier ordered his men ashore to build a small fortification in which to await the spring thaw. He traded provisions with local Indians, but he soon forbade the Indians to enter the fort because they showed signs of scurvy, and he did not want his men to catch this disease. Even then the Indians knew scurvy was not communicable. As the winter months slowly passed, scurvy soon began to stalk his men. They grew listless and weak. Their gums grew spongy and began to bleed, ugly splotches erupted on their skin, and they emitted a wretched stink. Of the 110 men, only ten showed no signs of the disease by February, and one by one the men died until twenty-five of his men were gone.

Cartier busily concealed the disease from the Indians for fear that they might attack the weakened men. Gradually, however, Cartier realized that the Indians who developed scurvy did not die but recovered their full health. He inquired cautiously about a cure, and the Indians readily showed him how to make a tonic from the bark and needles of an evergreen tree that the Hurons called *annedda* and was probably a hemlock or pine. This distasteful concoction carried a massive dose of vitamin C, the only cure for scurvy, and every man who took it recovered within eight days. Cartier dutifully recorded in his log that no amount of drugs from Europe or Africa could have done what the Huron drugs did in a week. In appreciation Cartier kidnapped the Indian chief Donnaconna and the other Indians in hopes that they could lead him to mountains of gold [Bakeless, pp. 115–16].

The world ignored this discovery of the cure for scurvy, but a fanciful legend did develop that the *annedda* tree of that area could cure syphilis. Sailors did sometimes pick up supplies of dried cranberries from the Indians of New England and use them to prevent scurvy, but sailors continued dying for the next two centuries. Not until James Lind (1716–1794), a Scottish naval officer, read of the incident with Cartier did European medicine take official notice that the Indians had found the cure for the disease. Based on Lind's research, the British Admiralty issued an order in 1795 to supply all naval ships with lime juice to prevent the disease. Lind then walked into history as the *discoverer* of the cause and cure of scurvy. His work finally led to the discovery of vitamins and to a fuller understanding of human nutrition [Driver, p. 399].

The Incas apparently knew how to prevent goiter problems as effectively as scurvy. The Incas harvested tons of Pacific Ocean kelp, *Macrocystis*, annually. They dried the seaweed and then transported it throughout the Andes for use as a food additive. The high iodine content effectively prevented most forms of goiter problems in the population. Today, all along the Pacific coast from California to Peru, large commercial ships harvest the underwater forests of kelp for a variety of foods, pharmaceuticals, and toiletries.

From the very first contacts between the Old and the New World, European doctors recognized that the Indians held the key to the world's most sophisticated pharmacy. Medicine in most of the world at that time had not yet risen far above witchcraft and alchemy. In Europe, physicians talked about the balance of body humors as they attached living leeches to the patient in order to suck out the "bad blood." Moslem doctors burned their patients with hot charcoals, and physicians in the Orient prescribed elaborate potions of dragon bones mixed with all types of flavorings.

By contrast the Indians of America had refined a complex set of active drugs that produced physiological and not merely psychological effects in the patient. This cornucopia of new pharmaceutical agents became the basis for modern medicine and pharmacology.

The Indians of northern California and Oregon gave modern medicine the most commonly used laxative or cathartic. They used the bark of the *Rhamnus purshiana* shrub as a cure for constipation. The Old World already had a number of such medical cures, but the Indian remedy, as advertisers still stress today, acts in an exceptionally mild manner. It evacuates the bowels completely within eight hours but with almost no discomfort to the patient. When the Spanish arrived in California and found this bark, they named it *cascara sagrada*, "sacred bark," because of its unique qualities. Because of its bitter taste, it had to be mixed with sugar or in some cases with chocolate to persuade people to use it. Even though scientists have failed to synthesize it in the laboratory and vast amounts of bark must be gathered annually for its manufacture, it has spread to become the world's most commonly used laxative since its first introduction by the American pharmaceutical industry in 1878.

When Francisco de Orellana made his river voyages down the Napo through what is now Ecuador and discovered the Amazon River, Indians along the way frequently attacked his heavily armed band. The simple wooden weapons of the Indians seemed to offer little threat against the sophisticated European arsenal of metal. The confidence of the Spanish suffered a serious challenge, however, when one of Orellana's men died from a minute Indian arrow that barely pierced the skin. This unknown soldier of Orellana's became the first European victim of the arrow tipped with the powerful poison that became famous as curare.

Not until 1807 did the German naturalist Baron Alexander von Humboldt discover that the source of curare originated in a group of plants growing in the Amazon jungle. The most important of these was the woody vines of the genus *Chondodendron*, which the Indians cooked into a gum and then painted onto their arrows and darts.

Even after the discovery of the plants, medical research took a long time to figure out how the poison worked. Unlike the poisons of the Old World, which invariably produced violent spasms and almost epilepsy-like seizures in the victim, curare produced a quiet, gentle, and quick death. Persistent research revealed that the patient died from asphyxiation. Further research finally unraveled the complicated process whereby the curare blocked nerve transmission to the muscles, leading to paralysis and death when the muscles no longer enabled the victim to breathe.

Initially, no one could imagine any practical application for such a powerful drug other than for illegal or unethical uses, but doctors soon found that small doses of curare acted as a muscle relaxant. In this way it served as the first treatment of tetanus or lockjaw, which caused a severe cramping of the muscles of the throat and jaw; curare relieved the cramping by relaxing the muscle. Doctors soon gave it to patients going into abdominal surgery to relax the strong muscles that could make surgery quite difficult. Doctors also found that curare relaxed a patient enough to permit insertion of a tube into the windpipe to facilitate breathing during operations. In due time curare was synthesized into a number of different muscle-relaxant drugs fulfilling a variety of medicinal purposes. In the 1980s, Dutch doctors introduced curare as a means of euthanasia for terminally ill patients (Ferrieri, p. 51).

Indians in the northeastern United States treated intestinal worms with the vermifuge pinkroot, *Spigelia marilandica*, a plant with red and yellow flowers. Trees of the genus *Cornus* of North America, known as dogwoods, were used by the Indians as a febrifuge, or fever reducer. They had a number of emetics in addition to ipecac; these included bloodroot—*Sanguinaria canadensis*, also called puccoon—and lobelia. The Indians made an astringent called alumroot from the wild geranium, *Heuchera americana*, and a stimulant from boneset, *Eupatorium perfoliatum* [Driver, pp. 557–58].

The Indians of North America used the bark of the poplar or willow tree to make a liquid capable of curing headaches and other minor pains. Only centuries later with the discovery of aspirin as a coal-tar derivative was it found that the active ingredient salicin closely resembled what we now know as aspirin or acetylsalicylic acid. Such a simple medication remains as a good example of the many American Indian gifts that western medical science failed to recognize and then had to invent independently through a laborious and expensive process of research.

Indian healers developed many drugs especially to treat the problems of women. They used a parasitic plant that grew on the roots of oak trees—blue cohosh or squawroot, *Caulophyllum thalictroides*—as an antispasmodic that helped induce menstrual discharge. They also used the bitter root of *Trillium erectum* to ease pain during childbirth, a practice that subsequently led the pioneers to name the plant "birthroot."

Indians of America developed a large number of ointments and salves to promote the healing of flesh wounds, and the pioneers usually called these medicines "balsams." In the western United States the Indians gave the pioneers a balsam root from plants of the genus *Balsamorhiza*, especially *B. sagittata*, which produces yellow flowers and an aromatic root. Tolu, or balsam of Tolu, the aromatic resin of the tropical tree *Myroxylon toluiferum*, became widely used in toiletries and pharmaceuticals. The North American tree tacamahac or balsam poplar, *Populus balsamifera*, produced fragrant resin-coated buds that Indians also made into a variety of ointments. An evergreen from northeastern North America, the balsam fir, *Abies balsamea*, produced very small needles and cones and was used to make Canada balsam. One of the best-known of all was the balsam of Peru made from the resin of the tree *Myroxylon pereirae*, which has an aroma prized in the manufacture of perfumes and some toiletries.

The Indians also developed the astringent that became known as witch hazel, made from the bark and leaves of the shrub *Hamamelis virginiana* and used to soothe tired or strained muscles. The Indians knew how to dry the flowers of plants in the genus *Arnica* to make a tincture of arnica that they applied to sprains and bruises to relieve the pain and swelling. The Indians gave the colonists the oil of wintergreen, which could be used in a similar way but has since become much better known as a flavoring for candies and medicines.

One of the most widely used skin ointments in the world today is known in English as "Indian petrolatum" or "petroleum jelly," a scientific name derived from Greek and thus obscuring the Indian invention of the ointment. In making this nearly colorless gelatinous material of olefin hydrocarbons and methane, the Indians found one of the first practical uses for petroleum. Indians applied it to human and animal skin to protect wounds, stimulate healing, and keep the skin moist. They also used it to lubricate the moving parts of tools.

Petroleum jelly is another of the American Indian products readily available for sale in Timbuktu and areas throughout the Sahara. Traditionally the nomads of the Sahara smear beef fat on their skin and hair as protection from the relentless sun, dry wind, and pounding sand. Today, many of them have replaced beef fat with petroleum jelly, which has proven to be a superior skin ointment. Petroleum jelly offers the same protective properties as fat, but since it uses an inorganic material, it does not attract insects as much as do animal fats. Petroleum jelly, like quinine water, meets such an important need in the Sahara that Tuareg traders transport it over thousands of kilometers to every corner of the desert.

In addition to employing the sophisticated medicine chest of the Indians, native doctors also understood and practiced many medical arts, some of which were still unknown in the Old World. One of the most unusual of these was the brain surgery or trephining performed by surgeons in varied Indian civilizations, particularly in the Andes. The surgeon drilled a hole in the skull, usually in the right parietal, and thereby relieved the compression that built up from some forms of concussion, particularly those resulting from severe blows to the head during combat. Archaeologists have excavated skulls showing that patients survived as many as five trephinations [Wissler, pp. 11–12].

The Aztecs developed a particularly sophisticated medical organization with different kinds of specialists for the diagnosis of a disease, for its treatment, and for the making of drugs. *Tlamatepaticitl* applied medicines to the skin and prescribed drugs somewhat like contemporary internists while *texoxotlaticitl* acted as surgeons. On a lower level of prestige and importance came the *temixiuitiani*, who performed as midwives, and *tezoctezoani*, who acted as bloodletters. *Papiani* served as herbal pharmacists and *panamacani* as the dealers who distributed the drugs [Guzmán, p. 13]. In this medical system, the Aztecs paralleled in many regards the European organization of medicine at that time, and in some ways they surpassed it. Even today no steel scalpel has ever been made that cuts sharper than the obsidian implements of the Aztec surgeons. Only the laser beam can cut a finer incision with less bleeding and less scarification than the Aztec surgeons. The fine Aztec scalpels allowed the doctors to cut with minimum blood loss, and the wound healed with fewer scars.

Indian surgeons sewed facial lacerations by using bone needles threaded with human hair. They set bones in plasters made of downy feathers, gum, resin, and rubber. They gave enemas with rubber hoses, and they invented the bulbed syringe for use in a variety of medical treatments as well as simple tasks such as cleaning the ears. In Amazonia, where rubber originated, they made syringes with rubber, but in the north, they made them from animal bladders. European doctors quickly adopted both the rubber hose and rubber syringe and continue to use them today.

Indian healers lanced boils and removed tumors by surgery. Surgeons amputated limbs, prescribed artificial legs, removed teeth, and castrated men and animals. They also understood the principles of sucking out the venom to treat snake bite, and they mastered the application and use of tourniquets and cauterization. *Papiani* concocted emetics, purges, febrifuges, and skin ointments as well as underarm deodorants, toothpaste, and breath fresheners.

The Aztecs may have had the most thorough understanding of human anatomy of any society in the world of the sixteenth century. In part this knowledge derived from the peculiar and varied nature of the human sacrifices they performed. They understood the role of the heart and blood circulation long before the Englishman William Harvey (1578–1657) proposed his theory of blood circulation. The Nahuatl-speaking doctors developed an extensive vocabulary that identified virtually all of the organs that the science of anatomy recognizes today.

One medical practice employed extensively by the Aztecs but abhorred by the Spanish was bathing. This included daily washing in a river, lake, stream, or pond as well as more elaborate medicinal baths. The Aztecs built *temazcalli*, steamrooms similar to ancient Roman hypocausts. These beehive-shaped structures of stone or brick were heated, and the patient rested inside while various combinations of drugs were burned in the smoke or added directly to the steam to treat the patient. Sometimes this was accompanied by body massage with various types of leaves and ointments. Every village had one or more *temazcalli*, and they were used to treat everything from fevers and boils to insect allergies and snakebites. They were also used to treat exhaustion and aching muscles as well as to speed the recovery of women following childbirth.

Apparently this practice extended over virtually all of the Americas in various forms. When Francisco Pizarro arrived in the land of the Incas, the emperor Atahualpa was in the mountains enjoying the thermal baths around Cajamarca and recovering from a long military campaign against his half brother Huascar. Throughout the Andes, hot springs were tried as sacred *huaca* by the Quechua speakers and used to promote good health.

The extensive use of baths by the Indians was viewed with great consternation by the Spanish, who thought that such frequent bathing was debilitating to the body and could lead to terrible diseases. Colonial officials repeatedly tried to outlaw such practices as harmful to the Indians, and the *temazcalli* disappeared in Mexico, but persisted in the remote areas.

Virtually all of the Indians of North America used steambaths similar to the Aztec *temazcalli*. Groups as widely separated as the natives of California and Delaware built semisubterranean earthen structures entered by a tunnel. The Alaskan natives built similar baths covered with logs, while the Creeks covered theirs with hides and mats. Many of the natives in the southeastern United States slept all night in the sweat lodges during the winter months and each morning upon awaking ran from the lodge to jump into the cold water of the river. The Plains Indians used a temporary structure made of branches and leaves covered in blankets [Driver, p. 132]. Still today, Indians throughout the United States and Canada use the sweat bath as a ritual part of religious ceremonies and powwows and for general physical and mental hygiene.

The widespread and persistent use of the steambaths and of water baths by the Indians paralleled the practices of ancient Mediterranean cultures, but stood in sharp contrast to the practices of the Europeans who arrived in the New World. The bathing probably served to reduce diseases among the Indians prior to the European arrival and thereby partly accounted for the general freedom from epidemic diseases. The destruction of the lodges by the Europeans and their denunciation of frequent bathing quite probably contributed to the rapid spread of Old World epidemics among the natives of the Americas.

The same Indians who gave the world quinine also gave it coca, which Indian farmers cultivated in approximately the same area at the foot of the Andes. One of the traditional uses of coca was as a ritual cleanser applied to the body of the patient by a healer. More commonly, the leaves of the coca bush are chewed or made into a tea that soothes the body and alleviates pain as well as the discomfort of thirst, hunger, itching, and fatigue. Even though it cured no diseases the way quinine did, it seemed to refresh the mind and spirit as much as quinine refreshed the aching body.

Coca arrived in Europe by 1565, when Nicolas Monardes of Seville made the first scientific descriptions and drawings of it. Not until the late 1850s did German chemists manage to isolate the active ingredient, which became known as cocaine. The first major medical use for it came in the 1880s as an anesthesia for painful eye surgery and later for dental surgery and other kinds of operations. Eventually chemists synthesized cocaine to make procaine. Under the trademark Novocain, it continues today as one of the most important anesthetics in the world. Even though cocaine cured nothing, it launched the medical use of local anesthesias that replaced the more common use of ether.

At the same time that medicine was exploring the surgical possibilities of cocaine, the young chemist Angelo Mariani introduced Mariani's Coca wine, a concoction for which the pope gave him a special medal. This wine made cocaine the fad of Europe not merely because of its medicinal properties but because of its recreational and refreshing qualities as well. In addition to Pope Leo XIII and Queen Victoria, customers included such celebrities as William McKinley, Thomas Edison, and Sarah Bernhardt.

During the same time in the United States, pharmacist and Confederate war veteran John Styth Pemberton of Atlanta devised a series of medicines using both native American ingredients and some foreign ingredients. He invented medications with names such as Flower Cough Syrup, Triplex Liver Pills, and French Wine Coca, advertised as the "Ideal Nerve and Tonic Stimulant" and an obvious imitation of Mariani's Coca wine. Realizing that the public most enjoyed the stimulant property of the drink and that they could buy mere alcohol anywhere, he dropped the wine and added some caffeine and the flavorings of the African kola nut. The result was Coca-Cola, which was released to the public in 1886 as a flavoring for water drinks. Soon the water of choice for mixing with the syrup became fizzy carbonated water, and thus was born the modern drink that has captured a world market.

Pemberton marketed the syrup through drugstores and soon attracted the interest of another pharmacist, Asa Griggs Candler, who bought up the Coca-Cola business to add to his small array of products that included De-lecta-lave dentifrice, Everlasting Cologne, and Botanic Blood Balm. Although he manufactured the products together and advertised them together, sales of the new drink soon surpassed those of all the other products, and Candler built a whole soft-drink empire around it [Kahn, pp. 55–59].

The connection between cocaine and Coca-Cola continued so closely even after the manufacturers removed cocaine from it that the nickname for Coca-Cola quickly became Coke, the same nickname used for cocaine. In the early part of the twentieth century in the south, where Coca-Cola was so popular, people often called the drink simply "dope" or more obliquely "a shot in the arm." Still today, hearing-impaired users of sign language express the same connotation in their slang sign for a cola drink. They make the gesture of inserting a hypodermic needle into the upper forearm.

Many of the roots and barks used to make Indian medicines tasted quite bitter or spicy. Because of this, many of the plants became known as peppers, and the drinks made from them bore such trademarks as Dr Pepper, emphasizing both the spicy taste and the medical origin. Of course, the emotional or physiological kick from these drinks originally came not from the misnamed "peppers" in them but from the alcohol, opium, caffeine, cola, and cocaine.

In common speech, however, the word "pepper" became closely associated with the notion of excitement, hyperactivity, and the amphetamine-like high produced from these supposedly Indian tonics. Young people soon shortened the word "pepper" to "pep" to signify the state produced by these drinks; and thus the English language acquired a new word. One of the first recorded uses of the new word appeared in the *Literary Digest* of August 21, 1915, when "pep" was written in quotes to refer to the power of a motor. "Pep" became one of the buzzwords of the twentieth century and was closely associated with the 1920s; in time it appeared in phrases such as "pep talk," "pep rally," and "pep pill." The popular word was also used as the basis for yet another cola drink, Pepsi.

The soft-drink industry in America grew directly out of the traveling medical salesmen who hawked various kinds of Indian tonics. Because of the association of the Indians with the medical knowledge in the nineteenth century, the sellers of every medicine tried to connect it as closely as possible with Indians. Advertisements proclaimed their medicines as Indian tonics or Indian cures. The traveling medicine hawkers often carried a living Indian with them as proof that their medicine sprang from genuine Indian medicine. The most famous of these included the Kiowa Indian Medicine and Vaudeville Company and the Kickapoo Indian Medicine Company, which sold for $250,000 in 1911 after over thirty years of performances. Documents show that at least 150 medicine shows featured one or more Kickapoo Indians, compared with 180 stock companies playing Broadway shows around the country in 1911 [Green and Laurie, p. 69].

In the nineteenth century, medical publishers brought out a series of books on Indian medicine. These started in 1813 with *The Indian Doctor's Dispensatory*, followed by *The Indian Guide to Health* in 1836 and *The North American Indian Doctor, or Nature's Method of Curing and Preventing Disease According to the Indians* in 1838 [Hallowell, p. 329]. The *United States Phar-*

macopeia, which first appeared in 1820, listed over two hundred drugs supplied by the Indians; of these about twenty-five are of South American origin [Driver, p. 557].

As American medicine became established and regulated by universities, hospitals, and medical associations, the Indian healer was pushed ever farther aside. The medicine shows became more vaudeville than medicine as they combined humor, tricks of daring, and a little sex to stimulate flagging sales of their Indian nostrums, which often contained more alcohol, opium, or cocaine than they did Indian medicines. Increasingly, Indian medicine became associated with shams and quackery.

At the same time these shows helped to build a new image of the Indian as a daring and savage fighter. Particularly in the show started by William F. "Wild Bill" Cody (1846–1917) in 1883, the Indians were presented not as healers but as expert horsemen and fierce warriors who performed feats to thrill the American and European masses. The wild west shows coincided with the development of the film industry, and Cody starred in one of the first such films depicting the action and drama of his traveling troupe. This gave birth to a whole new genre of entertainment as the cowboys-and-Indians movie was born. The Plains Indian in full warpaint became the symbol of the Indian that was then diffused around the world. The Indian as warrior replaced the Indian as healer.

By this time the Indian cures and medicines had circled the world and become fully integrated into cultures on every continent. The medicines became so taken for granted that it was easy to forget that they had not always been there and that they had not been discovered or invented by Old World doctors, pharmacists, and chemists. The Indian as healer lives on in only a few places such as Timbuktu, where the great Indian drugs arrived but the wild west show and the cowboy western films never came to change the image of the Indian from healer to warrior.

The accumulation of archaeological and medical evidence has slowly led to the conclusion that in addition to all the medicines that America gave the world, it contributed at least one dreaded disease—syphilis. The Old World had no knowledge of syphilis prior to 1493, and contemporary observers claimed that Columbus brought it back from Hispaniola, a claim given added weight with the publication in Spanish of *Treatise Called Fruit of All the Saints Against the Serpentine Malady of Hispaniola* by Ruiz Díaz de Isla in Seville in 1539. Each country it infected, however, named it for the country from which it received it. Thus the Italians and English called it the French disease, Poles called it the German disease, Russians called it the Polish disease, and so forth until the name "syphilis" was established in the early sixteenth century.

The first documented outbreak came in Italy in 1494 or 1495 during a French invasion led by King Charles VIII, who wanted to make himself king of Naples. In 1497, Gaspar Torrella published his *Treatise with Advice Against Pudendagram or the Gallic Malady*, giving one of the first medical accounts of this disease that struck so suddenly and so viciously. By 1495 the disease moved to Germany, and it followed to Britain in the next year. Carried by Portuguese sailors, it reached the Middle East and India in 1498, and it arrived in Russia and eastern Europe by 1499. By 1505, only a dozen years after Columbus's return to Spain from America, syphilis erupted in China on the farthest side of the Eurasian continent.

The disease in its early years acted much more virulently and rapidly than today. It killed fast and frequently. Its impact on the Old World was much like that of Acquired Immune Deficiency Syndrome, AIDS, in the twentieth century. There was no known cure, it spread easily, it attacked young, active individuals, and it usually proved lethal. Once again the Old World inhabitants turned to the pharmacy of the Americas for a cure, and they thought they had found it in the wood of trees of the *Guaiacum* genus. The oil guaiacol acted as an expectorant. According to European medical logic of the era, a patient would easily spit out the noxious infection in the pints of saliva which he expelled from his body after taking guaiacol.

Doctors claimed to have cured many people by this method only to have the patient infect others. In the meantime, merchant families such as the Fuggers made fortunes importing the wood from America and selling it in the form of various drugs. At the same time, British merchants claimed that they too had found the cure for syphilis in the sassafras plant, which made a very popular tea sold at high prices. Whether or not syphilis actually came from America and no matter what its early history, it proved to be one disease for which the Indians had no cure to offer.

Despite the sophistication of American medicine when the Europeans arrived, the healers succumbed to the onslaught of Old World diseases. Never in human history have so many new and virulent diseases hit any one people all at the same time. Smallpox, bubonic plague, tuberculosis, malaria, yellow fever, influenza, and the other major killers of the Old World had been totally unknown in America until the arrival of Columbus. These diseases swept rapidly through the people, who lacked all immunities against them. The Indians also lacked immunities to what are often called the childhood diseases of the Old World. Diseases such as measles, mumps, and whooping cough that provoked only a minor illness among Europeans and Africans proved deadly to whole villages of Indians who had never before encountered any of those germs.

In a few cases the Indian doctors could apply their old cures, such as quinine that proved to be a cure for malaria, but for most of the Old World diseases they had no protection at all. Even the medicine of quinine quickly became too precious to the Europeans for them to allow the Indians to use it. The whites monopolized it to eradicate malaria in Europe while leaving the Indians to die from this disease that soon found a new permanent home in the American tropics. The Indians died by the millions. Probably 90 percent of the American Indian population died within the first century after the European arrival in America. Both continents were left decimated again and again by wave after wave of the new diseases.

In this agonizing and slow genocide, the Indian doctors found most of their cures impotent and were thrown back increasingly on the meager resources remaining to them—prayer and magic. They chanted, danced, mumbled, and searched for magical solutions to ailments that they had never before encountered.

The great accomplishments of Indian medicine have been forgotten. In a few remote spots in North America, however, a small memorial still exists to the great power of Indian medicine in the English place-names. The faint memory of Indian medicine lingers in such seemingly quaint and obscure names as Medicine Lake, Montana, Medicine Bow Forest, Wyoming, and Medicine Hat, Alberta.

▲ ▲ 11 ▲ ▲
THE DRUG
CONNECTION

Sitting across from me on the back of the open truck crossing the Andes, an old Indian man reached into his pocket and pulled out a small plastic bag of leaves. He carefully extracted several crumpled leaves and a pinch of dark-brown paste and held them out to me. In the proper Quechua way I cupped my two hands together to receive them and bowed my head in a silent gesture of thanks. The Quechua Indians lack an equivalent of the European phrase "thank you," since their culture teaches that sharing is a requirement of life and that gratitude can only be shown in deeds and not in words. The old man then took a portion for himself, and the two of us began to chew the dusty-smelling leaves. The coca made my mouth feel as fresh as though I were chewing mint or had just left the dentist's office after having my teeth cleaned. After I had chewed a little longer my tongue and cheeks felt slightly numb.

The leaves produce no strong effect like drinking a cup of coffee, a glass of iced tea, or even a cola drink. Instead, they merely take the sting out of the cold and blunt the edge of discomfort that one feels on those endlessly long trips up and down the mountains of Bolivia. In the high passes, coca alleviates the discomfort of the reduced air pressure on the body and the thinned oxygen in the lungs. It is one of the few drugs that prevents *soroche*, or altitude sickness, one of the most common ailments in the Andes. When we descended into the tropical valleys, the coca relieved the discomfort of the sudden change in altitude and the heat that rapidly built in the unshaded back of the truck.

For centuries the lowland natives have grown coca and traded the leaves to the highland natives who chew them. In addition to lessening the discomforts of life, the mildly narcotic coca leaf supplies calcium and vitamins A, C, and D. This offers much-needed nutrients to a people who otherwise might lack calcium, since the altitude is generally too high to support either cows or many garden vegetables that contain much calcium. The coca strengthens their bones and teeth, and for some yet unclear reason it significantly retards cavities and related dental problems.

As our truck reached a small police shack at the edge of the Amazon jungle in the infamous drug region known as the Chapare, the soldiers motioned us off the road and began their slow search of the truck and people. Since I was a foreigner, they took me inside for further questions. There I saw three teenage boys tied together. The young men's hands showed large bleeding ulcers and like those of a leper were missing chunks of flesh. The police had tied the boys' hands in front of them, but even without the ropes, the boys could not have escaped very easily, since their feet were also covered in the same sores, making it difficult for them to stand, let alone walk. When the military police wanted to move them, each boy had to be lifted at the arms by two men to be half carried and half dragged. The police had just captured these young boys, who had been working as *pisacocas* in the cocaine kitchens of the Chapare. The *pisacocas* use their hands and feet to mix coca leaves with kerosene, sulfuric acid, and acetone in the first stages of extracting coca paste from the leaves. In the laborious process, the chemicals quickly eat away the flesh. Even in this condition, the boys continue working, rendered oblivious to the pain of their open wounds by the constant supply of cocaine-laced cigarettes that they smoke. Unable to flee, however, they become easy targets when the police or army raid the "coke kitchen" where they work.

In this southwestern edge of the Amazon Basin the Andes meet the tropical jungle, in an environment similar to that around the village of Genaro Herrera on the Ucayali in Peru a thousand miles to the northwest. The coca bush originated here. Half a millennium ago the Inca aristocracy received a steady supply of coca leaves from here and used them in their religious ceremonies. Archaeological evidence shows that Indians in the area used coca thousands of years ago. The first coca boom, however, was fueled by the European need for silver and by the opening of the mines on Cerro Rico in Potosí.

The mines of upper Bolivia, particularly the mines around Potosí, strain the limits of human endurance. They are so high and the oxygen content inside the labyrinth of small passages drops so low that the work is almost too strenuous even for the Indians already accustomed to hard labor at high altitudes. The conquistadores, however, found that the miners worked much longer and harder if they chewed the coca leaves. Not only could the men work with less oxygen, but they could work longer hours with less food. The workers continued working while chewing the coca and thus did not take breaks. To meet this new demand, the Spaniards expanded the plantations of coca growing in the humid lowlands and shipped tons of the leaves up to Potosí, which had become the world's largest consumer of coca.

Even though the mines no longer rely on forced labor, miners such as Rodrigo Cespedes continue the custom, since the coca helps them to survive the inhuman labor conditions, which have changed only a little in half a millennium. Unfortunately for them, however, the price of the coca leaves soared in the last century, forcing them to pay an ever greater percentage of their wages for this leaf that helps them breathe and work.

The rising price began when European scientists learned to extract cocaine from the coca leaves in the mid-1800s. The Europeans and Americans began buying the coca leaves to make cocaine, which they used as a medicine and as flavoring for wine and cola drinks. By the time the United States government outlawed the use of cocaine through the Pure Food and Drug Act of 1906 and the Harrison Narcotics Act of 1914, a small but loyal market of users had been created. Use of the drug grew slowly but steadily until the 1970s and 1980s, when it exploded in the United States and Europe as the drug of choice among the urban affluent and the poor alike. Soon the fad spread even to Rio de Janeiro, Mexico City, Bogotá, and the other cities of Latin America.

The Indians of South America never acquired an interest in using the cocaine itself, but with the attempted imposition of European culture, law, and religion on the people of the Andes over the past five hundred years, they rallied around the coca leaf as a focal point of cultural identity. It offers them physiological refuge from the demands of the white world, but it also offers a psychological relief. Indians offer coca leaves in sacrifice by burying them or burning them whenever they plow a new field, build a home, or want to offer thanks. They also offer coca leaves along with *chicha*, the fermented corn beer, to the Virgin Mary, who has been Indianized virtually beyond recognition to outsiders. As one of the most valued substances on earth, coca is the gift most frequently sacrificed to the gods. The only higher gift is to offer the leaves together with the fetus of a llama, which, having never been born into the corruption and sin of the world, is the purest offering an Indian can give.

The spirit of the coca, known as Cocamama, along with the earth mother, Pachamama, plays a major role in the pantheon of Indian gods, demigods, and spirits. Cocamama has power to foretell the future through native seers skilled in the reading of the coca leaves, and Cocamama supplies *curanderos*, Indian healers, with the power to cure a sick body of almost any ailment by washing it with the dry leaves.

As a symbol of resistance to the whites and to European culture, coca plays a role in the Andes analogous to that of peyote among North American Indians of northern Mexico and the southwestern United States. Unlike peyote, *ebene* of the Orinoco, and similar drugs throughout the Americas, coca produces no ecstatic conditions. It does not make the soul leave the body, put the user in trance, invoke visions, provoke dancing, or produce other dramatic effects. To the contrary, coca plays a quiet and calm role in Quechua society somewhat as tea plays a focal role in British society or ritual baths play in Scandinavian, Japanese, and traditional Jewish society. Coca use creates a communal act to separate "us" from "them."

Today the Indians can afford only a small supply of coca leaves, because most coca leaves go directly into making cocaine. Particularly in the Chapare, the leaves grow too big and bitter for the connoisseur of coca chewing, but these leaves concentrate the active ingredient for cocaine and therefore yield more money to the drug manufacturers. The cocaine fad greatly increased the demand for Chapare leaves from Bolivia when coca bushes transplanted to California, Colombia, and Indonesia proved much too weak to produce a high grade of cocaine.

During the 1980s, coca paste and cocaine emerged as the primary exports of Bolivia, surpassing the tin and zinc which themselves had long since surpassed the colonial export of silver. By the late 1980s as much as 40 percent of the gross national product of Bolivia came from cocaine. Grandchildren of the Indians who walked the ore and mercury mixture to make the *pasta* from which silver was extracted now walked the kerosene and coca *pasta* from which cocaine is extracted. Whole villages of miners left their homes and families in the villages around Potosí to move into the lucrative Chapare, where they could earn up to $3 a day, far more than Rodrigo earns working on Cerro Rico.

In the 1980s, Roberto Suárez exercised a loose but extensive control over the cocaine trade in an area of eastern Bolivia larger than France. Roberto Suárez was the nephew of Nicolas Suárez, who had controlled the rubber trade in the same part of Bolivia around the turn of the century [Kendall, p. 281]. Suárez supposedly sold some refined cocaine but dealt mostly in the *pasta*, which Colombians bought to perform the final steps of processing before smuggling the drug into the United States or Europe. The cocaine industrialists had to fight off occasional harassment by the U.S. drug agents, and from time to time they repulse another U.S.-funded invasion by Bolivia's crack army unit of Leopardes. Invariably, the Leopardes lose and withdraw in humiliation. When the government of Bolivia seems about to cause major problems for the cocaine business, Suárez and his associates have been known to overthrow it and substitute their own, as they did in the coup that installed Garcia Meza Tejada as president on July 17, 1980.

As we drove into the drug area, our truck was stopped at another blockade, but this one was not manned by police or soldiers. Angry Indian men and women sat and stood in the road to stop our passage. As the bystanders shouted insults at us, several young men with pistols and machetes climbed up on the sides of the truck. The old man stared silently ahead, chewing his coca and ignoring the crowd; I tried to follow his example. Some of the young men hanging on to the side of the truck climbed aboard and started poking into everything on the truck. One of the young men accused the Indians on the truck with us of working as *pisacocas*, and contemptuously called the rest of us *narcotraficantes*, drug smugglers.

The Indians made this impromptu strike on the road in order to disrupt the drug traffic. The week before, their village had been flooded by the rising river and their freshly planted fields of corn and potatoes had been washed away. Because the government of La Paz was too distant either to offer them help or to offer a convenient target against which they might protest, the Indians directed their protest at the only thing around them—the drug traffic passing on the dirt road through their village. They demanded financial assistance or, they threatened, they would disrupt the drug trade. The subtle distinction between the whites who ran the government and the whites who ran the drug trade escaped the Indians' understanding. They searched our truck for chemicals used in making cocaine, but they found nothing on board but a couple of car batteries on which someone had apparently vomited.

Not until we reached our final destination did I realize that indeed we were carrying sulfuric acid concealed inside the hollowed car batteries. Someone had vomited *chicha* on the batteries as an effective deterrent to anyone wanting to inspect them too carefully. The driver of the truck used the same batteries to smuggle the cocaine paste out of the area on the return trip to the city.

Several weeks later, back in the city of Cochabamba, I heard that the Indians ended their strike when they ran out of food. Having received no help from the government, and not having been able to outsmart the drug traffickers, most of the displaced farmers went to work in the coca fields and in the cocaine kitchens as *pisacocas*.

Cocaine is merely the most recent in an extended wave of native American drugs and mind-altering substances to sweep the world as a fad. The boom in coca cultivation in the Chapare and the luring of colonists from the mountains down to clear the lowlands to satisfy this drug need clearly echoes the founding of the United States. The first colony of the United States was settled by profiteering colonists, convicts, and indentured servants who arrived in Virginia to cultivate tobacco leaves for sale to Europeans, who ground it and snorted it up their noses in the form of snuff. Tobacco was the first of the New World drugs to be widely accepted in the Old World, and the European zest for it played a major role in opening North America to colonization.

Contemporary civic mythology of the United States overlooks this role of America as drug supplier to the world. The 1607 settling of Virginia receives short mention compared to the much later settlement at Plymouth in 1620 by the Pilgrims, who thought they were landing somewhere much farther south. This cash crop of tobacco played so important a role in the United States that when the Founding Fathers built the original Capitol in Washington, D.C., they decorated the Greek columns with tobacco leaves. Some of these remain visible today under the small dome between the old Senate chamber and the main dome of the building, but most of them disappeared in the subsequent campaigns to make the Capitol appear Greek and to obliterate native American influences.

Just as the United States fights cocaine smugglers in the twentieth century, world governments of the seventeenth century ardently fought against the use of tobacco. Even the English under the rule of James I banned its use until they realized how much money they could make from the trade of their American colonies. Over the next fifty years, tobacco was outlawed by the Ottoman Empire, the Mogul Empire, Sweden, Denmark, Russia, Naples, Sicily, China, the Papal States, and the Electorate of Cologne. Regardless of the law, tobacco use increased in popularity and spread to new parts of the world, and people found ever more ingenious ways to use it.

Despite anti-tobacco campaigns around the world, Maryland and Virginia exported thirty thousand kegs of tobacco a year by 1723, a trade requiring the services of two hundred ships [Braudel, Vol. I, p. 264]. In the succeeding decades this trade increased astronomically as the Carolinas, Georgia, Delaware, and even parts of New England joined the tobacco boom. Even though the colonists amassed fortunes from their drug trade and managed to build large slave estates in the middle of the forest, they greatly resented the British government and merchants for taking a share of the profits. American colonists also resented the increasing attention British merchants gave to the rival crop of tea, which they transported from India and Ceylon to all parts of the world. Eventually, the colonists declared and fought for their independence, thereby seizing full control of the increasingly lucrative American drug trade.

Like cocaine, tobacco proved versatile. Woodland Indians of North America smoked dried tobacco in pipes, and the Indians of Mexico and the southwestern United States rolled it into cornhusk cigarettes to smoke. Indians of the northern Pacific coast chewed tobacco with lime much as the Indians of the Andes chew coca leaves. Some Indians, such as the Aztecs, ate the leaves straight. The Creek Indians mixed it with the leaves of *Ilex cassine* and other ingredients to make their Black Drink for use in their rituals.

Eighteenth-century gentlemen enthusiastically snorted it, finely ground into snuff, in the belief that the nose was the shortest route to the brain. This followed nearly two centuries of pipe smoking, in which the nicotine had been vigorously inhaled directly to the bloodstream through the lungs, a technique as efficient as taking it through the nose. When adopted by westerners, tobacco had no culturally prescribed place as it did among the Indians. Its use grew indiscriminately and soon became pervasive, with people smoking, chewing, spitting, and snorting tobacco in the streets, at the dinner table, in bed, and in classrooms.

Tobacco use spread around the world more thoroughly than coffee, tea, betel, kola nut, cocaine, or any other drug, with the possible exception of chocolate. Apparently every culture in the world today has been introduced to some form of tobacco use, and very few cultures have rejected it. Even in Tibet, where I found the lowest penetration of American Indian foods and other crops, tobacco use was nevertheless widespread. Unlike the people of Nepal, who have gladly adopted the American potato, and unlike their neighbors in Sichuan, who eat a variety of chilies, corn, and American Indian garden vegetables, the Tibetans adhere tenaciously to their diet of barley, yak butter, tea, and meat seasoned primarily with salt and sugar.

Even on a remote Tibetan pass called Karo La at an elevation of 16,548 feet, I came upon two herders about fourteen years old who pleaded more desperately for tobacco than the monks in the monastery pleaded for pictures of the Dalai Lama. The two young boys were sitting in the dirt beneath a stone cairn decorated with colorful prayer flags that snapped in the breeze, while in the background we could see the sun reflected from a glacier creeping down the high peaks toward Yamdrok Yamatso, a lake of Caribbean blue water. I did not have any tobacco, but my Chinese guide tossed two cigarettes into the dirt, and the boys scrambled for them. Despite the high altitude and the reduction of oxygen by a third of its concentration at sea level, the boys smoked one cigarette with great relish while saving the other.

The Englishman George Bogle in 1774 had followed the same ancient trail I was on into Tibet from India in an unsuccessful attempt to open Tibetan markets for the British East India Company. He spent time with the Pachen Lama at Shigatse and introduced the American potato to unimpressed farmers, but he never reached the court of the Dalai Lama in Lhasa. Bogle arrived at a time when the British trade network included all of North America and strongholds around the world, but it was on the eve of a big change in British trade—the American Revolution, and the loss of tobacco revenues.

When the British merchants lost control of the American tobacco market after 1776, they searched for a substitute crop to sell. They found the substitute in the opium poppy grown in their newly acquired lands in India and Burma. For the British merchants, opium promised a special advantage, because new customers could smoke it in pipes like tobacco, and therefore they did not need any new equipment or skills to learn to use opium. But opium had an additional advantage for British merchants in that it quickly addicted the user much more thoroughly than tobacco. In this way the British captured a market of millions of Chinese even though the Chinese government outlawed its use.

The British opium trade eventually caused two wars that ended in bitter defeat for the Chinese, and it allowed the British to acquire the port colony of Hong Kong. Since the discovery of America, silver from Mexico and the Andes had poured into China in exchange for the luxury goods produced there. China had much to offer but desired nothing from the west except the steady supply of American silver and gold, which had accumulated in great quantities since the opening of America. Finally, with the opium trade the British had found the key to unlock this vast storehouse of silver. As peasants and aristocrats alike sold off their silver coins, ingots, and jewelry to supply their opium addictions, Britain extracted a fortune from China while still taking out Chinese silks and porcelains to the west. Not since Francis Drake and the other English pirates raided the Spanish caravels had so much of the silver from Potosí flowed into British hands.

While the British made fortunes selling opium to the Asians, and while the newly formed United States peddled tobacco to the world, the Spaniards pushed a seemingly much more innocuous drug found in America. This became known throughout the world as chocolate, the active ingredient in the beans of the cacao pod. Despite the similarity in names, the coca bush, from whose leaves cocaine is extracted, is different from the cacao bush, which produces the golden-green pods of chocolate. Neither the cacao bush nor the coca bush bears any relation to the tropical coco tree, also called the coconut palm, which bears the large coconut. This confusion of plants, like the dual use of such terms as "pepper" and "Indian," further illustrates the cultural complexities and errors arising from the coming together of America and the Old World.

Europeans encountered chocolate when Hernando Cortés conquered the Mayas and Aztecs, who cultivated it extensively. The cacao bean served as the primary form of currency among Aztecs, who also consumed it in various delightful ways. Aztec cooks commonly whipped the chocolate with water and sometimes with honey to make a frothy, refreshing drink that they called *chocoatl* in the Nahuatl language. What excited the Spanish most about this plant was its narcotic properties. Like the coca leaves in South America, the cacao bean lessened the pains of hunger, gave a shot of energy, and let the user continue marching or fighting for hours. Because of these properties, the conquistadores immediately adopted it as an indispensable aid during their long military campaigns across mountains and through jungles.

The people back in Europe proved far less eager to accept chocolate, which to them looked far too much like rabbit feces. The pure chocolate tasted too bitter, and by tradition Europeans preferred black pepper, horseradish, and mustard for seasoning their vegetables and meats. The Europeans tried mixing chocolate with various spices such as mint and cinnamon to make it more palatable, but reputedly some experimenting nuns first mixed it with hot milk and added sugar to create the chocolate rage that continues today. Hot chocolate became particularly popular in the Catholic countries of the Mediterranean, where it stimulated the faithful on the numerous fast days when the church forbade food but permitted drink [Schivelbusch, pp. 96–107]. The Protestants in the north of Europe preferred coffee until England took over the tea plantations of India and Ceylon, and then they substituted tea for coffee.

The jagged, almost nervous stimulation produced by coffee and tea contrasted sharply with the smooth, sensuous high of chocolate. Consequently, chocolate acquired a strong reputation as an aphrodisiac that invigorated men and stripped women of their inhibitions. Something of this reputation lingers even today in American and European culture; chocolates still serve as the traditional gift of Valentine's Day or of a suitor at any time. Chocolate serves as the gift of love and the appropriate dessert after a candlelight dinner.

Chocolate provoked such a strong response in Europe because it seemed so unlike any known food. Carolus Linnaeus classified it as *Theobroma cacao*, taking the genus name from the Greek phrase for "food of the gods." Scientists have since applied the word "theobromine" to designate the active ingredient in chocolate, the counterpart of caffeine in coffee or cocaine in coca.

Chocolate spread not merely because of its unusual qualities or because of its religious or sexual roles. Behind both types of propaganda, an efficient Spanish monarchy held a monopoly over cacao production in its Mexican and Caribbean colonies and worked diligently to increase sales. Wherever the Spanish monarchy could, it suppressed coffee and tea trade in favor of chocolate.

The Spanish monarchy pushed chocolate into the Spanish Netherlands, and the Dutch quickly created an array of foods that mixed chocolate with various combinations of sugar and spices. All types of chocolate candies, cakes and tortes, puddings and pies soon became a permanent part of the European diet. Up to this point chocolate had been sold in large bars, which were rich in the cacao oil or butter as well as in the chocolate taste. The Dutch developed a new way of processing the chocolate so that the oil was removed and only the dry chocolate remained. This new product, cocoa, was easier to transport and store, and it became a very popular drink for children, since in this more refined condition it lacked the aphrodisiac qualities thought to lurk in pure chocolate.

Once chocolate was mixed with sugar it became very difficult for the consumer to tell how much stimulation came from the chocolate and how much from the sugar. Consequently, bakers and candy makers frequently reduced the amount of real chocolate in favor of greater use of less expensive vanilla and artificial chocolate flavorings. Today the taste that most people associate with chocolate springs primarily from the vanilla and other spices mixed with the chocolate. Cocoa butter has yielded to flavored forms of vegetable shortening, and now people ingest real chocolate in such minute quantities that most of the narcotic effect has been sacrificed to the sugar rush that substitutes for it.

Not all the substances chewed by Indians could be made into stronger stimulants. Indians in different parts of the Americas chewed the saps of various trees. New England Indians chewed spruce gum, and the Indians of Mexico chewed the rubbery sap of the sapodilla tree, which they called chicle. Although tasty, it lacked the narcotic high that might have led the Europeans to refine it or distill it into a more potent drug. Still the whites were not satisfied merely to chew this substance without some type of extra stimulation from it, so they added massive amounts of sugar. New Yorker Thomas Adams managed to make it into a commercial product after the Civil War and built the first successful chewing-gum factory in the 1880s. In its new sweetened form, chewing gum joined tobacco and cola drinks as American products that spread around the world.

In Mexico and part of Texas, the peyote or mescal cactus grows wild. This spineless cactus, Lophophora williamsii, produces nine alkaloids, the most powerful of which is the mescaline that creates hallucinations when ingested by humans. Like many American drugs, peyote may be eaten raw or brewed into a tea. Most of the plant grows beneath the ground, but the usable part, called the button, protrudes above the surface. To preserve and transport it, the Indians usually dried the plant, but Indians in the areas where it grows prefer to eat it while it is fresh and green.

Aside from tobacco and chocolate, peyote probably remains the most used of the native American drugs in North America. Over the past few centuries, the use of peyote spread steadily from its original Mexican base. When the Spanish arrived in Mexico they found peyote in use by Aztec priests as a sacred substance and as a part of the sacred ball games. In the campaign to eradicate Aztec religion and power, the Spanish forbade use of peyote. The Spanish effectively ended the trade in peyote, and the Inquisition treated drug use as an act of heresy, but the Indians continued to use it over the next three centuries in northern Mexico, where the cactus grew wild, beyond the reach of Spanish priests and soldiers. In addition to peyote, the Indians used the milder cactus Doña Ana, *Coryphantha macromeris*, as well as *pipintzintli*, the leaves of *Salvia divinorum*, and *ololiuqui*, the seeds of the *Rivea corymbosa* vine, and mescal beans of *Sophora secundiflora*, known as Texas mountain laurel.

In the nineteenth century when the Mexican Indians achieved independence from Spain, the use of peyote increased. It spread across the southwestern part of the United States, reaching the Caddo Indians of Texas by the time of the American Civil War, and by the mid-1880s it reached north to the Comanche and Kiowa of the western Indian Territory (later Oklahoma), from which it spread to the Cheyenne, Osage, Arapaho, and other Plains Indians. By the twentieth century, Indians adopted it around the Great Lakes and the Canadian border. Having witnessed the destruction of their own social and cultural systems while being denied access to those of the whites, the lost reservation Indians turned to the religious use of peyote as a refuge from an increasingly hostile social environment. The use continued to spread, and despite the efforts of Christian missionaries, peyote became the focal sacrament of a new church, which was officially incorporated and recognized in 1918 and eventually became known as the Native American Church.

One of the primary beliefs of the church is that while Christ came to the whites, peyote came to the Indians. Peyote offered them the same escape from the strictures of white civilization that coca leaves offered the Quechua Indians. In their church, peyote heals and brings enlightenment within the context of a communal and spiritual ritual, but the peyote has too sacred a function to be used recreationally or to be abused through excessive or inappropriate use.

To separate themselves clearly from movements such as that of the Ghost Dance or the Red Sticks, the Native American Church inserted into its charter a clause of loyalty to the United States, pledging their lives for the defense of the United States Constitution and government. This certainly surpassed in loyalty the commitment of any Christian sect in America [Spicer, p. 288], but even so it did not prevent attacks on the church from the white legal and religious establishment.

Peyote found limited use among another alienated group, the American blacks, but they adapted poorly to the Native American Church, since they lacked the American Indian history of drug use and vision quest in their religious worship. The use of peyote in religion quickly died among the few blacks who tried it. Within another half century from the founding of the Native American Church, however, peyote use had spread into the white population via an alienated generation of American youth. As a drug with mystical associations, it first became popular in a burst of enthusiasm within the youth movement of the 1960s when it achieved acclaim as a psychedelic. This popularity grew with the publication of a number of books on the philosophical and mystical properties of the drugs as used by Indian shamans. In order to achieve the desired effect from the peyote, the user needed to chew a handful of the very bitter and unappetizing buttons. To ease this process during the late 1960s the active ingredient, mescaline, was made available in synthetic form in capsules that were both easier to consume and easier to hide, since the law forbade possession of the drug outside its use in officially recognized churches. Usage in both organic and capsule form continued to be popular among young people, in part because of its reputed lack of health risks and because it did not addict the user as would cocaine and some other mood-altering drugs. After a few years, peyote gradually lost the mysticism that had accompanied its first foray into urban America, and it became just one more drug used solely for secular purposes by whites.

Another common drug in America derived from the psychedelic mushrooms that grow in animal droppings. The mushrooms *Psilocybe mexicana* and *P. cubensis* produce psychoactive ingredients known as psilocybin or psilocin. Like peyote, the approximately twenty varieties of psilocybin mushrooms require virtually no processing to activate the hallucinogenic ingredients. A strong psychological reaction follows eating the mushroom, drinking it in tea, smoking it, or sniffing it in powdered form. The arrival of the Europeans in America greatly expanded the range of the mushroom, because it grows so well in the dung of the cow that the Europeans introduced to America.

Three and a half millennia ago, the Mayas used the mushrooms in their ceremonies. The Aztecs also used them, as in the coronation ceremonies for Moctezuma in 1502. The mushrooms, *Paneolus campanulatus*, were known as *teonanacatl*, "food of the gods," a name very close in meaning to what the Europeans later chose for the other Aztec drug, chocolate. The Spaniards quickly acted to suppress psilocybin mushrooms, but Indians continued to eat them until modern times, when they also spread into United States urban areas. Because of the similarity of psilocybin mushrooms to the toxic *Amanita* genus of mushrooms, poisoning sometimes occurs. In some cases, however, these other mushrooms may be prepared in a special way and taken in the right dosage to produce a different type of emotional and cognitive reaction.

Since the Indians were punished by the church and state for using these drugs, they often kept them secret. Only now do scientists know enough about some of these drugs to initiate systematic studies of them. The Indians of the Amazon Basin learned to strip the bark from the vine *Banisteriopsis caapi*, boil it, and make a hallucinogenic tea with reputed aphrodisiac value. The active ingredient, harmine, can also be extracted and snorted much as cocaine is used. The drug is called *yage* in the Andes or *caapi* in the jungle zones.

Probably the most common of Amazonian drugs outside of coca is *ebene* or *epena*, made from assorted jungle plants. The Yanomamo Indians of Venezuela use it by placing it in the end of a bamboo tube that may be up to a meter and a half in length. One Indian puts the tube to his nostrils, while another one blows hard on the other end. The drugs then force their way through the nasal membranes and into the bloodstream. Soon the recipient begins hallucinating and vomiting while a thick green mucus begins draining from his nose. In this way the Yanomamo commune with their *hekura* or forest spirits [Chagnon, pp. 50–51].

Several thousand miles north of the Amazon in the middle of the Canadian plains, the Indians developed a similar drug from the root of the marsh plant called cakanus, *Acorus calamus*. Jimsonweed was widely used in North America in much the same way. When settlers and soldiers in Jamestown, Virginia, cooked and ate this weed of the genus *Datura* in 1676, the hallucinogenic results gave rise to the name "Jamestown weed," since shortened to "jimsonweed" in English.

The people of the Old World were not satisfied with the drugs that the American Indians made, and so they quickly found ways to make drugs out of American plants that lacked narcotic properties. The Europeans took the common plants of maize corn from central America and the Andean potato and distilled them into alcoholic drinks that were mood- and sensation-altering. This process required massive amounts of corn and potatoes, but the new plants grew easily, offered high yields per acre, and could be easily produced in quantities large enough to support a corn liquor and vodka industry.

The Indians knew how to ferment various plants to make wines or beers, but they had no knowledge of distilling stronger spirits containing more than 3 or 4 percent alcohol. The ancient Mexicans fermented *Agave* and *Dasylirion* plants to make pulque, which was a vitamin-rich drink. The Pima and Papago Indians made a cactus wine, while other Indians in the same area made beer from mesquite, screwbeans, maize, and even the cornstalk. Tribes along the Atlantic coast of North America made persimmon wine, which later attracted a strong following among the colonists. Indians made at least forty alcoholic drinks from various fruits and plants, including palm, plum, pineapple, mamey, and sarsaparilla wines (Driver, p. 110). The most exotic of all was a type of Mayan mead called *balche* made from the fermented honey of a stingless bee.

Despite all these alcoholic beverages, intoxication remained rare among Indians. They used alcohol as they did other drugs, in a primarily religious context. As an indication of just how seriously the Indian cultures took the religious use of such substances, the Aztecs executed any noble, student, or priest found to be publicly drunk. A commoner would be beaten for the first offense and then executed for the second [Driver, p. 111].

The origin of the distilling process is not known, but it began somewhere in the Old World. European alchemists used it to make medicines well before the discovery of America. In addition to distilling various herbs and plants, they distilled wine as well; this produced the first brandy. From this the whole gamut of distilled alcoholic drinks evolved. Brandy soon escaped the confines of medicinal purposes and became a source of intoxication much faster, stronger, and more efficient than wine or beer. Brandy, however, remained a somewhat expensive luxury because of the limited amount of wine available for distilling. In its early years only aristocratic circles and the rising merchant class could afford the luxury drink; it remained well beyond the grasp of the common peasant or the emerging class of factory workers. Alcohol, however, could be distilled from many more substances than just wine. Enterprising apothecaries and monks soon applied the same technique to even the most humble and common of plants.

The first extensive liquor distillation took place in the Caribbean, where the Spanish and later the British made rum from the large quantities of sugar produced in the islands. Colonists in the United States sought to duplicate this grand success, but their land lacked suitable conditions for the cultivation of sugar cane. Instead they applied the same distillation process to what would grow on their land—corn. Corn grew so luxuriantly in American fields that the settlers harvested much more than either humans or animals could consume. They turned it into corn liquor. The process of distilling is technologically so simple that to this day the government has problems collecting its liquor taxes from many of the small-time producers who set up shop in remote areas. Corn liquor, however, did not find the world popularity of rum, because the British crown, which derived great revenues from its well-established rum trade, vigorously fought any competition from corn.

Resourceful colonists readily found new markets for their corn whiskey—the native Indians. The English, Dutch, French, and Spanish colonists all realized that distilled alcohol was a potent tool for subduing the Indians while making money from them. The Mexican viceroy Bernardo de Gálvez, for example, in 1786 noted that alcohol had been so effective in taming the Indians and in bringing money to the state that perhaps it could be used to conquer the unruly Apaches in the north. He claimed that this would make "a new need which forces them to recognize very clearly their obligatory dependence with regard to ourselves" [Braudel, Vol. I, p. 249].

Today Andean Indians use coca leaves very moderately even when surrounded by the cocaine trade; yet this moderation disappears when it comes to alcohol. The same Indian who would not consider snorting cocaine drinks himself into a coma on the village streets during the fiesta honoring the Virgin of Urkupina. Similarly, the North American Indian who uses tobacco moderately and with respect has no such cultural moderation when it comes to whiskey.

Indians have not been the only ones unable to handle their liquor. The Europeans themselves had a long history of using fermented drinks such as wine, mead, ale, and beer, which they consumed in great quantities, but until the last few centuries they had no tradition of using the much more potent distilled spirits of rum, whiskey, gin, and vodka that were quickly developed. As American plantations and American crops transplanted to Europe made alcohol cheap, the peasants substituted hard liquors for their traditional fermented drinks. The Russians learned to wash down their food with tall glasses of vodka in place of beer, while the Irish and Scotch drank more whiskey in place of their ale. This created a wholly new disease, alcoholism, which has spread steadily over the past few centuries. This rise closely parallels the development of industrialism; alcohol provided a psychic break from the monotonous and long work associated with industrial production.

When the Spaniards found that the Indians would work longer and harder if mildly drugged, they made a major discovery of extensive consequences for workers around the world—that factory workers want drugs to help them withstand the drudgery and monotony of their work. Just as the money factory of Potosí served as prototype for factories of all kinds, the use of coca by the workers in Potosí served as a prototype of the use of drugs of all types as a way to alleviate the painful and unnatural conditions of work. The industrial revolution could just as easily have been called the alcohol and drug revolution.

Henry Fielding and other writers chronicled the evils of the new alcohol epidemic caused by the more efficient distillation of gin in the eighteenth century. The engraver William Hogarth hammered home the same message, as did generations of pamphleteers, ministers, and reformers.

In the nineteenth century, the movement for women's rights fought hand in hand with the anti-alcohol movements, as the early feminists saw alcohol as often the greatest oppressor of women. In the home the abuse of women and children usually came at the hands of drunken men. Similarly, increased rape, seduction, and prostitution seemed closely tied to increased alcohol use by males and females. Many women became addicted to alcohol and thus damaged their own and their children's health as well as their personal finances. The changes brought to urban areas in the twentieth century by the spread of drugs was merely a small reflection of the extensive social, economic, familial, cultural, and sexual changes precipitated by the far more widespread use of alcohol in the eighteenth and nineteenth centuries.

Not content to use only the native products of the New World, the European colonists and companies realized very early that the fertile land of America was good for growing a number of Old World stimulants. Coffee, which could not be grown in Europe and therefore cost the Europeans dearly, took readily to the soils of the Caribbean and Brazil.

The Europeans also found that the Americas provided excellent growing land for marijuana, another Old World drug. Moist and mild zones along the California coast and in the Caribbean proved particularly hospitable to this plant. By the 1980s, marijuana apparently had become the primary cash crop of California as well as some smaller countries such as Belize. Through selective breeding, the American farmers strengthened the production of the active ingredient in the plant and thereby cultivated an ever stronger drug.

Because the crop remained illegal, farmers learned to grow it in heavily wooded areas where the plots were difficult to find and were camouflaged from air reconnaissance. Because of this the jungle areas of Belize and the redwood forest areas of northern California became primary production areas that were still relatively close to markets in urban areas of North America. The total land under cultivation for marijuana within the United States alone probably exceeded the most extensive coca cultivation ever in Bolivia. The United States government, with its tremendous financial and technological resources, found it impossible to control the cultivation of marijuana even within its government-owned and -operated park system, but still pressured Bolivia for not being able to control coca cultivation in its extensive and scarcely populated jungles.

Over the past five hundred years, the world has ransacked American pharmacology looking for ever higher highs, ever more complete forms of intoxication, and ever more altered states of consciousness. The quest for drugs continued from chocolate through a variety of tobacco forms, root beers, tonic water, peyote, cola drinks laced with cocaine, and finally to pure cocaine. Along the way, drugs such as marijuana and the poppy were introduced from the remote parts of the Old World, and when possible these were made into stronger substances such as opium and heroin.

By the twentieth century the quest for ever stronger drugs had replaced the earlier quests for gold and the fountain of youth. Many of the drugs of the New World have yet to be tried outside of their native settings. Perhaps they too await the appropriate technology to transform them into even stronger substances which might foster sufficient appeal to become the cocaine of a future generation.

▲ ▲ 12 ▲ ▲

ARCHITECTURE AND
URBAN PLANNING

The oldest signs of human habitation in Nicaragua appear in the hardened mud along the edge of Lake Managua, which the Indians called Xolotán. Along this shore in the northwestern part of Managua, seventeen men, women, and children left footprints indelibly marked into once soft mud. Jaguar paw prints and deer hoofprints crisscross the human tracks, adding a sense of dramatic urgency to the mute artifacts as though the people and animals had all been fleeing something quite frightening. The depth of the adult prints suggests that the men and women struggled under the weight of heavy burdens, which may have been young children, loads of food, or prized possessions, as they ran toward the possible safety of the water. Whatever danger threatened them must have been quite awesome to scare not only these seventeen people but the animals as well. Perhaps the nearby volcano Masaya erupted at that undetermined moment thousands of years ago, throwing these people and animals into a panic.

The people around Lake Managua have always faced peril at the whim of an unpredictable and often cruel Mother Nature. Even more recent prints of disaster scar the lake shores today. Downtown Managua still looks like a battle zone long after its destruction in the Christmas earthquake of 1972.

The Bank of America skyscraper and the Intercontinental Hotel with its 210 luxury rooms survived the catastrophe to stand like sentinels at two ends of a plain of devastation. Office buildings crumbled, but because the quake struck in the middle of the night the white-collar workers escaped injury; cleaning crews, night guards, and homeless people curled in the doorways died. Fellow anthropologist Götz von Houwald, who lived in the area for many years, pointed out to me the ruins of a hotel where several people had died in their beds. He told me of the less fortunate group that had just started ascending in the hotel elevator when the quake struck. They survived the destruction of the building, protected inside the metal elevator in the cement-block elevator shaft, but their protection became their tomb. Even though rescuers could hear their muffled screams, they could not reach the shaft before all the victims had died of slow suffocation and trauma.

Houwald also guided me through the cathedral, whose roof had collapsed, littering the center of the city with chunks of broken marble and leaving virgins and saints on the altars staring at the sky and exposed to tropical rains, dusty winds, and the degradations of birds. Near the still-standing Intercontinental Hotel, he took me to a street corner to show me the ruins where a foreign friend of his had lived and told me of going to her home after the quake and seeing people loot it while her body lay kicking and half exposed but trapped alive beneath the rubble.

Managua bears the marks of the earthquake far more vividly than the marks of the political revolution that followed, and in some ways the earthquake probably caused the revolution. The quake virtually destroyed the city. Ten thousand died, and hundreds of thousands lost their homes. An outpouring of world assistance, money, and supplies followed the earthquake, but the greedy family and allies of dictator Anastasio Somoza diverted much of the assistance into private accounts. Rather than using the funds to rebuild the city, they used it to create and speculate on new suburban projects. By the time the revolution reached the streets of Managua, the city center stood open, the buildings already lying in ruins. The rock throwing and shooting in the streets that marked the final days of the general uprising of the lower classes against a widely despised dictatorship added little to the devastation already caused by the earthquake.

Even cursory examination of a relief map of the Americas reveals a peculiar feature. A chain of mountains runs from Alaska in the north to Tierra del Fuego at the tip of South America. The mountains start well above the Arctic Circle at 70 degrees north and 160 degrees west, run from Alaska down the western side of Canada, fan out to pass through the United States, and then run down through the middle of Mexico and Central America, becoming ever narrower. Jumping over to Colombia, the mountain range hugs the western coast of South America before widening to a dramatic climax in the massive Andes of Bolivia and finally tapering off south of Patagonia at 52 degrees south latitude and 65 degrees west longitude. This ten-thousand-mile-long chain stretches approximately halfway around the world and boasts a disproportionate share of the world's volcanoes, geysers, hot springs, and salt flats as well as all of the Andes and the Rockies. A large number of fault lines radiate across and out from these mountains like cracks in dried mud.

Through centuries of pushing and pulling at the land along the lines where several continental plates intersect, this stretch of the earth's surface gave rise to major deposits of mineral wealth. Potosí dominated the mountains as the most lucrative site of all, but this same long chain also supplied the silver mines of Mexico and was the source of the gold rushes in Alaska, California, and the Canadian Rockies. The mountains have also given up a bounty of base metals, including copper, tin, and zinc.

Earthquakes in this part of the world occur with such frequency that most people outside of the area allocate them little notice. Managua itself toppled once before in 1931, and long before that the nearby capital of León collapsed in an earthquake in 1609 and had to be moved to the site of present-day León. The former capital for all of Central America once stood in Antigua, Guatemala, but earthquakes destroyed it so many times that finally in 1775 the government abandoned it and moved the capital to a new site now known as Guatemala City.

A major quake hit Ecuador in 1797, killing an estimated forty thousand people. In April 1906 an exceptionally severe earthquake destroyed the city of San Francisco with a Richter-scale reading of 8.3. Four months later a quake of 8.6 magnitude struck Valparaiso in Chile, killing over twenty thousand. In 1964 a major quake hit Alaska. On May 31, 1970, a quake hit off the coast of northern Peru, destroying the towns of Huaraz and Yungay while burying Callejón de Huaylas under a torrent of icy mud from the surrounding mountains. In February of the following year a major quake shook the area around San Bernardino, California. In 1976 an earthquake with a Richter-scale reading of 7.5 flattened Guatemala City, killing twenty-two thousand. In the autumn of 1986 a quake rocked San Salvador, capital of El Salvador, killing thousands and leaving tens of thousands homeless and further destabilizing a nation already in a civil war. A few months later in 1987 a similar quake struck eastern Ecuador, destroying the nation's meager oil industry and plunging the nation into the depths of economic crisis.

Mount St. Helens blew its top in Washington State in 1983, destroying thousands of acres of forest and sending dust and debris into the jet stream, which spread it around the world. The mountain arc along the Pacific coast of the Americas boasts the world's highest volcanoes, running the length of the mountains from Alaska to Chile. At 9,677 feet, Mount St. Helens ranks in the middle between some of the small Alaskan volcanoes of only a few thousand feet up to the Andean giants that hover just under twenty thousand feet. Part of the Pacific coast's Ring of Fire, these volcanoes are traditionally among the most active in the world.

The oddest fact about this mountainous chain of destruction may be cultural rather than geological, for despite this precarious situation, nearly every major Indian civilization was built on or very near this mountain range. The mountain chain abounds with the ruins of Indian cities, temples, and pyramids that seem little affected by the devastation around them. This unstable territory became home for the Aztecs of highland Mexico, the Mayas of Guatemala, the Chibcha of Colombia, the Inca civilization, and the culture of Tiahuanaco on Lake Titicaca. The Indian constructions endure the earthquakes while the more modern cities built by the whites must be frequently rebuilt. Ironically, the Intercontinental Hotel in Managua was built to resemble a Mayan temple pyramid and decorated in Mayan motifs. This had nothing to do with its durability, but it stands tall in the European ruins around it as a defiant symbol of Indian continuity amid the chaos of natural and political turmoil.

Part of the reason the buildings survive seems to be that the Indian architects over the centuries consciously developed their edifices to withstand the shock and frequent movement of these cataclysms. Inca stones fit together snugly, but the masons allowed flexibility in the walls. Thus through all the quakes of the last half millennium these walls have never fallen.

The tapering shape of the temple pyramids of central Mexico and their nearly solid construction also enabled them to withstand tremendous earth movements without collapsing into themselves or shedding their outer layers of stone. In lowland and more stable Indian sites such as Tikal in Guatemala and Uxmal in the Yucatan, the pyramids could be taller and built at a much steeper angle with less volume. Thus, at 228 feet, the pyramids of Tikal are the highest in the Americas. The slope rises so sharply that the ascent more closely resembles climbing a mountain than a set of stairs. Modern governments had to add chains to help modern climbers get up or down the pyramid. Even though such steep pyramids could be built in stable areas, the architects knew enough to build lower ones with more gradual ascents in unstable areas. Probably for this reason the great pyramid of Cholula in the less stable highlands of Mexico rises to only half the height of the tallest Egyptian pyramid but exceeds the Egyptian pyramid in volume by 15 percent [Driver, p. 115]. Not until the United States built its space-shuttle facilities at Cape Canaveral, Florida, did America see any structures more massive than the pyramids of Cholula and Teotihuacán.

The tallest structure standing in the nation of Belize even into the twentieth century was still the Maya pyramid of Altun Ha. The pyramids of Tikal still rank among the tallest structures in Central America, and until the twentieth century the pueblos of Mesa Verde and Chaco Canyon survived as the largest, albeit deserted, apartment buildings in the United States.

The Indians in different parts of the Americas mastered the technology for making concrete and the use of lime mortar, and they developed plaster and stucco. But none of these seemed to have had an impact on the subsequent skyscrapers and apartment buildings built in America. Most of the techniques of monumental construction used by the Indians have been lost.

Even though a building such as the Intercontinental Hotel in Managua, the university in Mexico City, an art museum in Santa Fe, or even an idiosyncratic skyscraper in Los Angeles may take stylistic nuances from the Indian cultures of the past, none of them uses Indian principles of architecture or science. Unlike native American agriculture, medicine, and political ideas, Indian architecture never influenced Europeans, and it failed to survive on a very large scale even in America.

One reason that the Old World settlers coming into America did not adopt the monumental architecture of the Indians was the fanatical European obsession with the arch. Old World architects of churches and public buildings arched the entryways and lined the walls with arched windows. They vaulted the interior of churches by a series of arches, or they capped the building with a dome, an architectural device which is nothing more than a hemisphere of arches. The Europeans used the arch frequently not only in churches, schools, and monasteries, but also in government buildings of all types from courts and palaces to prisons and arenas.

By contrast, the architecture of America, like that of ancient China, Egypt, and Greece, generally ignored the arch, using instead the more sturdy angles, straight lines, and parallels. Of all the American groups, only the Mayas used a type of arch in their monumental architecture. This was the corbeled or false arch that they used to make entries, vaulted passageways, and interiors. The Mayas derived an array of arch types from this, including a trefoil arch that had a Moorish appearance, but none of these functioned as a true arch, since they used the cantilever principle to direct the stress downward rather than to the sides as in a true arch. Because of this the Mayas could not build structures of several floors without using massive support walls, but the Mayan buildings still stand from the Yucatan to Honduras even after the European buildings with their heavy dependence on the arch have long since crumbled into ruins.

The Gate of the Sun at Tiahuanaco adjacent to Lake Titicaca in Bolivia illustrates the American tradition. This monolith rises approximately ten feet in height and stretches to twelve and a half feet wide. Unknown Indians carved it from a single block of andesite weighing approximately ten tons. The form appears typically American in its perfectly angular shape. By contrast, the carvings decorating it exhibit much more fluidity, and the angles of the form contrast nicely with the roundness of the sun that forms the centerpiece of the gate. This more stable door survived earthquakes even when arched doorways collapsed. The lines and angles of the ruins suggest Athenian temples much more than the architecture brought in by European conquerors. Perhaps because of the similarities of architectural style among American Indian, Egyptian, and Greek architecture, all of these civilizations have bequeathed to the world impressive ruins, while so many other civilizations have passed away with barely an architectural trace.

Even though the Europeans loved the arch and the vaulted ceilings and domes derived from it, they used it primarily in large public buildings and only sparingly in their homes. By an odd contrast, the native Americans almost never used the arch or any of its derivatives in their public, or monumental, architecture, but frequently used it in their homes and in the less important buildings. Some of the first longhouses encountered by the settlers in North America relied primarily on arched construction. These buildings consisted of a single long room with an arched ceiling. In form they more closely resembled European churches than homes. Other North American structures such as the wigwam, wickiup, hogan, pit house, kiva, sweat lodge, and, above all, the igloo incorporated some form of the arch or a real dome as the primary feature of its construction.

In South America as well, the natives employed the true arch in simple constructions of homes but not in the monumental constructions of public buildings. Around the River Plate or Plata in Argentina, the natives built small mud-and-wattle huts with thatched roofs that had arched doorways. Several thousand miles away on the Peruvian coast, the Indians also used arched entrances, but these never diffused up into the earthquake zones of the Andes. Simple constructions of wood and supple materials would survive an earthquake or would do only minimal damage if they collapsed.

Sometimes the great pyramids, temples, and other monumental constructions blind us to simpler but even more important architectural achievements of the Indians. The village of Acoma in New Mexico probably holds as much valuable information for us as do Cuzco, Tikal, and Teotihuacán.

Acoma springs up before the visitor in the middle of the high desert about fifty miles east of Albuquerque and over a mile above sea level. Acoma, which is often called Sky City but means "people of the white rock," sits atop a large sandstone mesa that rises dramatically from the plain surrounding it. No gentle slopes or rolling hills make the transition from the plain to the mesa top. Instead, the Acoma mesa rises with essentially vertical walls like those of a European castle. Centuries ago the residents carved a narrow path into the living rock to connect the village on top of the mesa with their cornfields on the plain. They carefully concealed the path from the curious glances of passersby and thoroughly protected it from the sight of unwanted visitors.

The buildings of Acoma climb up another two or three stories above the mesa top. Buildings that look like so many brown blocks stacked on top of one another carefully adhere to the traditional pueblo design. The Indians still make their homes from mud bricks and mud topped by roof timbers that also serve as the patio to the next story above. Wooden ladders connect to other stories that usually house relatives. These Keresan-speaking Indians must transport not only the timbers up to the top of the mesa but also the bricks and the mud plaster. The rocky mesa lacks the simplest materials; the residents must even haul up dirt in order to bury their dead in the cemetery.

Acoma has adopted few modern conveniences even today. The residents banned electricity as well as water pumps. They collect and store rainwater in stone cisterns on the mountain, and they transport it by hand. Women bake bread in oval earth ovens much like the ones used in places as varied as Timbuktu in the Sahara and Kahl in the middle of Europe. Firewood is the only fuel allowed for this baking as well as for all other cooking and for heating on cold nights.

Those villagers who prefer a more modern life live a few miles away and out of sight of Acoma in a governmental housing project called Acomita adjacent to the interstate highway. There they have unlimited access to radios, video recorders, refrigerators, stoves, and the other necessities of modern life. Many families maintain residences in both Acomita and in Acoma in order to participate in both styles of life.

Acoma and its approximately three thousand residents preserve much of the past, but its importance derives from more than mere nostalgia. Acoma and the other Indian pueblos of New Mexico are the oldest continuously inhabited communities in the United States. When Captain Hernando de Alvarado first visited Acoma in 1541, the village housed about six thousand people, and according to his description, it looked then much as it does now except for the church.

Indian settlers built the community of Acoma around the year A.D. 900, at a time when Europe was suffering through the Middle Ages. About this time Charles III, also known as Charles the Fat, ruled the Frankish kingdom and had to deal with the Vikings, who took over his province of Normandy; the Moors were conquering Spain; the Huns were moving into Hungary; and Alfred the Great was fighting to bring order to the barbarian tribes of England. Tikal had already reached its height of development and no one had yet imagined either the Aztec or the Inca empires that followed much later.

The great pageant of the last millennium of world history left little mark on Acoma. Armies came and went, marching under the flag of the Spanish kingdom, the Holy Roman Empire, the Mexican Republic, and more recently the United States. From time to time these invaders devastated the pueblo, starting in 1599, when Vicente de Zalvidar avenged the death of his brother Juan by enslaving most of the villagers and chopping off one foot of all males over twenty-five years of age. Despite violent episodes of conquest, revolt, and subjugation, the people of Acoma found a way to continue their traditional life in the same village without changing the building style.

Long before the Puritans dreamed of building a colony in North America, Spanish settlers moved into this area, and they adopted Indian architecture and construction techniques to make their homes. When the Spanish priests arrived they built their massive church in a European shape but of mud and brick like every other building in the community. They built Santa Fe, the early

capital for the area, in much the same way that the people of
the pueblos built their homes. They added Spanish tiles and
metal fixtures, increased the number of windows, and built interior walls dividing the buildings into rooms, but the Indian
nature of the style endured for several centuries after the initial
conquest.

Throughout not only the southwest but all of North America,
the colonists borrowed Indian building techniques. The Algon-
quian-speaking Indians along the Virginia coast surrounded their
villages with a row of posts buried firmly in the ground and
sharpened at the top. These barriers offered protection against
surprise attack. The Europeans immediately adopted the same
technique, and this evolved into the stockade and finally the
wooden fort that became an emblem of the white expansion and
conquest of North America.

Early settlers on the Great Plains of North America built their
semisubterranean sod houses in imitation of Indian pit houses or
earth lodges. These well-insulated homes withstood the ravages
of the severe continental winters and summers and provided
protection from tornadoes that plow across the plains. Later, when
the pioneers became more prosperous, they bought lumber shipped
in from the woodland zones, and they left the sod homes in favor
of more traditional European-style wooden houses built aboveground. Heating and cooling costs for such houses have proved
very high, and annually a few hundred of them must be replaced
because of the destructive tornadoes.

On the northern Pacific Coast the Europeans had no problem
adopting the plank house of the Indians, since it was rectangular,
built well above ground with gables, and made with dressed
lumber, usually cedar or redwood. It looked much like the dwellings to which the whites were accustomed.

In the twentieth century, native American architecture once
again received attention both for its functional form and for its
practical building techniques. In an effort to create a new American architecture that blended in organic unity with nature, Frank
Lloyd Wright returned to some basic Indian principles. He min-
imized the number of interior walls in favor of free-flowing space,
and he used warm earth tones. Even though he introduced new
engineering concepts and integrated new materials into his con-

structions, his homes maintained low, linear profiles that nestled into the earth like the pueblos of Arizona and New Mexico.

An Indian or Eskimo of a millennium ago could easily recognize his igloo or wigwam in the modern geodesic dome that Buckminster Fuller popularized in his writings and in the United States exhibit he designed for the 1967 World's Fair in Montreal, Canada. Similarly, the "habitat" style in the same fair introduced modular apartment units stacked together with private entrances and patios resembling closely the pueblo-style construction of the southwest. At the same time in the extremely cold areas of Canada and the northern parts of the United States, modern builders experimented with a variety of semisubterranean constructions for houses, factories, and schools. These too appear as modern versions of the traditional Indian constructions in the same area. In the southwest there has been a resurgence of the use of adobe as the ideal insulator in that hot, dry climate.

The valley of Pocona in Bolivia is littered with the remains of the Incas. The site, called Inkallajta, which means "place of the Incas," contains ruins of the largest room known to have been built by the Incas. It sits on a clearing just above a small waterfall that flows even during the long dry months of December through March. Nearby is the village of Pocona, with ruins that were probably a lookout or guard station on the mountain overlooking it. The present adobe houses of Pocona have the traditional Spanish colonial format of a household of buildings clustering around an open courtyard. Like the homes of Timbuktu, they mostly show blank walls to the outside world while guarding trees, flowers, and whatever beauty they may have for the people on the inside.

Looking closely at the buildings of Pocona, I soon realized that even though they were Spanish in form, many of them were built on stone foundations that were clearly Incan. The large cut stones had been rearranged to form new shapes, and then the adobe walls and tile roofs were built on top.

Early settlers destroyed or altered most of the native American architecture. The great Inca fortress of Sacsahuamán became the quarry from which the conquistadores built a new and more Spanish version of Cuzco on the stone foundations of the Inca city. Cortés ordered the Aztec capital of Tenochtitlán pulled down and the debris of the buildings and pyramids used to fill in the extensive canal network. Above this newly leveled ground, he built the new plazas, streets, and churches of Mexico City. Most of the monumental sites of America were razed, and only the abandoned or remote ones such as Machu Picchu in Peru, Tikal in Guatemala, Chichén Itzá in the Yucatan, and the Anasazi cliff dwellings of the United States survived. These complexes had little impact on the building styles of the new settlers, and they certainly did not influence builders in other parts of the world.

Incan urban planners adhered tenaciously to the grid concept in laying out cities. While the cities of Europe grew up pellmell around narrow and twisted alleys, the Inca emperor directed a careful plan to all cities, towns, and villages throughout his empire. The towns always centered on a large plaza around which stood the major religious and political buildings of the community. In turn each block of buildings centered around an open *cancha*, or courtyard.

Where the topography demanded some changes in this rectangular arrangement, the Incas showed great ingenuity. The planners of Cuzco made the city in the form of a puma with its head centered on the great fortress of Sacsahuamán.

Even though the colonists arriving in America built on top of Indian sites, they did not follow Indian building patterns. To find the model for most colonial cities from San Francisco to Buenos Aires, one need not look at the great Indian cities such as Cuzco or Tenochtitlán nor at the smaller villages such as Pocona. The model for the American cities came instead from the small Andalusian village of Santa Fé in Spain.

Entering Santa Fé today, one would hardly take it to be the model for anything. It is a small settlement of eleven thousand people. As I walked through the streets of Santa Fé, I could have been in any one of a thousand Mediterranean villages. Along one street, an elderly woman dressed in black awkwardly whitewashed the front wall of her house with a paintbrush tied to a long stick. An even older woman, also dressed in black, sat in a chair pulled up close to the same wall so that she could paint the bottom ledges of the windows. All of the houses of the village had the same whitewash, but the two feet of the house just above the ground had been painted a very dark green.

Santa Fé has no large boulevards or open park areas to make it appear an appropriate model for a city. Young men on motorcycles and workmen in small trucks and vans made the streets of Santa Fé much louder than the rather meager traffic warranted. On the smaller streets, women on their errands could walk safely down the middle of the street and pause to talk with one another without fearing any greater danger than a stray ball tossed by one of the numerous children playing in the same area.

Santa Fé cannot boast any palaces, castles, ancient fortifications, gardens, or even a church any more grand than the usual parish edifice. By Spanish chronology, it does not even have a particularly ancient pedigree, having been founded on October 2, 1491, almost exactly one year prior to Columbus's discovery of America. But therein lies an odd coincidence that makes Santa Fé such an important spot for anyone studying American urban design of the last five hundred years.

When Queen Isabella and King Ferdinand laid siege to the Moors in the Alhambra, they assembled an army of sixty thousand camped on the plains outside Granada. To impress the Moors with their determination to sustain the siege until victory and with their strength and resources, Isabella built a camp of brick and stone rather than a flimsy one of tents and woods. This camp on the Genil River she named Santa Fé, "Holy Faith," in recognition of her faith in victory through the guidance of the Christian God.

The army laid out this town like a Roman camp rather than like the towns then being built in Europe. Santa Fé was made in the form of a rectangle, with two major streets crossing in the middle at a plaza. Each of the four streets terminated in a gate on one side of an otherwise walled rectangle that protected the camp. This rectangular shape contrasted with the more circular shape common to urban areas that centered on a main castle or other edifice and had several main arteries radiating from the center like spokes on a wheel. The best example of this survives in the form of Paris. The new form probably appealed to Isabella and Ferdinand's medieval superstitions, since the town assumed the shape of the sacred cross.

While the Catholic monarchs stayed at this new village during their Moorish war, Christopher Columbus arrived to petition them to finance his planned trip of exploration to Asia. After great indecision and vacillation, Ferdinand and Isabella granted him the Capitulaciones de Santa Fé on April 17, 1492, giving him both the permission and the financing for his journey.

When Columbus and the subsequent conquistadores arrived in America they used the plan of Santa Fé for virtually every city they founded. Each American enclave became an armed camp in stone crossed by two major arteries and divided into a sequence of blocks centered on the plaza, which housed the church and the chief municipal building or governor's palace. From Santo Domingo to Lima, all American cities had the same form as the humble village of Santa Fé. Some of the Spanish explorers also carried the name of the village to America and gave it to such places as Santa Fé de Bogotá, Colombia, as well as Santa Fé del Rosario, Argentina, and Santa Fe, New Mexico.

In order to make the newly established settlements conform to their urban pattern, the Spanish destroyed many Indian cities such as Tenochtitlán as well as small towns such as Pocona. When settlers arrived a century later in what would be the United States, they too followed this new grid model of city planning. Washington, D.C., is one of the few exceptions to this pattern. Designed by the Frenchman Pierre Charles L'Enfant in 1791, the city used the older Parisian design of spoked avenues radiating from fixed points.

Aside from this notable exception, the North Americans not only embraced the grid for urban planning but extended it to rural organization as well. Grids show on the map where most of inland United States and Canada is divided into nearly precise squares or rectangles such as Colorado, Wyoming, and Manitoba. The planners further divided these squares into smaller squares which became counties. The obsession with this grid overcame planners, who then built roads and tried to lay out all towns precisely on this one principle. Planners marked off the newly conquered or purchased territories of the United States into squares or townships. The legacy of this looms prominently to any passenger on a transcontinental flight crossing the American heartland, which appears neatly farmed in a checkerboard fashion of squares.

Even though European settlers imposed new architectural styles and new ideas of urban planning on America, they usually built over existing Indian settlements rather than clearing out new areas of settlement. Subsequent generations of Americans usually forgot that their towns and cities had been founded by Indians. Myths rose about how the colonists literally carved their settlements out of the uninhabited forest. Nowhere does contemporary civic mythology elaborate on this theme more than in the case of Washington, D.C.

According to this story, George Washington himself, the father of his country, surveyed this virgin land astride the Potomac River as a place to build a new capital equidistant between the northern and southern halves of the country. The location on the Potomac also gave the city a potential water link into the Ohio River system. Few American books bother to mention that the city of Washington arose on top of Naconchtanke, the main trading town of the Conoy Indians. At the time of their first contact with the Virginia colonists in 1623, the site served as home and headquarters to Chief Patawomeke and his followers. The name of the chief evolved in the present name Potomac, and Naconchtanke survives only in its Latinized corruption Anacostia, one of the subdivisions of the city of Washington.

In the 1975 excavation on the White House lawn for the presidential swimming pool, builders found Indian relics that pointed to the commercial prosperity of a former Indian group. Only a few blocks away from the White House, the Indians had operated one of the largest Indian quarries for steatite or soapstone. Numerous manufacturing sites surrounded it where Indian craftsmen made dishes, pipes, and implements from the soft stone. From here the Indians traded the manufactured goods all along the eastern coast in what may have been the last productive enterprise practiced by humans along this stretch of the Potomac.

In nearly every case the European colonists built a city that eventually stretched to hundreds and even thousands of times the size and population of the original Indian settlement, but nevertheless they built on top of a previous settlement rather than starting a new one. Even the Puritans took over fields already cleared by the Indians but abandoned when European diseases decimated the native population.

Like the city of Washington, most American capitals arose atop Indian communities. Some capitals such as Mexico City and Quito were built on the ruins of cities that were already major administrative, trade, and religious centers. Other cities such as Lima, Ottawa, and Buenos Aires arose from much more modest Indian settlements.

The new settlers of America continued on a much more expansive scale the same settlement patterns already firmly established by the Indians. The Europeans concentrated on building in the same places that the Indians had built before them. In North America the Indians built along the rivers and coast with only minimal settlement of the plains or mountains, but in South America the Indians built primarily in the mountains, secondarily along the coast, and almost not at all in the large inland river areas and the plains. Precisely the same patterns hold today. North Americans live along the two coasts and the Mississippi and St. Lawrence river systems while leaving much of the remainder of the country virtually vacant. The Mexicans crowd the highland plateau and mountains, avoiding the lowland areas. In South America the population also concentrates itself in the Andes and along the two coasts, but despite centuries of government pressure avoids the vast interior drained by the Amazon and Orinoco rivers and the great plains of Argentina, Paraguay, and Uruguay.

The importance of the Indians in shaping contemporary cultural geography in America shows clearly in the names of American rivers, mountains, cities, and states. The first white arrivals in America named most of the eastern lands after places in the Old World; the American lands became New Granada, New York, Nova Scotia, New Brunswick, and New England. The British colonists also named other new areas after sovereigns whom they wanted to honor or flatter, as in Maryland, Carolina, Georgia, Alberta, and Virginia. The Spanish usually preferred to use the names of saints rather than sovereigns, as in San Francisco, Santo Domingo, San Antonio, and San Diego.

At first it appeared that the Indian names would soon be dropped entirely and the map of America would read like a thoroughly scrambled map of the Old World. To the contrary, however, the Indian names often showed great tenacity. From very early, the name Massachusetts stuck, as did names for smaller places, such as Nantucket, Roanoke, Tallahassee, Poughkeepsie, and Oswego. As the colonists moved west, they made far less use of foreign names and stuck to American ones, either adopting the existing Indian names, as for Chicago, Minnesota, and Tennessee, or accepting the name of the Indians already in the area, as for Kansas, Dakota, Utah, and Texas. Even after three centuries as a Spanish colony under the name New Spain, Mexico reassumed its older Indian name after winning independence in 1821.

The cultural geography of the modern Americas combines many varied characteristics from both the Old and the New World. Even though much of the Indian heritage has been lost or buried, some of it still shows through—enough to make America very different from Europe, Africa, or Asia.

▲ ▲ 13 ▲ ▲

THE PATHFINDERS

Late one January afternoon I arrived with five other people at a
cluster of houses beside Mango
Creek on the Caribbean shore of Belize. We were en route to
the offshore village of Placentia. The road ended at the water's
edge, and the few local fishermen had already hauled in their
equipment and settled down for the evening. One young man
about sixteen years old volunteered, for a price, to take us over
to Placentia in his dugout. While waiting for him to borrow an
outboard motor and some gasoline, our group divided. Three
people made camp and stayed with the Land Rover, while three
of us prepared for the trip over to where we were to meet an
archaeologist who was excavating coastal Mayan sites.

Hurrying so that we could cover as much distance as possible
before dark, the boy returned with the motor, and we set off
down the winding creek that opened into Placentia Bay. Even
after dark, he piloted the dugout expertly through the small
channels in the mangrove thickets and between the tiny islands,
some of which lurked just below the surface of the water at high
tide.

We spoke English with the pilot, but his native language was
Garifuna, the mother tongue of approximately 100,000 Black Caribs who live on the coast of Belize, around the Gulf of Honduras
and along the Mosquito coast. The descendants of shipwrecked

and escaped slaves who intermarried with Carib Indians on the island of St. Vincent in the western Caribbean, the Black Caribs of Central America were brought to the island of Roatán in the Gulf of Honduras by the British in 1796. From Roatán the Black Caribs soon settled neighboring islands and the deserted parts of the mainland shore as far north as Dandriga in Belize and south as far as the Mosquito coast of Nicaragua, where they intermarried with some of the Miskito Indians and to a lesser extent with Sumu and Rama. These black Indians look like Africans, but they speak a Cariban language and they follow the traditional lifestyle of their Carib Indian ancestors.

In subsequent years other blacks emigrated both voluntarily and through compulsion from Jamaica and neighboring islands to work as loggers in the primeval jungles along the Honduras coast, as construction workers building the railroad of Costa Rica, and as laborers in the banana plantations spread throughout the area. The new wave of blacks brought the English language with them and added new ingredients to the already rich and colorful cultural heritage of the region. From these later migrations, the Spanish-speaking countries of Central America acquired Caribbean ports with quite Anglican names, such as Livingston, Guatemala; Bluefields, Nicaragua; and Penshurst, Costa Rica.

Even though our pilot was descended from the Black Caribs, the village of Placentia to which he was taking us was a creole village of blacks who spoke mostly English creole; they did not claim to be Indians. Had we continued north another four miles we would have landed in Seine Bight, a Black Carib village. Villagers in Seine Bight and Placentia lead similar economic lives, but a cultural gulf divides them. The Garifuna language of the Black Caribs draws sustenance from deep roots in the Indian culture from which it descends, while the English creole culture draws more widely from the Anglo-African traditions of the Caribbean and from the English-speaking world at large. The villagers in both communities live in small wooden houses built up on stilts about five feet off the ground. The traditional palmetto thatching has given way to corrugated tin roofs, and most houses have a small porch with a railing. Numerous windows allow the air to circulate, but ventilated wooden shutters keep out the bright sun and the prying eyes of passersby.

At least one male in every home owns a boat and fishes. Twenty miles offshore lies the Great Barrier Reef, the largest reef in the Americas and second in the world only to the Great Barrier Reef of Australia. The reef off the Belize coast, however, teems with much more sea life than that of Australia. The fishermen harvest a wide variety of fish, conch, spiny lobster, and one of the local favorites, sea turtle. The women know dozens of ways to prepare the turtle, such as cutting it into thin turtle steaks that they pan-fry or grating the tougher pieces of meat and mixing them with spices and hot peppers to make turtle balls that are served over rice or with fried cassava bread and a plate of fried plantains.

After turning into a narrow black opening in the mangrove trees, the pilot carefully steered the boat up to the beach. Because of the black sand and the thick vegetation, the beach absorbed rather than reflected the moonlight, thus creating a very dark scene. The next day I found that the black sand becomes even more of a problem in the sun, for it quickly becomes too hot for human feet to walk in it. To move from one house to another in the daytime, the villagers balance on a series of thin wooden walkways crisscrossing the community.

The next day the fishing cooperative of the community ran out of gasoline; this landlocked most of the men, who relied on outboard motors for their dugouts or who fished from larger boats. The only exit that day was by walking up to Seine Bight or by paddling a canoe to either Seine Bight or back up to Mango Creek. Despite modern technology and nearly half a millennium of contact between the people of this coast and the Old World, the canoe still served as the most reliable transport in the area. Newer technology had brought in faster vehicles, but they depended on outside lines of supply that flowed only sporadically. By contrast, the canoe always worked.

Prior to the arrival of the Garifuna Indians, the Mayas and a few other Indian groups inhabited this coast while the Arawak and Carib Indians occupied most of the islands in what we now call the Caribbean. All of them used the canoe as their primary means of transportation. It is from the Arawakan and Cariban languages that we today have the word "canoe." Columbus exported the first canoe, taking it to Europe after seeing how agilely and swiftly the sleek boats moved across the water.

Along the edge of Mosquitia, south of Belize, the natives developed a narrow boat with steep sides and a sharp prow. Known in the Miskito language and adapted into English as the "dory," this vehicle still serves as a common fishing boat on the open seas.

The Mayas hauled trading goods in their canoes up and down the coast of the Yucatan and Central America, and around the Gulf of Mexico possibly as far north as the Mississippi River. The canoe served as the perfect vehicle along the many shallow rivers and creeks of the area. Indians throughout the coastal and riverine parts of North and South America used the canoe as the primary vehicle of travel and transport. Indians in various areas constructed it of diverse materials. On the coast of Central America and throughout much of lowland, tropical South America where large trees flourished, the Indians most commonly made dugouts.

In the northern part of the United States, which lacked appropriate trees for making dugouts, the Indians constructed a light frame from thin branches and covered it with strips of bark about one-eighth of an inch thick, the thickness of a penny. The best canoes used the bark from the birch tree, *Betula papyrifera*, sewn together with spruce roots and sealed watertight with spruce gum. This light vehicle glided easily over the many lakes and streams of the area, and the paddlers easily lifted it to carry it from one body of water to another.

Early explorers report that the larger Iroquois canoes carried up to thirty warriors. Three men could easily handle one of these canoes even after they had loaded it with goods. Despite the delicacy of its hull, it could be repaired with very few tools and with materials gathered anywhere in the forest. The major disadvantage of this exceptionally light craft was that on land it needed to be securely tied to prevent the wind from blowing it away.

Small European boats of that time seemed by contrast heavy and bulky, requiring the added power of oars to propel them. In order to use the oars, the oarsman sat with his back toward the bow, and this left him unable to see where he was going. The paddles used in canoes allowed the paddler to face the direction of travel, making the canoe ideal for even a solitary traveler.

Even after the introduction of sailing craft into the American rivers, the Europeans found that the canoes provided faster and more reliable transport. As the experiences of Cartier had already shown in the St. Lawrence River, speed was very important in order to penetrate an area and get out again before all of the water routes froze and trapped the traveler. For this reason, canoes continued as a major source of transportation of people and goods throughout North America until well into the twentieth century, when the railroads proved able to haul people and goods faster and more reliably.

In the Arctic, where no birch trees grow to provide bark for this type of canoe, the Eskimo made a similar boat by stretching animal skins over a framework. The Eskimos waterproofed the boat by covering the top so as to allow only a small opening in which the operator could sit. Even lighter than the birch canoe, this boat, the kayak, could be easily carried and proved excellent at maneuvering among the chunks of ice that constantly clogged Arctic water routes. This boat had the unusual characteristic of capsize recovery; the kayaker could turn right side up after capsizing without having to get out of the boat. This feature, the "kayak roll," allowed the Eskimos tremendous maneuverability in hunting walruses, seals, whales, and other sea mammals.

The Eskimo also used a large boat made from skins but applied to a frame more in the shape of a large tub. This umiak transported whole groups of people and their possessions. It often relied on women paddlers and for that reason was known as the women's boat.

The Kwakiutls, Quinaults, and other groups along the northern Pacific coast of the state of Washington and the Canadian province of British Columbia constructed the largest oceanic canoes in America. Made from durable red cedar and over forty feet long with about the width of a man's arm span, these whaling canoes carried eight men and all of the equipment necessary to catch and haul a whale.

On Lake Titicaca, twelve thousand feet high in the Andes between the nations of Peru and Bolivia, the Aymara Indians made a boat entirely of totora reeds. The Indians propelled it by a long pole. In form and design the boat is very similar to those made in the Middle East in the marshy parts of the Tigris and

Euphrates rivers, as well as those made on the shores of Lake Chad in northern central Africa.

In the lowland Inca areas, the people made inflated rafts from sealskins. They used these to float piles of guano back to the mainland from the bird islands dotting the coast [Von Hagen, p. 143]. This custom parallels a similar practice from Mesopotamia as recorded by Xenophon in the *Anabasis*; he describes the Greek army inflating goat skins in order to float across a river.

Although not usually accorded much importance as transport vehicles, the rafts of the Indians often surpassed similar constructions in other parts of world. In addition to the inflated rafts of the Peruvian coast, Indians of the area made large rafts of balsa, *Ochroma lagopus*, which grew in the jungles of South America. These were the largest water transports constructed in the Americas and could be used on the ocean as well as on the larger rivers. This tree proved so ideal for making rafts that in Spanish the word *balsa* came to mean "raft."

Norwegian anthropologist Thor Heyerdahl claimed that the Indians of South American probably used these rafts as ocean vehicles that connected them with Polynesia. To prove his thesis he had such a raft constructed, and under the name *Kon-Tiki*, he sailed it to Easter Island. Whether or not such commerce actually existed still arouses debate among historians and anthropologists. None of them, however, denies the importance of such rafts for coastal and river trade.

These five boats, the canoe, kayak, umiak, dory, and reed boat, together with the rafts functioned as excellent small vehicles for their particular ecological niches, but nowhere in America did any Indian group make the transition from boats and rafts to ships. Even though some of the oceangoing vehicles spaciously accommodated several tons of trade goods and had to be paddled by a crew of up to a dozen men, they never became ships. Although the Indians mastered paddling they never mastered sails, oars, or a rudder, nor did they have any of the navigational equipment of the Old World, such the compass, astrolabe, or sextant. Consequently, the Americans never became sailors of the high seas, and their civilizations remained inward-looking. For them the sea served only as a source of food and as a convenient way to move from one coastal village to the next, such as from Seine Bight to Placentia or from island to island in the Caribbean.

After the European settlement of America, Indian boats, particularly the canoe and the kayak, spread to prosperous areas around the world for recreational use. No better boats have ever been developed for traveling over white water, into unexplored territory, into shallow waters, or into areas requiring portage of the boat. They became toys of the leisure class with little more practical application than the surfboard invented by the Polynesians. None of these had a significant impact on the lives of most working people.

Where water transport proved impractical in America, the Indians relied almost exclusively on transport by foot over trails and roads. The native Americans invented few transport vehicles for land use. In the far north, Eskimos trained dogs to pull a sled over snow and ice. Indians south of there also invented the toboggan, which could be pulled by humans or dogs. On the plains of North America, the dogs pulled a small travois, which is something like a primitive sled. Farther south around the Gulf of Mexico, people sometimes used litters to carry the sick and palanquins to carry leaders. Such very meager and unsophisticated contraptions contrast markedly with the diversity of Old World land vehicles such as coaches, chariots, carts, wagons, wheelbarrows, and sleds.

America lacked these other vehicles because America lacked the animal power to pull them. Aside from the dogs that pulled sleds or travois, the only domesticated animal in America able to carry even a small load was the llama in the Andes, and its legs and ankles were too frail to transport an adult rider. America lacked horses, cows, oxen, elephants, camels, donkeys, or goats to pull land vehicles. Without draft animals, the Indians never developed the wheel for use on anything more complicated than toys. Yet even though they lacked wheels and draft animals, the Indians built the best roads known in the world.

The first piece of Inca road I saw was the section that snaked through central Ecuador. The Incas opened this stretch of road about 1493, just after Columbus landed in the West Indies but still two generations before the whites found Peru. The road leaves the high city of Quito, which served as administrative capital of Chinchasuyu, the Inca land of the Puma, and heads south toward the mountains of Cotopaxi and Chimborazo, which rise to 20,561 feet and 19,347 feet respectively. In the nineteenth century, scientists counted these as the highest peaks in the world. Indeed they are the highest if one measures distance from the center of the earth rather than from sea level. Located at the equator, which bulges out slightly from a true sphere, they poke out about two miles farther from the earth's center than do the much more northerly Himalayas. For several days' walk, the road twists among these giant mountains.

Chimborazo is an extinct volcano, but Cotopaxi is one of the world's highest active volcanos, and when the first Spanish traveled this road in 1534 the volcano erupted in full force. The volcano erupts periodically for several successive years but then remains quiet for several decades as a new cone of ice and snow forms about its massive summit. The Inca road crosses the dry plain at the foot of Cotopaxi. Odd forms of plants dot the landscape, and at the lower altitudes herds of mustangs abandoned by the Spanish still ravage the meager flora.

Even though the Inca highway does not ascend Cotopaxi, the gentle slope makes it an inviting excursion. The steep but persistent slope of Cotopaxi resembles a cold lunar landscape. Climbing up it my feet sank to my ankles in the fine volcanic powder, and I gasped for breath with every step. Above fourteen thousand feet, breathing becomes increasingly difficult and the bitter wind ever colder. The wind blasts so persistently that it sweeps the raised volcanic ribs clear of snow and turns every drop of moisture in the air into pelting ice that stings the mouth and nose like a swarm of bees. The Quechua (or Quichua, as they prefer in Ecuador) Indians breathe without difficulty, but I, unaccustomed to the altitude, struggled for air. At this altitude cigarette lighters will not flame because of the lack of oxygen, and only the Indians can coax a smoldering slow fire to burn the precious pieces of wood that they have lugged up the slopes.

When Cotopaxi explodes, it spews down a flood of mud from the suddenly melted snows trapped on its top. The mud sweeps away surrounding villages and towns, the closest of which is Latacunga, about twenty miles away. According to the early

Spanish chronicles, Latacunga boasted gold-encrusted figures of llamas on its temple, making it one of the most magnificent resting places along the highway.

The road continues south through the volcanoes, following a route roughly parallel to but ten miles from the Pan American Highway. The ancient route had a *tambo* every fourteen miles. These were combination storehouses and inns, offering shelter and food supplies for the traveling Inca army or officials. The Incas maintained over a thousand *tambos* along the entire length of the highway. Unlike Old World armies, the Inca armies did not march with large supply trains in tow, nor did they have to forage off the land and exploit the peasants in their path.

At selected spots along the highway, Incas built larger complexes such as the one at Ingapirca, or "Inca walls," high above the steep gorge of Intihuaynca. These ruins have the only Inca room left aboveground in Ecuador. The site began as a major *tambo* and reputedly as a fortified palace where the Inca emperor always rested on the 1,230-mile journey along this road from Cuzco to Quito. Still today the road to Ingapirca is guarded by a megalithic Intinahui, sometimes called the Eyes of the Road. The Indians also carved into the living rock what appears to be a large chair or possibly throne called the Ingachunguna. Local Quechuas make the apocryphal claim that the ancient Incas made human sacrifices on this spot, and they point to small stone gullies where the human blood supposedly drained.

Today the Inca road lies largely untended and crumbling, but local farmers on foot, on horseback, and with their llamas still use stretches of it. Most parts of the road, however, remain inaccessible to wheeled vehicles, because the Incas built the highway literally on high ground. Building the roads up high discouraged lowland Indians from invading and also made it easier for the Incas to keep watch on the surrounding countryside as they moved.

The Inca highway through Ecuador twists along the top of ridges and at times leaps over deep gorges via several kinds of bridges, including the suspension bridges constructed from twenty-two thousand feet or more of handmade rope. Even though the Incas wove their cables from natural fibers, they used the same techniques later used to make steel cables for such modern structures as the Brooklyn Bridge. Where necessary the Inca engineers cut into the side of the very mountains and reinforced the road with large retaining walls of stone. In places the road feels almost like a tunnel because it slices so deeply into the mountain, and in one spot on our way to Ingapirca, the road passed on the underside of a waterfall which fell into a small pool at our feet. Usually the highway is broad enough for several people to walk abreast in each direction, but in the higher mountain passes and along the steeper escarpments it narrows to only enough room for two lines of people to pass without one of them having to stop.

Called the Capac Nan or Beautiful Road by the Incas, this paved, all-weather road had gutters and curbs in areas where it rained and draining ditches where necessary. In hot areas, the Incas lined the road with trees to supply shade. In addition to the swinging suspension bridges, plank bridges were built on stone supports where possible, and the Incas devised a complex system of aerial ferries consisting of a small gondola attached to ropes and propelled over gorges and rivers by pulleys. In arid valleys, the Incas built underground cisterns called *puquios* and kept them filled with fresh water for the travelers. In flood zones, the Inca engineers built causeways of stone or built the road over stone culverts. The type of road varied with the terrain and the requirements of each ecological zone.

The road stretched for approximately three thousand miles, but including its major arteries it surpassed five thousand miles. The Beautiful Road was by far the longest road in the world. The main branch of it covered a distance equal to that from London to New York or from London to Jerusalem, while the total system roughly equaled the distance from Beijing to San Francisco. This highway system also tied in with small road systems throughout the empire, uniting an area larger than western Europe. So far fourteen thousand miles of primary and secondary routes have been charted by archaeologists, and the total may never be known.

In some of the lower valleys, the jungle vegetation now obscures the road and makes passage difficult without a machete to hack the lianas, bushes, and small trees clogging the route. In other lowland areas, the Inca road has been absorbed into modern highways, including the Pan-American Highway that runs from Alaska to Chile.

Parallel to the great highway, the Incas incorporated a number of lowland roads near the ocean into a single coastal highway. This highway stretched to over twenty-five hundred miles, a distance longer than the Mississippi River. Wherever possible the engineers maintained a standard width of twenty-four feet on the coastal highway. Because most of it crossed deserts to link the small river valleys of the coastal area, Inca engineers built adobe walls to the side to keep out drifting sands. They also added road markers or *topos* at intervals just under five miles.

The Inca highways served as the communications network of the empire through a system of messenger runners called *chasquis*. Operating out of the *tambos*, they carried government messages quickly from one end of the empire to the other through a relay system, each *chasqui* running about two miles. These runners endured harsh training from childhood to make them capable of running at altitudes up to fifteen thousand feet. The *chasquis* carried messages all the way from Quito to Cuzco in five days, averaging about 250 miles a day. This is about the same rate of travel achieved by the Pony Express in the United States several centuries later, but whereas the Pony Express relied on horses, the Incas used only human power. The similarity in speeds is partly due to the excellent training of the *chasquis*, but it is also a tribute to the quality of the road on which they ran. A message sent by *chasqui* five hundred years ago traveled faster than a letter mailed today from Quito to Cuzco. The *chasquis* also connected towns that have never again had regular message delivery service since the Spanish abandoned the runner system in the nineteenth century.

Without the expert highway system in place, the European conquest of America would have been significantly slower than it was. The horse would have been useless and the heavy cannons would have quickly become mired in the mud without the paved road. Ironically it was the very superiority of the American highway system that made the native civilizations so vulnerable. Those areas with the best roads were conquered first. The areas that lacked good roads did not see conquest until much later. Still today the people of the Old World have failed to penetrate some of the isolated parts of the Amazon Basin where there are no Indian roads or navigable rivers.

The Indians of North America constructed fewer and less sophisticated highways than did the Incas. One of the best-preserved but least-understood highway systems radiates from the ruins of Chaco Canyon in the southwestern part of the contemporary United States. Stretching over an area roughly the size of Ireland, the road system weaves together the Four Corners areas of Arizona, New Mexico, Colorado, and Utah, with many of the roads crisscrossing the present Navajo Nation. The roads run in nearly straight lines, slicing through long stretches of desert, and all focus on the settlement at Chaco Canyon. The so-called Anasazi Indians built these roads around the twelfth century of the present era. The roads widened to about thirty feet in some areas, and the builders added causeways and stairways cut into the living rock to connect settlements in the canyons with the road system in the desert above them. Parallel to the roads the Anasazis built and maintained signal relay stations on top of hills and mesas. From these spots the Anasazis telegraphed messages by smoke signal or light reflection from one town to another almost instantly.

Archaeologists do not know why the Anasazis built such a sophisticated system in an area that lacked the wheel or pack animals. The increased efficiency that it provided for walking did not justify the labor required to build such roads. They may have been ceremonial avenues used in rituals, emergency roads for hurrying bands of warriors to distant communities, or trade routes for merchants, or they may have combined these and other unknown functions. Even though the Anasazis abandoned these roads before Columbus arrived in America, the dry climate preserved them until the present day. Nothing superseded them in technical efficiency until the recent introduction of paved roads in the twentieth century.

Most of North America lacked such complex systems of roads. In those parts of the country where river and creek transportation proved insufficient, the Indians used a network of interlocking trails. More than merely haphazard footpaths crisscrossing the continent, these trails were built and consciously maintained for the transportation of trade goods and passage of warriors. The

Iroquois maintained one of the best trail networks, by which they easily dispatched armies deep into Canada or down to the Carolinas at the slightest provocation.

The white colonists settling America always had a distinct advantage in their travels westward from the Atlantic Ocean because they pushed the Indians before them. The Indians constantly opened up new paths and widened old paths as they went. The expulsion of eastern Indians opened up the lands of Georgia, Alabama, and Mississippi in the south and Ohio, Indiana, and Illinois in the north. The Indians were truly the pathfinders of America. Just as the Inca highways of South America facilitated the movement of the Spanish conquistadores, the trails of North America facilitated the settlement of the British pioneers.

The European settlers who arrived in America did not have to hack their way through the thick forests of America or wander forlornly around the Great Plains. The Indians had already blazed clearly marked paths for them. The trails of the Indians deteriorated rapidly after the arrival of the colonists. The trails had been built for human passage, but the hooves of horses and oxen pulling wagons destroyed them and reduced them to muddy bogs in many places. Eventually colonists rebuilt the system to facilitate passage of heavy vehicles and motorized vehicles. The present road and highway system, railroad network, and even the canals of the United States and other American nations largely follow Indian trails and roads.

The Indians maintained a major trail west from the Mississippi River to the northern edge of Mexico. The two ends of this trail became the modern cities of St. Louis, Missouri, and Santa Fe, New Mexico, and the road between them was the Santa Fe Trail, which by 1850 supported regularly scheduled stagecoach service once a month. This continued on from Santa Fe to California by the Old Spanish Trail, which terminated at Los Angeles. A northern route left Kansas City, Missouri, heading northwest. From there one branch continued on as the Oregon Trail and another headed for San Francisco as the Central Overland Route, following roughly the same route chosen for the Pony Express riders in 1860. Today the Interstate Highway System follows essentially these same paths.

****

Despite some significant achievements by the Incas in road and bridge construction, the Americans had not developed very diverse transportation technology. The Old World systems showed a much wider array of travel techniques using a variety of animals and contraptions as well as oceangoing vehicles. As in the case of architecture, Indian transportation systems offered little to the remainder of the world.

It should be equally clear that every explorer, conquistador, and settler who arrived in America used the existing transportation systems, which proved well suited for their needs and the requirements of the terrain and climate. Despite the many self-serving and self-glorifying accounts of brave adventures written by white explorers and pioneers, America was by no stretch of the imagination an overgrown continent through which the Europeans had to hack their way searching for new settlements. Over tens of thousands of years, Indians had already opened the land, built roads or paths, and developed a system of canoes and small boats to reach every corner and crevice of the Americas from the Bering Straits to Tierra del Fuego.

▲ ▲ 14 ▲ ▲
WHEN WILL AMERICA
BE DISCOVERED?

The old Yuqui woman jerked her head up toward me and stared blindly into my face. As flies crawled across her eyes and drank from the only moist place left on her body, her left hand scratched habitually at the lice and filth encrusted into her hair. No one knew her age, but she was the oldest survivor of a band of Yuquis living in the rain forest of the southern Amazon region. Most of her life she had wandered through the forest with her fellow Yuquis following the same culture as unknown generations had done before them. She had lived most of her life without knowledge of whites or other outsiders except that they lurked on the edges of her forest world. Like the evil spirits of the dead, the whites brought disease and death to the Yuquis, the real people.

Not until 1968 did her band make its first contact with a white, when the Protestant missionaries Bob and Mary Garland arrived in their world. In time the small band settled around the base camp of the missionaries on the Chimore River, and they wandered less and less to hunt. Anthropologist Allyn Stearman raced to record their way of life as it dissolved around her. The missionaries taught them to grow a few crops and helped them to hunt more efficiently and to use canoes. They taught them to make fire so that they would no longer have to raid another band each time their fire was lost, and they helped the women in childbirth rather than letting them disappear alone into the jungle to bear their babies as had been their tradition.

Had this woman not been contacted by the missionaries she most assuredly would have been dead long before I came across her. If the lumbermen had not captured or killed her in their periodic shootouts with the Yuquis, then perhaps the coca growers or the ranchers would have seized her in a raid and made her a cook and prostitute for the mestizo workers. Even if she had been spared all of these indignities from outsiders and managed to live alone with her band, the group would have deserted her along the trail as soon as she became too ill to travel. As nomads who traveled strictly by foot, they never developed the knowledge of how to deal with the infirm or elderly. Anyone unable to walk through the jungle was left to die alone.

Now she sits deserted all day beneath a mosquito net in her hut wrapped in a filthy rag of a dress. She lost her sight, her hearing deteriorated, and she grew too weak to walk or crawl. Gradually she became deranged and delirious. The missionaries feed her and care for her most basic needs, but her own relatives who live nearby have no idea what to do for her. In their harsh jungle life, they never had to minister to anyone like this.

When I appeared at her net with the missionary, her bony hand reached out, groping for food. She clutched my arm, and her jagged fingernails scratched my hand as her cool but dry skin rubbed against mine with a sound like sandpaper against bark. She mumbled a few words that were incoherent to me, but the missionary said she was just naming foods and uttering the names of relatives, some living and some dead. Finally in defeat, she withdrew her hand, her jaw dropped, oblivious to the gnats crawling in and out of her mouth, and she seemed to return to the stupor and the scratching that occupied most of her dying weeks.

There was nothing heroic about the poor old woman. She was now at the end of her days, and all she sought was another morsel of food, some water, and some relief from the heat and the insects that plagued her now as they had all her life. Like so many Indians today from Canada to Chile, she seemed to be the truly wretched of the earth, the abandoned, the abused, the suffering who merited nothing but pity or charity from outsiders.

She lay dying as a miserable outcast from the contemporary American society that had gradually and persistently consumed her land over the past five hundred years.

This dying woman contrasted painfully with the image of the Indians as the world's greatest farmers and pharmacists, as the noble savage of Rousseau or the practical administrators who inspired Benjamin Franklin. I could not help but wonder why, if these people were really so great, they had fallen so low and been so oppressed. If they could build great cities and roads, why couldn't they defend themselves from the waves of Europeans who washed across their land?

Even though the Indian civilizations surpassed the Old World in a few areas, they lagged behind in others. The Indians developed superior agricultural skills and technology, and they surpassed the Old World in their pharmacology. They had far more sophisticated calendars than the Europeans, and the Indians of Mexico had a mathematical system based on place numbers superior to the numerical systems then in use by the Spaniards.

In their exhaustive attention to agriculture, medicine, mathematics, and religion, the Indians neglected the domestication of animals, which proved so decisive for the Old World civilizations. Because farmers in Europe, Asia, and Africa were so much less efficient in growing crops, they relied extensively on eggs, milk, cheese, and dozens of other animal products as well as on the meat of these animals. This made their Old World diet no better than that of the Americans, but it gave the people who domesticated animals a distinct advantage in that they easily learned to harness animal energy in place of human energy. The Europeans arrived in America with strong horses to help men in battle as well as oxen to pull heavy carts laden with supplies and cows and goats to give protein-rich milk to marching armies of soldiers and later to hordes of settlers.

The Indians built an elaborate civilization on human energy, but the Old World had thoroughly exploited animal energy sources that helped them in their endeavors. Additionally, the people of the Old World had begun tapping inanimate energy sources in ways that foreshadowed the coming industrial revolution. The sophisticated use of ships and sails, of windmills and waterwheels, and of cannons and gunpowder gave them a decisive advantage over the Indians.

All of these skills made the invaders better soldiers and gave them better instruments of war. Indian metallurgy lacked the variety of the Old World's and was directed mostly toward decoration rather than tools of production or war. The European invaders, however, had learned to make steel into swords and lances and to cast metal cannons, which they mounted on wheels to be pulled by animals. The Indians still fought with arrows and spears tipped with stone, and they had no war machine more sophisticated than a simple *atlatl* or spear thrower.

Together with their animals and machines, the Europeans brought horrendous epidemic diseases that had been unknown to the New World. These diseases traveled through the Indian population faster than through the European. By the time the Europeans arrived in Tenochtitlán or Cuzco or on the plains of North America, their microbes had preceded them and thoroughly decimated and weakened the native population.

The Indian civilizations crumbled in the face of the Old World not because of any intellectual or cultural inferiority. They simply succumbed in the face of disease and brute strength. While the American Indians had spent millennia becoming the world's greatest farmers and pharmacists, the people of the Old World had spent a similar period amassing the world's greatest arsenal of weapons. The strongest, but not necessarily the most creative or the most intelligent, won the day.

The inevitable defeat of Indian groups such as the Yuqui seemed so overwhelming and so final that in the process we have overlooked the contributions that they made to the world. They mined the gold and silver that made capitalism possible. Working in the mines and mints and in the plantations with the African slaves, they started the industrial revolution that then spread to Europe and on around the world. They supplied the cotton, rubber, dyes, and related chemicals that fed this new system of production. They domesticated and developed the hundreds of varieties of corn, potatoes, cassava, and peanuts that now feed much of the world. They discovered the curative powers of quinine, the anesthetizing ability of coca, and the potency of a thousand other drugs, which made possible modern medicine and pharmacology.

The drugs together with their improved agriculture made possible the population explosion of the last several centuries. They developed and refined a form of democracy that has been haphazardly and inadequately adopted in many parts of the world. They were the true colonizers of America who cut the trails through the jungles and deserts, made the roads, and built the cities upon which modern America is based.

Over the past five hundred years, human beings have sculpted a new worldwide society, a new political and economic order as well as a new demographic and agricultural order. Indians played the decisive roles in each step to create this new society. Sometimes they acted as prime movers, other times they played equal roles with a set of actors, and sometimes they were mere victims. But in all cases they acted as necessary although not sufficient causes. Somewhere in the telling of modern history, the writing of the novels, the construction of textbooks and instructional programs, attention drifted away from the contribution of the Indians to the heroic stories of explorers and conquistadores, the moral lessons of missionaries, the political struggles of the colonists, the great and impersonal movements of European history, the romance of the cowboy. The modern world order came to be viewed as the product of European, not American, history. The Americans became bit players, and only their role as pathetic victims remained visible.

The Indians, such as the woman crouched before me, disintegrated into peripheral people. They became little more than beggars on the world scene, pleading for food, for the redress of land and treaty rights, for some attention. In ignoring the Indian cultures, however, we are doing far more than merely slighting the American Indians of their earned place in history. We may be hurting ourselves because of what we have all lost.

In staring at that ancient woman from the time before the white man came, I could not help but wonder what practical knowledge we were losing with her impending death. Through grubbing in the woods did she know of some plant that might serve as a key to feeding the starving masses in the tropics? From poking in ponds and bogs did she know of a concoction that might cure multiple sclerosis? From countless nights under the stars did she know of some weather-forecasting device that we had missed, or did she know something about the anatomy of the night birds that helped them to see through the dark? Had she incorporated something into her diet that prevented stomach cancer? Did her language have the capacity to express some idea more easily than ours, or could it help in the writing of new computer codes? She lived in an environment that few people in the world have ever been able to survive. What knowledge did she have that made that possible? How did she survive for so long in a place that would kill most of us within days? Soon after my visit the old woman died, and now we may never know.

When she died a treasure of information went with her, for she was one of the last Yuquis to live their traditional life. In losing her and the Yuqui culture, we lose more than just a small band of people. We lose a whole world view, for each culture creates the world in a different way with unique knowledge, unique words, and unique understandings. While most of this cultural knowledge may be of no importance to us today, we have no idea what value it may yet hold for our children in generations to come. For centuries our ancestors saw no value in the potato or rubber or the Huron concoction of vitamin C to cure scurvy, but in time all of these came to have important roles to play.

The world has yet to utilize fully the gifts of the American Indians. Hundreds of plants such as amaranth and quinoa are hardly even known, much less fully utilized. Who knows how many more plants might be out there waiting to serve humans? We still do not understand the complex mathematical systems of the Mayas and the sophisticated geometric science of the Aztecs. Who knows what completely different systems of computation and calculation now lie buried in the adobe of Arizona or beneath the rocks of Inkallajta? The civilizations of Mexico and Guatemala developed a more accurate calendar than the one used in Europe, but it took decades of work for us to understand its superiority. Who knows what additional knowledge they had about the stars, the planets, the comets, and who knows how much knowledge still lies locked in the stone monuments yet to be discovered in the jungles of Guatemala or Belize?

We often know even less about the millions of American Indians surviving today, speaking their language and preserving at least some of their traditional cultural knowledge. The Quechuas of Bolivia, the Crees of Canada, the Guaranis of Paraguay, the Yanomamos of Venezuela, the Hopis of the United States, the Zapotecs of Mexico, the Sumus of Nicaragua, the Guajiros of Colombia, the Shuars of Ecuador, the Mayas of Guatemala, the Cunas of Panama, the Shavantes of Brazil, and a thousand other Indian nations are not dead. They are only ignored.

In the five hundred years since Columbus's voyage to America, the people of the world have benefited greatly from the American Indians, but the world may have lost even more than it gained. Some information that died with the old Yuqui woman and with the hundreds of exterminated tribes, nations, and cities may be lost forever. Some of it may be retrieved by coming generations of scholars who have the opportunity to study our past. Sadly, however, we know much more about the building of the pyramids of Egypt, thousands of miles and years from us, than we know about the pyramid builders of the Mississippi. We know more about the language of the long-gone Hittites than we do about the still-living Quechua speakers descended from the Incas. We know more about the poetry of the ancient Chinese than about the poems of the Nahuatls. We can decipher the clay tablets of Mesopotamia better than we can the stone tablets of Mesoamerica. We understand the medical practices of ancient Babylon better than those of the living Dakotas. We understand more about the interbreeding of the Angles and the Saxons than we do about the mixing of the Indians in America with the European and African immigrants. We know more about the Greeks' mythological tribe of Amazons than we know about the dying Yuquis of the Amazon. The history and culture of America remains a mystery, still *terra incognita* after five hundred years.

Columbus arrived in the New World in 1492, but America has yet to be discovered.

REFERENCES

Chapter 1

Braudel, Fernand. *Civilization and Capitalism, 15th–18th Century.* 3 vols. Translated by Siân Reynolds. New York: Harper & Row, 1982–84. Vol. I, *The Structures of Everyday Life.* Vol. II, *The Wheels of Commerce.*

Berdan, Frances F. *The Aztecs of Central Mexico.* New York: Holt, Rinehart & Winston, 1982.

Crow, John A. *The Epic of Latin America,* 3rd ed. Berkeley: University of California Press, 1980.

Erasmus. Epistle 530, in *The Epistles of Erasmus.* Translated by F. M. Nichols. London: Longmans, Green, 1901.

Fehrenbach, T. R. *Fire and Blood.* New York: Collier, 1973.

Galeano, Eduardo. *Open Veins of Latin America.* New York: Monthly Review Press, 1973.

Garraty, John A., and Peter Gay, eds. *The Columbia History of the World.* New York: Harper & Row, 1972.

Guicciardini, Ludovico. "Antwerp, the Great Market." Translated by J. B. R. and C. Pennock. In James Bruce Ross and Mary Martin McLaughlin, eds., Renaissance Reader. Viking, 1953. Pp. 185–202.

Newby, Eric. The World Atlas of Exploration. London: Mitchell Beazley, 1975.

Pendle, George. A History of Latin America. New York: Penguin Books, 1963.

Ross, James Bruce, and Mary Martin McLaughlin, eds. Renaissance Reader. New York: Viking, 1953.

Smith, Adam. The Wealth of Nations. New York: Random House, 1937. Originally published in 1776.

Vega, Garcilaso de la. The Incas: The Royal Commentaries of the Inca. Translated by Maria Jolas. New York: Avon, 1961.

Webb, Walter Prescott. "The Frontier and the 400-Year Boom," in The Turner Thesis. Lexington: Heath, 1949. Pp. 131–43.

Weber, Max. Religion of China. New York: Free Press, 1951.

Werlich, David P. Peru: A Short History. Carbondale: Southern Illinois University Press, 1978.

Wolf, Eric R. Europe and the People Without History. Berkeley: University of California Press, 1982.

Chapter 2

Bourgois, Philippe. "The Miskitu of Nicaragua." Anthropology Today, II, 2 (1986), pp. 4–9.

Brandon, William. Indians. New York: American Heritage, 1985.

Braudel, Fernand. Civilization and Capitalism, 15th–18th Century. 3 vols. Translated by Siân Reynolds. New York: Harper & Row, 1982–84. Vol. III, The Perspective of the World.

Davis, K. G. The North Atlantic World in the Seventeenth Century. Minneapolis: University of Minnesota Press, 1974.

Hecht, Robert A. Continents in Collision. Washington, D.C.: University Press of America, 1980.

Helms, Mary W. Middle America. New York: University Press of America, 1982.

Krech, Shepard III, ed. *The Subarctic Fur Trade*. Vancouver: University of British Columbia, 1984.

MacLeod, William C. *The American Frontier*. New York: Knopf, 1928.

MacShane, Frank, ed. *Impressions of Latin America*. New York: Morrow, 1963.

Morison, Samuel Eliot. *The Great Explorers*. New York: Oxford, 1978.

Newman, Peter C. *Company of Adventurers*. Ontario, Canada: Viking, 1985.

Pretty, Francis. "We Took the Silver and Left the Man." In Frank MacShane, ed., *Impressions of Latin America*. New York: Morrow, 1963.

Smith, Adam. *The Wealth of Nations*. New York: Random House, 1937.

Turner, Frederick Jackson. *The Frontier in American History*. New York: Holt, Rinehart & Winston, 1920.

Wallerstein, Immanuel. *The Modern World-System. I: Capitalist Agriculture and the Origins of the European World-Economy in the Sixteenth Century*. New York: Academic Press, 1974.

Williams, Eric. *Capitalism and Slavery*. New York: Russell & Russell, 1961.

Wolf, Eric R. *Europe and the People Without History*. Berkeley: University of California Press, 1982.

Wright, J. Leitch, Jr. *The Only Land They Knew*. New York: The Free Press, 1981.

Chapter 3

Braudel, Fernand. *Civilization and Capitalism, 15th–18th Century*. 3 vols. Translated by Siân Reynolds. New York: Harper & Row, 1982–84. Vol. II, *The Wheels of Commerce*. Vol. III, *The Perspective of the World*.

Burke, James. *Connections*. Boston: Little, Brown, 1978.

Cole, Jeffrey A. *The Potosí Mita: 1573–1700*. Stanford: Stanford University Press, 1985.

Crosby, Alfred W., Jr. *The Columbian Exchange*. Westport, Conn.: Greenwood, 1972.

Crow, John A. *The Epic of Latin America*, 3rd ed. Berkeley: University of California Press, 1980.

Hobhouse, Henry. *Seeds of Change*. New York: Harper & Row, 1986.

Kropotkin, Peter. *Fields, Factories, and Workshops*. New York: G. P. Putnam's Sons, 1901.

Mintz, Sidney W. *Sweetness and Power*. New York: Viking, 1985.

Parrington, Vernon L. *The Romantic Revolution in America*. New York: Harcourt, Brace & World, 1927.

Picon-Salas, Mariano. *A Cultural History of Spanish America*. Translated by Irving A. Leonard. Berkeley: University of California Press, 1966.

Poatgierter, Hermina. *Indian Legacy*. New York: Julian Messner, 1981.

Weatherford, Jack M. "Millennium of Modernization: A Changing German Village." In Priscilla Copeland Reining and Barbara Lenkerd, eds., *Village Viability in Contemporary Society*. AAAS Selected Symposium Series 34. Boulder, Colo.: Westview, 1980.

Wolf, Eric R. *Europe and the People Without History*, Berkeley: University of California Press, 1982.

Chapter 4

Braudel, Fernand. *Civilization and Capitalism, 15th–18th Century*. 3 vols. Translated by Siân Reynolds. New York: Harper & Row, 1982–84. Vol. I, *The Structures of Everyday Life*.

Crosby, Alfred W., Jr. *The Columbian Exchange*. Westport, Conn.: Greenwood Press, 1972.

Drummond, J. C., and Anne Wilbraham. *The Englishman's Food*. London: Cape, 1957.

Farb, Peter, and George Armelagos. *Consuming Passions: The Anthropology of Eating*. New York: Washington Square Books, 1980.

Kalinowski, Luis Sumar. *Kiwicha, el pequeño gigante*. Lima, Peru: UNICEF.

National Academy of Sciences. *Amaranth: Modern Prospects for an Ancient Crop*. Washington, D.C.: National Academy Press, 1984.

Petersen, William. *Population*, 3rd ed. New York: Macmillan.

Salaman, Redcliffe N. *The History and Social Influence of the Potato.* Cambridge, England: Cambridge University Press, 1949.

Smith, Adam. *The Wealth of Nations.* New York: Random House, 1937.

Stea, Vikkie. "High-Yield Corn from Ancient Seed Strains." *Christian Science Monitor,* August 20, 1985, p. 29.

Weatherford, Jack M. "Millennium of Modernization: A Changing German Village." In Priscilla Copeland Reining and Barbara Lenkerd, eds., *Village Viability in Contemporary Society.* AAAS Selected Symposium Series 34. Boulder, Colo.: Westview, 1980.

Chapter 5

Bryant, Carol A., Anita Courtney, Barbara A. Markesbery, and Kathleen M. DeWalt. *The Cultural Feast.* St. Paul: West, 1985.

Chacon, J. C., and S. R. Gliessman. "Use of the 'Non-Weed' Concept in Traditional Tropical Agroecosystems of South-Eastern Mexico." *Agro-Ecosystems* 8 (1982).

Gliessman, S. R., R. Garcia, and M. F. Amador. "The Ecological Basis for the Application of Traditional Agricultural Technology in the Management of Tropical Agroecosystems." *Agro-Ecosystems* 7 (1981).

Sauer, Carl O. *Selected Essays 1963–1975.* Berkeley: Turtle Island Foundation, 1981.

Stea, Vikkie. "High-Yield Corn from Ancient Seed Strains." *Christian Science Monitor,* August 20, 1985, p. 29.

Vega, Garcilaso de la. *The Incas.* Translated by Maria Jolas. New York: Avon, 1961.

Werlich, David P. *Peru: A Short History.* Carbondale: Southern Illinois University Press, 1978.

Chapter 6

Aziz, Khalid. *Indian Cooking.* London: Hamlyn, 1974.

Escoffier, A. *The Escoffier Cook Book.* New York: Crown, 1941.

Gumpert, Anita von Kahler. "One Potato, Two Potato." *Americas,* May 1986.

Hansen, Barbara. *Mexican Cookery.* Tucson: HP Books, 1980.

Morris, William, ed. *The American Heritage Dictionary of the English Language.* Boston: Houghton Mifflin, 1969.

Rogers, Robert E. "The Incredible Potato." *National Geographic,* May 1982.

Wernick, Robert. "Men Launched 1,000 Ships in Search of the Dark Condiment." *Smithsonian,* February 1984.

Chapter 7

Berkhofer, Robert F., Jr. *The White Man's Indian.* New York: Knopf, 1978.

Brandon, William. *New Worlds for Old: Reports from the New World and Their Effect on the Development of Social Thought in Europe, 1500–1800.* Athens, Ohio: Ohio University Press, 1986.

Clastres, Pierre. *Society Against the State.* Translated by Robert Hurley. New York: Urizen, 1977.

Commager, Henry Steele. *The Empire of Reason: How Europe Imagined and America Realized the Enlightenment.* Garden City, N.Y.: Doubleday, 1978.

Johansen, Bruce E. *Forgotten Founders.* Ipswich, Mass.: Gambit, 1982.

Lehning, Arthur. "Anarchism," in *Dictionary of the History of Ideas.* New York: Scribner's, 1968. Vol. I, pp. 70–76.

Montaigne, Michel de. *Essays.* Translated by J. M. Cohen. Middlesex, England: Penguin.

Paine, Thomas. *Representative Selections.* New York: American Book, 1944.

Parrington, Vernon L. *The Colonial Mind 1620–1800.* New York: Harcourt, Brace & World, 1927.

Tocqueville, Alexis de. *Democracy in America.* 2 vols., Henry Reeve text, edited by Phillips Bradley. New York: Random House, 1945.

Chapter 8

Burton, Bruce A. "Iroquois Confederate Law and the Origins of the U.S. Constitution." *Northeast Indian Quarterly,* Fall 1986, pp. 4–9.

Cappon, Lester J., ed. *The Adams-Jefferson Letters,* Vol. II. Chapel Hill: University of North Carolina Press, 1959.

Commager, Henry Steele. *The Empire of Reason: How Europe Imagined and America Realized the Enlightenment.* Garden City, NY: Anchor, 1978.

Goldenweiser, Alexander A. "Iroquois Social Organization," in Roger C. Owen, James J. F. Deetz, and Anthony D. Fisher, eds., *The North American Indians.* New York: Macmillan, 1967.

Hecht, Robert A. *Continents in Collision.* Washington, D.C.: University Press of America, 1980.

Hu-DeHart, Evelyn. *Yaqui Resistance and Survival.* Madison: University of Wisconsin Press, 1984.

Jefferson, Thomas. *Notes on the State of Virginia.* Chapel Hill: University of North Carolina Press, 1955.

Johansen, Bruce E. *Forgotten Founders.* Ipswich, Mass.: Gambit, 1982.

Morgan, Lewis Henry. *League of the Iroquois.* Rochester: Sage, 1851.

Paine, Thomas. *Rights of Man.* Middlesex, England: Penguin, 1969. Originally published 1791.

Parrington, Vernon L. *The Romantic Revolution in America.* New York: Harcourt, Brace & World, 1927.

Thomson, Charles. "Appendix 1," in Thomas Jefferson, *Notes on the State of Virginia.* Chapel Hill: University of North Carolina Press, 1955.

Tocqueville, Alexis de. *Democracy in America.* 2 vols. Henry Reeve Text, edited by Phillips Bradley. New York: Random House, 1945.

Turner, Frederick Jackson. *The Frontier in American History.* New York: Holt, Rinehart & Winston, 1920.

Waldman, Carl. *Atlas of the North American Indian.* New York: Facts on File, 1985.

Weatherford, J. M. *Tribes on the Hill,* rev. ed. South Hadley, Mass.: Bergin & Garvey, 1985.

Weatherford, J. M. "Kongresskultur." *Freibeuter* 12. Berlin: Wagenbach Verlag, 1982.

Wilson, Edmund. *Apologies to the Iroquois.* New York: Farrar, Straus & Giroux, 1959.

Chapter 9

Arnade, Charles. *Bolivian History*. Cochabamba: Editorial Los Amigos del Libro, 1984.

Engels, Frederick. *The Origin of the Family, Private Property, and the State: In the Light of the Researches of Lewis H. Morgan*. New York: International Publishers, 1942.

Fehrenbach, T. R. *Fire and Blood*. New York: Collier Books, 1973.

Galeano, Eduardo. *Open Veins of Latin America*. New York: Monthly Review Press, 1973.

Guzmán, Augusto. *Historia de Bolivia*, 6th ed., Cochabamba: Editorial Los Amigos del Libro, 1981.

Halbert, H. S., and T. H. Ball. *The Creek War of 1813 and 1814*. Tuscaloosa: University of Alabama Press, 1969.

Harris, Fred R. "Mexico: Historical Foundations." In Jan Knippers Black, ed., *Latin America: Its Problems and its Promise*. Boulder, Colo.: Westview, 1984.

Hoxie, Frederick E., ed. *Indians in American History*. Arlington Heights, Ill.: Harlan Davidson, 1988.

Hu-DeHart, Evelyn. *Yaqui Resistance and Survival*. Madison: University of Wisconsin Press, 1984.

Picon-Salas, Mariano. *A Cultural History of Spanish America*. Translated by Irving A. Leonard. Berkeley: University of California Press, 1966.

Riding, Alan. *Distant Neighbors*. New York: Random House, 1986.

Spicer, Edward H. *A Short History of the Indians of the United States*. New York: Van Nostrand Reinhold, 1969.

Werlich, David P. *Peru: A Short History*. Carbondale: Southern Illinois University Press, 1878.

Wolf, Eric R. *Peasant Wars of the Twentieth Century*. New York: Harper & Row, 1973.

Chapter 10

Bakeless, John. *The Eyes of Discovery*. New York: Dover, 1961.

Driver, Harold E. *Indians of North America*, 2nd ed. Chicago: University of Chicago Press, 1969.

Green, Abel, and Joe Laurie, Jr. *Show Biz from Vaudeville to Video*. New York: Holt, 1951.

Ferrieri, Giuliano. "Death by Choice." *World Press*, Dec. 1987.

Guzmán Peredo, Miguel. *Medical Practices in Ancient America*. Mexico City: Ediciones Euroamericanas, 1985.

Hallowell, A. Irving. "The Backlash of the Frontier." In Paul Bohannon and Fred Plog, eds., *Beyond the Frontier*. Garden City, N.Y.: Natural History Press, 1967. Pp. 319–45.

Hobhouse, Henry. *Seeds of Change*. New York: Harper & Row, 1986.

Kahn, Ely Jacques, Jr. *The Big Drink: The Story of Coca-Cola*. New York: Random House, 1950.

Lira, Jorge A. *Medicina Andina: Farmacopea y Ritual*. Cusco: Centro de Estudios Rurales Andinos "Bartolome de las Casas," 1985.

Taylor, Norman. *Plant Drugs That Changed the World*. New York: Dodd, Mead, 1965.

Wissler, Clark, Wilton M. Krogman, and Walter Krickerberg. *Medicine Among the American Indians*. Ramona, Calif.: Acoma, 1939.

Chapter 11

Braudel, Fernand. *Civilization and Capitalism, 15th–18th Century*. 3 vols. Translated by Siân Reynolds. New York: Harper & Row, 1982–84. Vol. I, *The Structures of Everyday Life*. Pp. 264–65.

Chagnon, Napoleon. *Yanomamo*, 3rd ed. New York: Holt, Rinehart and Winston, 1983.

Driver, Harold E. *Indians of North America*, 2nd ed. Chicago: University of Chicago Press, 1969.

Kendall, Jonathan. *Passage Through El Dorado*. New York: Avon, 1985.

Pacini, Deborah, and Christine Franquemont, eds. *Coca and Cocaine*. Cambridge: Cultural Survival, 1986.

Schivelbusch, Wolfgang. *Das Paradies, der Geschmack und die Vernunft*. Munich: Carl Hanser Verlag, 1980.

Slotkin, James S. "The Peyote Way." In Roger Owen, James Deetz, and Anthony Fisher, eds., *The North American Indians*. New York: Macmillan, 1967. Pp. 647–54.

Spicer, Edward H. *A Short History of the Indians of the United States*. New York: Van Nostrand Reinhold, 1969.

Weatherford, J. M. "The Cocaine Boom and the Economic Deterioration of Bolivia." In James Spradley and David McCurdy, eds., *Conformity and Conflict*. Boston: Little, Brown, 1987.

Young, Lawrence A., Lynda C. Young, Marjorie M. Klein, Donald M. Klein, and Dorianne Beyer. *Recreational Drugs*. New York: Berkley, 1977.

Chapter 12

Céspedes, Guillermo. *América Indígena*. Madrid: Alianaza, 1985.

Mays, Buddy. *Ancient Cities of the Southwest*. San Francisco: Chronicle Books, 1982.

Coe, Michael, Deand Snow, and Elizabeth Benson. *Atlas of Ancient America*. New York: Facts on File, 1986.

Driver, Harold E. *Indians of North America*, 2nd ed. Chicago: University of Chicago, 1969.

Haberland, Wolfgang. *Das Geben Sie Uns*. Hamburg: Museum für Völkerkunde, 1975.

Helms, Mary W. *Middle America*. Boston: University of America Press, 1982.

Morley, Sylvanus G. and George W. Brainerd. *The Ancient Maya*, 4th ed. Stanford: Stanford University Press, 1983.

Chapter 13

Adney, Edwin Tappan, and Howard I. Chappele. *The Bark Canoes and Skin Boats of North America*. Washington, D.C.: Smithsonian Institution, 1964.

Olson, Ronald L. *The Quinault Indians and Adze, Canoe, and House Types of the Northwest Coast*. Seattle: University of Washington Press, 1967.

Von Hagen, Victor Wolfgang. *The Royal Road of the Inca*. London: Gordon and Cremonesi, 1976.

INDEX

achiote, 46
Acoma, 224–225
Adams, Thomas, 208
Africa, 6, 17, 65, 71, 72, 74, 75
agricultural research projects, 77–78,
    80–82, 95, 97
agricultural technology, Indian,
    61–63, 70, 73, 80–97
    influence of, 83–84, 87–88, 89, 92,
    93, 95
Alaykin, 127
alcohol, 212–215
alcoholism, industrialism and,
    214–215
Algonquian Indians, 129–130
Alvarado, Hernando de, 225
amaranth, 63, 75–76, 254
American Revolution, 125, 126, 130
amoebic dysentery, 181
anarchism, 123, 130–131
Anasazi Indians, 246
anesthetics, 190
animals, domesticated, 93–94, 241,
    251
Antwerp, 15
APRA (Popular Revolutionary
    American Alliance), 169–170
Arango, Doroteo (Pancho Villa), 164
architecture, 10, 12
    Greek, 146–147, 223
    Indian, 59, 60, 220–228
    Old World, 222, 223, 225–226,
    228–230
Armelagos, George, 67, 71, 73
Arnade, Charles, 166
arrows, poisoned, 184–185
Asia, 16–17, 71, 72, 74, 75, 76, 103
asphalt, 48
Astor, John Jay, 23
Atahualpa, 8, 189

avocado, 114–115
Aymara Indians, 1, 239
Aztec Indians, 7, 46, 60, 204, 206,
    209, 211, 220, 254
    diet of, 75
    medical organization of, 187–190
    political organization of, 143–144

Bakeless, John, 183
Bakunin, Michael, 130
Ball, T. H., 158
balsams, 186
Banderas, Juan de la Cruz, 160
banking system, 37
barbecuing, 109
Barnwell, John, 139
baths, bathing, 189–190
beans, 72
beaver pelts, 24–25, 33
Belize, 235–238
Berdan, Frances F., 7
berries, New World, 114
Bingham, Hiram, 59
Black Caribs, 235–236
Bodin, Jean, 15
Bogle, George, 205
Bolívar, Simón, 36
Bolivia, 1–5, 19, 89, 166–169, 173,
    201–202
Brandon, William, 122, 123, 124
Braudel, Fernand, 10, 14, 16, 27, 36,
    44, 65, 66, 69, 70, 203, 214
Brazil, 45, 47
brazilin dye, 45
breakfast cereal industry, 93
bridges, suspension, 243–244
British companies, 22–26, 32, 33–35,
    38, 205
    in Latin America, 36–37
    quest for silver and gold by, 27–31

Burke, James, 48
Burton, Bruce A., 141

cacao, 81, 90–92, 206
Calhoun, John C., 56
Canassatego, 135, 136
Candler, Asa Griggs, 191
canoes, canoe building, 24, 237–241
capitalism, silver's role in rise of, 13–20, 37–38
Caribbean Sea, 28, 31, 33, 34, 36
Carolinas, 31–32, 33–35
Carranza, Venustiano, 165
Cartier, Jacques, 182–183, 239
cassava, 74–75, 80–81, 93
Castro, Fidel, 168
Catherine the Great, 66, 69, 129
caucus, political, 145
Caventou, Joseph, 177
Cayuga Indians, 136
Cerro Rico Mountain, 2–5, 6, 12, 13, 18, 36
Cervantes, Miguel, 5, 15
Cespedes, Rodrigo, 1–5, 199, 201
Chaco Indians, 127
chacras, defined, 80
Chagnon, Napoleon, 212
Charles II, King of England, 22, 33
Charles III, Frankish Emperor, 225
Charleston, 33–35
Charles V, King of Spain, 10, 14
chayotes, 111–112
Cherokee Indians, 44, 148, 159
chewing gum, 208
Chibcha Indians, 9
Chickasaw Indians, 44
China, 16–17, 64, 75, 76, 103, 203, 205–206
chocolate, 206–208
Choctaw Indians, 44
Churchill, John, 31
Clastres, Pierre, 126–127
clothing, water-resistant, 47–48
coca, 3–4, 60, 61, 190–191, 197–198, 199–203
Coca-Cola, 191
cocaine, cocaine trade, 190–192, 198, 199–203
cochineal dyes, 45–46
Cody, William F. "Wild Bill," 193
coffee, 215
Cole, Jeffrey A., 50
Columbus, Christopher, 6–7, 10, 47, 52, 94, 101, 193, 229, 230, 255
Commager, Henry Steele, 127, 128, 129, 137, 142
communism, Indian social system and, 162, 172

companies, chartered, 22–26, 27–31, 215
    colonial policies and, 32, 37–38
    competition among, 33–35
    land, 35–36
Condorcanqui, José Gabriel, 171
constitutions, political, 135, 138
conuco agriculture system, 87–88
Cooper, Anthony Ashley, 31–32
Córdoba, 10, 11–12
corn, 73–74, 84–85, 92–93, 95, 108, 213–214
Coronado, Francisco Vásquez de, 8
corporations, rise of, 22, 26, 27–38
Cortés, Hernando, 7, 143, 206, 228
cotton, cotton production, 42–44
cotton gin, 44
Crawford, Thomas, 149
Creek Indians, 44, 113, 154–159, 189, 204
crops, New World, 41–49, 62–78, 80
    development of regional cuisines and, 101–115
    diffusion of, 64, 68–69, 72, 80, 94–95, 103
    impact on Old World of, 64–74
Crosby, Alfred W., Jr., 70, 71, 72, 75
Crow, John A., 14, 17, 50
Cuauhtémoc, 7
Cuban-style revolution, 168–169, 171
culinary history, New World foods and, 101–115
curare, 184–185
Custer, George, 163
Cuzco, 8, 10, 59, 63, 228

Dakota Indians, 93, 163
Davis, Jefferson, 149
Davis, K. G., 25
debate, principles of, 140–141
Deganwidah, 135
Delaware Indians, 137
democratic forms, 128–130, 134–143
    Greek model for, 145–147
    Indian model for, 134–143, 145, 147–148, 253
Diderot, Denis, 66
Dogon tribe, 175–176
Drake, Francis, 28–30
Drevetière, Delisle de la, 123
Driver, Harold E., 183, 185, 189, 193, 212, 213, 221
drugs, 197–216
Dutch companies, 27–28, 32, 33, 37
dyes, 45–46

earthquakes, 217–221
Eastern European cuisine, 105
El Dorado, 7, 8

electoral college system, 140
electricity, 48
Elizabeth I, Queen of England, 28, 29, 30
Engels, Friedrich, 161–162
England, 19–20, 44, 49, 70, 89, 105–106, 129, 134, 135, 143, 183, 194, 207, 213, 236
   chartered companies of, 22–26, 27–31, 32, 33–35, 36–37, 38, 205
Enlightenment, Indian liberty and, 124–128, 129
Eskimos, 239, 241
European cuisine, 104–107, 108, 115

factories, plantation model for, 54–55, 57
famines, 65, 66, 70
Farb, Peter, 67, 71, 73
federalism, 137
Fehrenbach, T. R., 19
Ferdinand V, King of Spain, 6, 229–230
Ferrieri, Giuliano, 185
fertilizers, 88–89, 96, 97
Fielding, Henry, 215
food preservation, 64, 90, 93
food processing, 90–93
Fort William, 22–25, 27, 35
France, 16, 19, 27–28, 32, 33–35, 36–37, 70, 106, 135, 181, 182, 194
Franklin, Benjamin, 135–136, 141–142, 145, 251
Frederick the Great, King of Prussia, 66, 69, 129
French Revolution, 125–126
frontier settlements, 147–148
fruit and vegetables, New World, 101, 104, 105, 111–113, 114–115
Fuller, Buckminster, 227
fur trade, 23–26, 33

Galaeno, Eduardo, 19, 164
Gallo, Mujica, 8–9
Gálvez, Bernardo de, 214
Gandhi, Mohandas K., 131
Garifuna Indians, 236, 237
Garland, Bob and Mary, 249
Garraty, John A., 13, 16
Gay, Peter, 13, 16
Genaro Herrera, 79–80, 95
Ghost Dance movement, 160, 210
gold, 6–12
   European supply of, 10, 12, 14
   quest for, 6–8
Gold Coast, 6, 17
Golden Man, legend of, 7, 8
Goldenweiser, Alexander A., 139

gold treasures, collections of, 8–12
Goodyear, Charles, 47
grain crops, 62–63, 65, 66–67, 68, 69, 73, 75–76
grave robbers, 9
Green, Abel, 192
guano deposits, 88–89
Guatemala, 151–154, 172, 219
Guevara, Ernesto "Che," 168–169
Guicciardini, Ludovico, 15
Guzmán, Abimael, 170–171
Guzmán Peredo, Miguel, 188

Halbert, H. S., 158
Hallowell, A. Irving, 178, 192
hallucinogens, 208–211
Harris, Fred R., 165
Harvey, William, 188
Hawkins, John, 28, 30
Haya de la Torre, Victor Raul, 169
Hecht, Robert A., 136
Helms, Mary W., 28
Helvetius, Claude Arien, 182
Helvetius, Jean Adrien, 181–182
Heyerdahl, Thor, 240
Hiawatha, 135
Hobbes, Thomas, 127
Hogarth, William, 215
hominy, 93
Hopi Indians, 73–74, 95
House of Trade (Casa de Contratación), 27–28
Houston, Sam, 148
Houwald, Götz von, 218
Huayna Capac, 5
Hu-DeHart, Evelyn, 144, 160
Hudson's Bay Company, 22–26, 27, 31, 33–35, 38
   labor policy of, 24, 25–26
Humboldt, Alexander von, 184
Huron Indians, 122–123, 124

impeachment, 138–139
Inca Indians, 5, 7–8, 49–50, 59–63, 94, 199
   agriculture of, 61–64, 70, 73, 88
   architecture of, 59, 60, 220, 227–228
   medicines of, 177, 189
   road system of, 241–246
Indian Removal Act of 1830, 159
Indians, 46, 155–156
   agriculture of, 61–63, 70, 73, 80–90, 95–97
   cuisine of, 63, 72, 94, 107–109, 110, 112, 113
   disease transmitted to, 28, 195, 249, 252

Indians (continued)
    domestication of animals by, 94,
        241, 251
    dye technology of, 45–46
    enslavement of, 5, 17–18, 63, 139,
        159, 160, 171
    food processing techniques of,
        90–93
    gold treasure of, 8–10
    medical practices of, 177, 181–196,
        252
    political organizations of, 120–123,
        126–127, 129, 135–144, 147–148,
        155
    present-day condition of, 1–5, 18,
        96–97, 249–251, 253–255
    religious ceremonies of, 7, 157,
        188, 199, 200, 204, 209–211, 212,
        213, 243
    religious conversion of, 32, 34
    revolutions of, 154–173
    waterproofing techniques of, 47,
        48–49
    women, political rights of, 138–139
industrialization, 41–58, 252
    impact of New World crops on,
        41–49
    manpower shortage and, 49–52
insecticides, 81, 83, 96–97
International Potato Institute, 77–78,
    97
intestinal worms, 185
ipecac, 181–182
Ireland, potato farming and, 64, 66,
    68–69, 70
Iroquois Indians, 125, 126, 129, 135,
    155, 172, 238, 247
    political organization of, 135–143,
        149, 162
Isabella I, Queen of Spain, 6,
    229–230
Ishi, 163, 172
Italy, 104–105, 106–107, 194, 203

Jackson, Andrew, 158–159
James II, King of England, 31
Jamestown, 31, 32
Jefferson, Thomas, 36, 138, 142, 161
Johansen, Bruce E., 125, 135, 140
Juárez, Benito, 37

Kahl, Germany, 39–42, 46, 48, 54,
    56–57, 66–67
Kahn, Ely Jacques, Jr., 191
Kant, Immanuel, 127
kayaks, 239, 240, 241
Kellogg, Will K., 93
Kendall, Jonathan, 201
King, Martin Luther, Jr., 131
Kon-Tiki, 240

Kropotkin, Peter, 54–55, 130
La Condamine, Charles de, 47
Lafitau, Joseph François, 124
Lahontan, Baron de, 122–123, 124,
    130
land companies, 35–36
Laughlin, Charles, 61
Laurie, Joe, Jr., 192
Laveran, Charles, 178
laxatives, 184
League of the Iroquois, 135–143, 149
L'Enfant, Pierre Charles, 230
liberty, notions of Indian, 120–128
Lind, James, 183
Linnaeus, Carolus, 178, 207
liquor distillation, 213–214
Little Big Horn, Battle of, 163
Locke, John, 31–32

Machu Picchu, 59–63, 77, 228
Macintosh, Thomas, 47
Magellan, Ferdinand, 30
Magna Carta, 128
malaria, 28, 176–179
Managua earthquake, 217–219,
    220–221
Mao Tse-tung, 171–172
Mariani, Angelo, 190
Mariátegui, José Carlos, 170
marijuana, 215–216
Marx, Karl, 38, 161–162
Massacre of Tohopeka or Horseshoe
    Bend (1814), 158
Massacre of Wounded Knee (1890),
    160
Maya Indians, 60, 151, 160, 163, 211,
    220, 221, 222, 238, 254
McGillivray, Alexander, 155–156
McLaughlin, Mary Martin, 15
medical practices, Indian-based, 177,
    181–196, 252
medicine shows, 192–193
Mexico, 14, 37, 45, 160, 163–166,
    168, 173
Milfort, LeClerc, 155, 156, 161
mills, 41–42, 48
milpa agriculture system, 82–84
miners, Indian, 1–5, 17–18, 166, 167,
    171, 199, 201
mining technology, 49–52
mints, coin, 12, 19, 51–52, 58
Mintz, Stanley, 53
Moctezuma Xocoyotzin, 7, 143–144,
    211
Mohawk Indians, 124, 136
Monardes, Nicolas, 190
money economy, silver and, 7,
    13–16
Montaigne, Michel de, 122

Moore, James, 139
Moors, 6, 225, 229, 230
More, Sir Thomas, 122
Morgan, Lewis Henry, 137, 138, 161–162
Morison, Samuel Eliot, 29, 30

Napoleon III, Emperor of France, 37
Narraganset Indians, 107
National Academy of Sciences, 47, 75, 76
Native American Church, 209–210
Navajo Indians, 63
Netherlands, 19, 27–28, 32, 33, 37, 49, 128, 129
noble savage, notion of, 124, 127–128, 129–130
North West Company, 23, 26
nuts, New World, 72, 103, 104, 113–114

Ojibwa Indians, 76, 110, 117
Oneida Indians, 136
Onondaga Indians, 136
opium, opium trade, 205–206
Orellana, Francisco de, 8, 184
Osceola, 159
Ottoman Empire, 16, 64, 203

Paine, Thomas, 125–126, 130, 142, 145
Parrington, Vernon L., 56, 146
Patiño, Simon "Tin King," 2
Paz Estensoro, Victor, 2, 167
peanuts, 72, 103, 104
pear cactus, 85–86
Pelletier, Joseph, 177
Pemberton, John Styth, 191
Pendle, George, 7, 13
peppers, 101, 104, 105
Pérez, Alan Garcia, 169–170
Peru, 8, 63, 80, 89, 96–97, 169–171, 172
Peruvian bark, 177–178
Petersen, William, 68
petroleum jelly, 187
peyote, 208–211
Picon-Salas, Mariano, 52, 171
piracy, 27, 28–31, 34, 38
Pizarro, Francisco, 8, 64, 189
plantations, 31, 33, 36, 45, 52–54, 199
Poatgierter, Hermina, 47
Pocahontas, 134
political systems, Indian model for, 120–131, 135–144, 147–148, 155
population growth, nutrition and, 70–71, 74, 253
potatoes, 41–42, 62–72, 74, 75, 77–78, 103, 105

Potosí, Bolivia, 1–5, 12, 14, 19, 36, 50, 51, 52, 89, 199
powwow, contemporary, 117–121
precious metals, New World, 5–20
inflation and, 15–16
Pretty, Francis, 29
protein supply, 72–73, 75
Proudhon, Pierre Joseph, 130
psilocybin mushrooms, 211
pyramids, 221

Quechua Indians, 1, 5, 46, 166, 197, 242, 243
quinine, 177–181, 195
quinoa, 63, 76, 254

rafts, 240
Raleigh, Sir Walter, 68
Rankin, Jeannette, 148
Ratsell, John, 122
Red Eagle, 156, 157, 159
Red Stick movement, 156–160, 172, 210
Revolutionary National Movement (MNR), 167
revolutions, Indian, 154–173
Ribera, Francisca Henrique de, 177
rice, 73, 74, 75, 76–77
Riding, Alan, 163
roads, highway systems, 241–248
Ross, James Bruce, 15
Ross, Sir Ronald, 178
Rousseau, Jean Jacques, 124, 251
Royal African Company, 31
Royal Fisheries Company, 31
Royal House of Money, 51
rubber, 46–48
Russia, 64, 65, 69, 70, 71, 73, 194, 203

Sahara, cuisine of, 99–101
Salaman, Redcliffe N., 63, 69
Sánchez, Elias, 87–88
Sandinista movement, Indians and, 169, 171
Santa Fe, N.M., 225–226
Santa Fé, Spain, 228–230
Sauer, Carl O., 82, 84
Schivelbusch, Wolfgang, 207
scurvy, 182–183
Seminole Indians, 44, 159
Sendero Luminoso, 170
Seneca Indians, 136
silver, 5, 11, 12–20
European economy and, 13, 14–17, 19–20, 64
silver mines, 5, 14, 17–18, 36, 50, 52, 164
Sioux Indians, 160
sisal, 46

slave factory system, 55–56
slavery, 5, 17–18, 63, 100, 121, 139,
    145–147, 159, 160, 171
  technological innovation and, 49,
    53
slave trade, 17, 27, 28, 30–32, 34, 35,
    38
Smith, Adam, 16, 37–38, 66, 67
snack foods, 110–111
Socrates, 145
soft drinks, 181, 191–192
soil management, 88–89
Somoza, Anastasio, 218
Sorel, Georges, 130
Soto, Hernando de, 8, 155
South Asian cuisine, 104
Spain, 6–12, 17–18, 19–20, 27–28,
    33–36, 45, 49–50, 63, 70, 75, 88,
    105, 128, 143, 144, 151, 184, 189,
    199, 206, 207, 209, 211, 213, 225
Spicer, Edward H., 156, 210
Stearman, Allyn, 249
Suárez, Nicolas, 201
Suárez, Roberto, 201
sugar plantations, 52–54
sunflowers, 72–73
surgery, 187–188
syphilis, 193–195

Taino Indians, 109
tar, 48–49
Tayasal, 151–152, 172
Taylor, Norman, 177
Tejada, Garcia Meza, 201
Temple, Edmund, 36
textile industry, 43–46
Thomson, Charles, 137–138, 142
Thoreau, Henry David, 131
Thunder Bay, Ontario, 21–23, 27
Tibet, 76, 204–205
Tikal, 151, 221, 225, 228
Timbuktu, 6, 17, 64, 179–180, 227
tin mines, 2, 19, 36
tobacco, tobacco trade, 203–205
Tocqueville, Alexis de, 126, 148
Toledo, Francisco de, 50
Tolosa, Juan de, 14
tomatoes, 101, 103, 104–105
Transcendentalism, 147
transportation:
  overland, arteries for, 241–248
  water, vehicles for, 237–241
Treaty of Cusseta, 159
Treaty of Fort Jackson, 158
Treaty of Ghent, 159
tree girdling, 84
Trotsky, Leon, 166
Tupac Amaru, 171

Turner, Frederick Jackson, 32, 36
Tuscarora Indians, 139

United States, 82, 84–85, 89, 199,
    201, 215–216
  Indian revolutions in, 154–160, 163
  models for government of,
    134–143, 145–148, 253
  regional cuisines of, 107–111
urban design, New World, 228–233
Ursua, Martin de, 152

van der Heyden, Herman, 178
vanilla, 92
Vega, Garcilaso de la, 7, 8, 88
Vegetable and Fruit Boutique,
    111–113
Villa, Pancho (Doroteo Arango), 164
Virginia Company of London, 31, 32
volcanoes, 220, 242
Voltaire, 127
Von Hagen, Victor Wolfgang, 240
voyageurs, 24, 25–26

Waldman, Carl, 139
Wallerstein, Immanuel, 38
Washington, D. C., 230, 231
Washington, George, 142, 156, 231
wealth, basis of, 15, 16–17
Wealth of Nations, The (Smith), 16,
    37–38
Webb, Walter Prescott, 14
Weber, Max, 16
Werlich, David P., 18, 89, 170
Whitney, Eli, 44
wild rice, 76–77
wild west shows, 193
Williams, Eric, 31
Wilson, Edmund, 136
Wissler, Clark, 187
witch hazel, 186
Wolf, Eric R., 6, 14, 15, 32, 44, 45,
    47, 54
wools, 43
Wright, Frank Lloyd, 226–227

Xenophon, 240

Yahi Indians, 163
Yanomamo Indians, 211–212
Yaqui Indians, 144, 160
yellow fever, 28
Yuqui Indians, 249–251, 254, 255

Zalvidar, Vicente de, 225
Zanzibar, cuisine of, 101–102
Zapata, Emiliano, 163–167, 169, 172
Zuni Indians, 143